From Good Faith to Utmost Good Faith in Marine Insurance

Johan Hendrik Botes

From Good Faith to Utmost Good Faith in Marine Insurance

PETER LANG
Frankfurt am Main · Berlin · Bern · Bruxelles · New York · Oxford · Wien

Bibliographic Information published by Die Deutsche Bibliothek
Die Deutsche Bibliothek lists this publication in the Deutsche Nationalbibliografie; detailed bibliographic data is available in the internet at <http://dnb.ddb.de>.

Zugl.: Hamburg, Univ., Diss., 2005

This publication was made possible by the kind support of the Deutscher Akademischer Austauschdienst.

D 18
ISBN 3-631-55549-0
US-ISBN 0-8204-8717-1

www.peterlang.de

Vir Ou Grote

ACKNOWLEDGEMENTS

One day more than a dacade ago, my friend and I, being bright-eyed matric *laaities* in the small *Swartland* town of Mooreesburg visited the local State Prosecutor. Somewhere in the corridor of the little magistrate's court, one of the only two attorneys then practicing in our town wanted to know what we were doing there. We said we were planning to study law and that the Prosecutor was going to let us sit in at a court case. The attorney merely sniggered and suggested we rather consider becoming policemen, since there was no future for us in law. Fortunately, we did not heed his advice and went on to study and obtain our law degrees. And fortunately, there were many people who cheered me on during my legal studies, a marathon session of 10 years that took me to 5 Universities in South Africa, Belgium and Germany.

A German doctoral student refers to his supervisor as "*Doktorvater*", which in the English language translates into "doctor father". Mine was Prof. Marian Paschke of the *Universität Hamburg* who took keen interest in my choice of topic from our first encounter in Hamburg in 2002 and immediately set out to assist me in finding a sponsor for my research. He fought alongside me in the bureaucratic trenches and, when finally I could settle down and begin my research, allowed me the freedom to develop the critique of "utmost good faith" that is contained on the following pages.

The *Deutscher Akademischer Austauschdienst*, or DAAD, sponsored my research by means of a more than generous scholorship and also financed this publication. A personal word of gratitude must go to my consultant at the DAAD, *Frau* Theresia Heinen for her friendly assistance, particularly when my father passed away suddenly on 9 September 2003. Within 15 minutes of my giving her the news she managed to arrange for my return to Cape Town. The partners of Hamburg shipping law specialists, *Lebuhn und Puchta*, also contributed financially and provided invaluable experience of German and European legal practice. Prof. John Hare of the University of Cape Town Shipping Law Unit kindled my interest in marine insurance law. In Germanic terms, I might well call him my academic father. My partner, Anna Busch, is in a certain sense the *sine qua non* of this academic adventure, which started out simply as an adventure. Her family, the Buschens of Berlin, became my substitude family during my research in Germany. Then, of course, there is my family who had to put up with my absensce and shortly thereafter with the loss of our anchorman. They kept on supporting me, regardless. To all these people I am most obliged.

And, to my dad, who now is amongst the very stars he told his children to reach for, this book is dedicated.

Contents

From Good Faith to Utmost Good Faith in Marine Insurance

1. Introduction *13*

2. The History of Good Faith in Marine Insurance *17*

2.1 Introduction to *Bona Fides* **17**

2.1.1 Of contracts *stricti iuris* and *bonae fidei* 17

2.1.2 *Bona Fides* and the aedilitian remedies 20

2.1.3 The role of *bona fides* in the writings of the medieval and natural lawyers 24

2.1.4 *Bona Fides* in England 31

2.2 History of the Marine Insurance Contract **33**

2.2.1 Of travelling money and premiums 33

2.2.2 Early codifications and treatise 38

2.2.3 Early classification of marine insurance contracts 39

2.3 The History of Good Faith in Marine Insurance Law **45**

2.3.1 *Stricti iuris* or *bonae fidei* 46

2.3.2 Duties flowing from *bona fides* 50

2.3.3 Extent of the duties to disclose and not to misrepresent 55

2.3.4 Excursus: Insurance on *good or bad news* 56

2.3.5 Remedies 64

3. Good Faith and the Marine Insurance Contract on the Continent *69*

3.1 Disclosure and Misrepresentation on the Continent **73**

3.2 Post-Contractual Duty of Good Faith **78**

4. The History of the Principle of "Utmost Good Faith" in Marine Insurance *83*

4.1 INTRODUCTION 83

4.2 CALLING A SPADE A SHOVEL? 85

4.3 A METAMORPHOSES OF PRINCIPLE 89

4.3.1 Signs of Good Faith in Early English Contract Law 89

4.3.2 The Law Merchant and the English Court of Admiralty 91

4.3.3 Lord Mansfield and the remains of *Carter v Boehm* 96

4.3.4 Misrepresentation 110

4.3.5 Remedies 112

4.3.6. Toward codification 114

5. THE MODERN PRINCIPLE OF "UTMOST GOOD FAITH" 117

5.1 THE PRINCIPLE OF "UTMOST GOOD FAITH" 117

5.2 IMPLIED TERM OR A DUTY ARISING EX LEGE 125

5.2.1 Fraud 126

5.2.2 Misrepresentation 127

5.2.3 Non-Disclosure 128

5.3 NON-DISCLOSURE 135

5.4 MISREPRESENTATION 141

5.5 MATERIALITY OF FACT AND INDUCEMENT 147

5.5.1 Materiality 147

Materiality – the *prudent underwriter* and the *reasonable man* 147

Materiality – the degree of knowledge 151

Types of material facts 159

Fraud and Materiality 160

5.5.2 Inducement 163

5.6 EFFECT OF BREACH OF THE DUTY OF UTMOST GOOD FAITH 171

5.6.1 Remedy of the Insurer 171

5.6.2 Remedy of the Assured 175

5.7 TIME OF THE DUTY OF UTMOST GOOD FAITH **179**

5.7.1 Variation of the Insurance Contract 183

Materiality and inducement 187

Remedy 190

5.7.2 The Claims Context 193

The fraudulent claims rule 194

The Litsion Pride and the application of section 17 199

Materiality and Inducement in the claims context 204

Remedy 209

6. CONCLUSION: IN THE MATTER BETWEEN GOOD FAITH AND "UTMOST GOOD FAITH" ***215***

7. BIBLIOGRAPHY ***223***

7.1 ESSAYS **223**

7.2 LITERATURE **227**

7.3 DICTIONARIES **233**

7.4 TABLE OF CASES **235**

1. INTRODUCTION

That the wolf was, in fact, not her grandmother was not all that apparent to Little Red Riding Hood. Wearing the old lady's glasses and nightgown with the blanket pulled up to under his chin, the wolf fooled Little Red Riding Hood. Whom she believed to be her grandmother with improved senses of seeing and hearing, turned out only to be the wolf, who boasted bigger eyes and ears than her grandmother.

In the field of marine insurance law, maritime lawyers have been confronted with a similar dilemma in relation to the civilian principle of good faith, and the problematic common law principle of utmost good faith as entrenched in section 17 of the English Marine Insurance Act of 1906. This work asks the question whether utmost good faith is in fact an enhanced grandmother, or whether it is only a peculiar legal principle clothed in *Justitia*'s robe *bonae fidei.*

According to *Hansell*, all contracts are subject to good faith, since the law cannot support fraud.[1] Although there do exist individual cases[2] in which it exhibits an element of good faith, English contract law does not require contractual duties to be performed in accordance with an overriding and general positive duty of good faith.[3] Though under English law there is neither room for dealings in bad faith, nor for fraud, as *Hansell* suggests, it remains hesitant about the implication of positive duties other than that contained in the contract.[4] In a limited class of contracts which includes insurance, partnership and fiduciary relationships, the

---

[1] HANSELL, D.S.: **Introduction to Insurance** p. 175.

[2] POWELL: *Good Faith in Contracts: An Inaugural Lecture delivered at University College London* pp. 10-12, where the author mentions the following examples: (1) the use of the standard of the ordinary man as a general rule in the interpretation of the express words of a contract, or (2) to fill gaps in the express terms, (3) the remedies for misrepresentation, mistake duress and undue influence, (4) the doctrine of part performance in terms of which a party to a contract can ask the court for specific performance of his contract even where he can produce only oral evidence of a contract which is required to be in writing, (5) the equitable doctrine that a party to a contract cannot go back on a promise which was intended to be binding and to be acted upon, and had in fact been acted upon, despite the general rule that a promise cannot be enforced unless it is under seal or consideration has been given for it, (6) the discretion of the court to refuse an action for specific performance where the plaintiff's conduct was inequitable, (7) in contracts *uberrimae fidei* where one party alone knows fully all the material facts which would affect the other party's decision to contract, (8) in certain contracts where the parties are in a fiduciary position, e.g. partnership and suretyship.

[3] BAATZ: *Utmost Good Faith in Marine Insurance Contracts* **Marine Insurance at the Turn of the Millennium** Vol. 1, p. 15; POWELL: *op. cit.*, *p.* 112.

[4] McKENDRICK, Ewan: *Good faith, A Matter of Principle?* **Good Faith in Contract and Property** p. 39; RHIDIAN THOMAS, D. (editor): **The Modern Law of Marine Insurance** p. 32, who goes even further, stating that the fundamental elements of the concept of good faith "stands in opposition to the philosophical outlook underpinning the main stream of the common law tradition." Also see LOWRY and RAWLINGS: *Insurers, Claims and the Boundaries of Good Faith* (2005) 68(1) M.L.R. 82, at pp. 83-84.

parties are required to act in what is called the "utmost good faith". Such contracts have also been called contracts of the utmost good faith, or contracts *uberrimae fidei*.[5]

The principle of utmost good faith is established as a fundamental tenet of marine insurance contracts[6] in English law.[7] Since a right of avoidance or rescission for material misrepresentation inducing a contract is part of the general law of contract, the distinctive feature and practical implication of a contract being of the utmost good faith is that the contractual parties are obliged to disclose all material facts that might induce the making of the contract.[8] The general position in English contract law is that only a misstatement of – and not a mere failure to disclose – a material fact by one contractual party, through which his counterpart is induced to conclude the contract, entitles the latter to rescind the contract.[9] Thus, Lord Atkin stated in *Bell v Lever Brothers Ltd*[10] that "[o]rdinarily the failure to disclose a material fact which might influence the mind of a prudent contractor does not give the right to avoid the contract."[11] This is so since in English law contracting parties adhere to the principle applicable to most commercial contracts, namely *caveat emptor*[12], i.e. the contracting parties will try to negotiate at arms length. Contracts of the utmost good faith, requiring the duty to disclose all material facts, detract from this general principle: "a description of a contract as being *uberrimae fidei* primarily connotes that it is one where there is a duty of disclosure, to which *caveat emptor* does not apply."[13] It is often said that these contracts require a "higher standard of good faith"[14] between the parties and that the contract may therefore be rescinded for failure to observe the requirement.[15] The logic appears, therefore, at least in modern English law, to be that since marine insurance contracts are of the utmost good faith, the assured in concluding a contract for insurance, is obliged to disclose facts which in general, as contracts are concluded at arm's length in English law, need not be disclosed to the insurer. But then, on the high authority of Lord Scrutton, it has also been held that as regards insurance contract, the assured is required to make a full disclosure of material circumstances, and that this is

[5] SOYER: *The Star Sea – a lode star?* [2001] LMCLQ 428, at p. 428.

[6] This is, of course, also the case in relation to non-marine insurance contracts in English law.

[7] RHIDIAN THOMAS, D. (editor): op. cit., p. 26; also see PARK, Semin: **The Duty of Disclosure in Insurance Contract Law** p. 8, where he cites the *dictum* of Kennedy L.J. in *London General Omnibus Co. Ltd.. v Holloway* [1912] 2 K.B. 72, at pp. 85-86: "No class of case occurs, to my mind, in which our law regards mere non-disclosure as a ground for invalidating the contract, except in the case of insurance. That is an exception which the law has widely made in deference to the plain exigencies of this particular and most important class of transaction".

[8] GILMAN: **Arnould's Law of Marine Insurance and Average** Vol. III, par. 579J.

[9] COLINVAUX, R.: **The Law of Insurance** p. 92; PARK, Semin: op. cit., p. 8.

[10] [1932] A.C 161.

[11] Ibid., at p. 227.

[12] Directly translated into English, the maxim reads: "Let the buyer be aware."

[13] GILMAN: op. cit., Vol. III, par. 579F.

[14] COLINVAUX, R.: op. cit., p. 92.

[15] PARK, Semin: op. cit., p. 8.

expressed by saying insurance is "*uberrimae fidei*".[16] Clearly, this amounts to a *petitio principii*, as *De Smet* has pointed out.[17]

The ground for the application of this principle in marine insurance has very often been reduced to the disparity between the various degrees of knowledge of the parties in relation to the risk to be insured against,[18] e.g. Lord Justice Scrutton's explanation of the legal position in *Greenhill v Federal Ins. Co.*[19]:

> "Insurance is a contract of the utmost good faith... the underwriter knows nothing of the particular circumstances of the voyage to be insured. The assured knows a great deal, and it is the duty of the assured to inform the underwriter of everything that he is not taken as knowing, so that the contract may be entered into on an equal footing."[20]

Good faith, at least as Lord Mansfield understood the principle to operate in the context of an insurance contract, was designed to bring equality into a bargain, which depended to a great extent on an accurate estimation of the risk to be insured.[21] In the next chapter, the historical role of the principle of good faith in marine insurance contracts will be described, at least as it is manifested in the works of the civilians. The first part of that chapter attempts to delineate the origins of good faith and *bona fides* in Roman and civilian law, and thereafter the development of the marine insurance contract is discussed. The principle of good faith has of course more than one application, and more than one meaning. One of these applications, in particular, is relevant to insurance law, namely "the use of good faith as a restraint upon self interest in deference to the interest of others".[22] The second part introduces the principle of *bona fides* to the marine insurance contract. The early treatise on commercial law and marine insurance law are scrutinised for traces of the principle in order to find out what its function was and how it operated in the context of marine insurance.

In the third chapter, this effect of the principle of good faith in marine insurance on the continent is demonstrated by a short excursus into the German and French laws of marine insurance.

In the fourth chapter, we travel across the English Channel to have a closer look at the principle of "utmost good faith" in English marine insurance law. The use of the principle of the "utmost good faith" in the law of marine insurance is to be contrasted with the general position of English law which favours the freedom to

---

[16] *Rozanes v Bowen* (1928) 32 Ll.L.R. 98 at p. 102; cf. p. 83 *infra* for the full quotation.
[17] Cf. p. 70 *infra*.
[18] PARK, Semin: op. cit., p. 10.
[19] [1927] 1 K.B. 65.
[20] Ibid., at p. 76.
[21] GILMAN: op. cit., Vol. III, par. 579J.
[22] FRIEDMANN, Daniel: *The Transformation of "Good Faith" in Insurance Law* **Good Faith in Contract, Concept and Context** p. 312.

contract and the idea of *caveat emptor* instead of the concept of good faith.[23] Under the *caveat emptor* rule, the person who is about to conclude a contract is usually free from any obligation to disclose information which might be disadvantageous to himself. The position in insurance law is different since the insured (and the insurer to some extent) is required to disclose material facts "which in order to obtain the best bargain it is in his interest to avoid pointing out".[24] Fletcher-Moulton L.J. described this duty of disclosure in *Joel v Law Union and Crown Insurance*[25] as a duty between the parties "to help each other come to a right conclusion, and not to hold each other at arm's length in defence of their conflicting interests". The duty of disclosure has been said to be the "cornerstone of the concept of good faith in insurance law".[26]

In the concluding chapter, the development of the concept of utmost good faith is put into context. It will be suggested that although the concept of utmost good faith in English marine insurance law initially was not much more than a signifier of a particular kind of contract to which the duty of disclosure applied, and subsequently did not have much to do with the concept of good faith, there is a continuing process in English law to redefine utmost good faith. This is facilitated by a new appreciation of old English authority on this point, as well as a willingness to give content to the concept of utmost good faith outside the limitations of section 17 of the Marine Insurance Act of 1906. However, before engaging in a discussion of this controversial notion as it stands today, it needs to be placed in its historical context.

---

[23] FRIEDMANN, Daniel: op. cit., p. 311.
[24] Ibid., p. 312
[25] [1908] 2 K.B. 863 (C.A.).
[26] FRIEDMANN, Daniel: op. cit., p. 312.

2. THE HISTORY OF GOOD FAITH IN MARINE INSURANCE

2.1 INTRODUCTION TO *BONA FIDES*

2.1.1 Of contracts *stricti iuris* and *bonae fidei*

The origins of the concept of good faith can be traced back to Roman law, which first recognised that a promise could create an obligation in law.[27] Roman contract law stood on two pillars, namely the *stipulatio*, which was governed by the *iudicium stricti iuris*[28], and the consensual contract. In relation to the former, the concept of *bona fides* found its way into the procedural *formula*[29] by way of a standard clause, inserted on request of the defendant.[30] This clause, the *exceptio doli*, read as follows:

> "*si in ea re nihil dolo malo A' A' factum sit neque fiat*"[31]

The phrase *factum sit* related generally to fraud before institution of the action, against which the *exception* was aimed, and in particular to fraudulent behaviour during the conclusion of the contract.[32] The inclusion of the phrase *neque fiat* in the *formula* instructed the judge to turn the search for *dolus* away from the personal conduct, or rather *mis*conduct, of the litigants to focus on the question whether equity and justice would be served if the action were to be allowed. By the phrase *neque fiat*, the judge was given an equitable discretion that enabled him to come to a decision that would be fair and reasonable.[33]

The other cornerstone of Roman contract law, the consensual contract, evolved as a result of the particular commercial expectations of the time.[34] In contrast to the *stipulatio* being *stricti iuris*, i.e. based on relationships of strict legal engagement,[35] "promissory obligations were defined by assumptions of good faith performance."[36] In these consensual contracts, the specific device of *exceptio doli* was not necessary in order to ensure the proper exercise of contractual rights. The reason was that the judge had the discretion to take into account all the circumstances and the relationship of the parties in terms of *bona fides* in any

[27] NEHF, James: *Bad Faith Breach of Contract in Consumer Transactions* **Good Faith in Contract, Concept and Context** p. 117.
[28] I.e. claims which have to be adjudicated upon according to strict law.
[29] The *formula* defined the issue which the judge was to adjudicate.
[30] WHITTAKER and ZIMMERMANN: "Good faith in European Contract Law: Surveying the Legal Landscape" **Good Faith in European Contract Law** p. 16.
[31] "if in this matter nothing has been done, or is being done, in bad faith by the plaintiff".
[32] ZIMMERMANN: "*Good Faith and Equity*" in **Southern Cross** p. 218.
[33] WHITTAKER and ZIMMERMANN: op. cit., p. 16.
[34] NEHF, James: op. cit., p. 117.
[35] AMOS, S.: **The History and Principles of the Civil Law of Rome** p. 55.
[36] NEHF, James: op. cit., p. 117.

event[37], as the *formula* provided that the defendant be condemned to whatever he should give to, or do for the plaintiff in good faith[38] –

> "*Quod A° A° N^m N^m hominem Stichum emit (vendidit), quidquid ob eam rem N^m N^m A° A° dare facere oportet ex fide bona, eius index N^m N^m A° A condemnato, si non paret, absolvito*"[39]
> (Emphasis added)

Accordingly, the action would fail for lack of good faith.[40] The content of the *exceptio doli* was thus enveloped in the requirement of *bona fides*. Since these particular claims were to be adjudicated in terms of the requirements of good faith, it became known by the phrase *iudicia bonae fidei*.[41] In these actions, the judge not only measured the performance of the contract in terms of good faith, but also had to take into consideration all the arrangements between the plaintiff and defendant in assessing whether the defendant should be ordered to perform.[42] The phrase *oportere ex fide bona* invited the judge to give effect, in accordance with good faith, to the provisions upon which the parties agreed that related to, supported and detailed the main contract, irrespective of whether they were favourable to the plaintiff or to the defendant.[43]

In summary, in the *iudicia stricti iuris*, the judge only had to decide whether the claim was in conformity with the *formula* prescribed by the *Praetor*, whereas in *iudicia bonae fidei*, the judge had more authority to go into the merits of the case and had the discretion to decide whether or not the contract had been performed as promised.[44] It was the duty of the judge in both these actions to let himself be guided by justice and equity, rather than by strict legal distinctions.[45]

The *bonae fidei iudicia* were particularly important in the sanctioning of fraudulent behaviour.[46] *Cicero* argued that the requirement of *bona fides* was the conceptual antithesis of fraudulent behaviour, giving the principle a clear ethical character.[47]

---

[37] AMOS, S.: op. cit., p. 56.
[38] WHITTAKER and ZIMMERMANN: op. cit., p. 16; ZIMMERMANN: **The Law of Obligations** p. 509 .
[39] ZIMMERMANN: **The Law of Obligations** p. 277, quoting the *formula* for the *actio empti* (action of the purchaser against the seller) and *actio venditi* (action of the seller against the purchaser) for the sale of the slave Stichus.
[40] ZIMMERMANN: "*Good Faith and Equity*" in **Southern Cross** p. 230.
[41] WHITTAKER and ZIMMERMANN: op. cit., p. 17.
[42] In an *actio stricti iuris*, the judge were bound by the formula; thus if the defendant did not insure that his *excptiones* (defences) were included in the formula, the judge would not take notice thereof during the trial.
[43] ZIMMERMANN: **The Law of Obligations** p. 509.
[44] EMéRIGON: **Treatise of Insurances** p. 15; NEHF, James: op. cit., p. 117.
[45] Translation in EMéRIGON: **Treatise** pp. 15-16.
[46] SCHERMAIER: *Bona Fides in Roman Contract Law* **Good Faith in European Contract Law** p. 86.
[47] Ibid., pp. 86- 87.

An act of *dolus*, whether arising during formation of the contract or by instituting the action, would have led to judgement against the guilty party. The action for *dolus in contrahendo* was also available where the contract was invalid due to initial impossibility of performance. Furthermore, as has been noted above, the judge would not give relief to a fraudulent plaintiff, i.e. the judge would keep an eye on whether the claim or the bringing of the action had been based on *dolus*.[48] In those instances, which fell outside the sphere of *bonae fidei iudicia*, the Roman jurists employed "equivalent notions like *aequitas* or *bonum et aequum*".[49] *Pomponius*, for instance, thought that, since the aedilitian actions were not *bonae fidei iudicia*, it would be *aequum*, i.e. in accordance with equity, to allow the seller's exception and dismiss the action where the buyer knew of a defect.[50] But it is in the writings of *Cicero* that the ethical character of *bona fides* and its function in deterring fraud are best explained. Certainly the most famous of *Cicero*'s case studies, in which he was concerned with honesty and fairness in performing a contract,[51] is the following: a *vir bonus* brought a large shipment of grain from Alexandria to Rhodes, which had been struck by famine, as a result of which provisions were selling at very high prices there. In these circumstances, *Cicero* was interested to know whether, if this man had known that several other grain merchants had set sail from Alexandria and if he had sighted vessels heading for Rhodes with grain on board, "*dicturusne sit id Rhodiis an silentio suum quam plurimo venditurus?*"[52], i.e. he, being a virtuous and upright man, would tell the Rhodians, or whether he might keep silent in order to sell his own stock at the highest price possible.[53] In this case, *Cicero* was concerned with the unequal relationship between seller and buyer in so far as the latter enjoyed an informational advantage over his counterpart, and the difficult problem of how a virtuous and upright man would think in considering whether it would be immoral to conceal the facts from the Rhodians.[54] Indeed, *Cicero* thought that the Rhodians should be informed of the approaching relief,[55] his reason being "*[n]eque enim id est celare, quicquid reticeas, sed cum, quod tu scias, id ignorare emolumenti tui causa veils eos, quorum intersit id scire.*"[56] His portrayal of the merchant as a *bonus vir*, i.e. a virtuous and upright man, as well as the fact that he considered this case as

[48] Ibid., pp. 86-87.

[49] Ibid., p. 87; Indeed, equity (*aequus*) and *bona fides* appear to have been two sides of the same coin: see e.g. Dig. 16, 3, 31, where it is stated that good faith, which is required in contracts, requires the highest measure of equity (*Bona fides quae in contractibus exigitur aequitatem summam desiderat*).

[50] Dig. 21, 1, 48, 4; SCHERMAIER: op. cit., p. 87.

[51] SCHERMAIER: op. cit., p. 91.

[52] CICERO: ***De Officiis*** 3, XII ff.

[53] SCHERMAIER: op. cit., p. 91.

[54] *Cicero* was not concerned with the fairness of the rise in price as a result of a high demand and low supply: see CICERO: ***De Officiis*** 3, XII – 50; also SCHERMAIER: op. cit., p. 91.

[55] CICERO: ***De Officiis*** 3, XIII – 57; SCHERMAIER: op. cit., p. 92.

[56] CICERO: ***De Officiis*** 3, XIII – 57; see footnote 572 *infra*.

equivalent to not disclosing defects in an object of sale[57], is a reflection of his perception of the function of *bona fides* to limit the extent to which a party to a contract may take advantage of such an informational advantage.[58] It was this function of good faith which facilitated the reception of the aedilitian actions into the civil law and the liability i.a. for latent defects in the law of sale.

2.1.2 *Bona Fides* and the aedilitian remedies

As we have seen above, fraud or deceit militated against the implied condition of *bona fides*, upon which all consensual contracts, including the contract of sale, or *emptio et venditio*, were founded by reason of the *actiones bonae fidei*.[59] The *actio empti* was available at those instances "where the vendor had acted in such a way that not to make him liable would have seemed in conflict with good faith"[60] i.e. where he acted fraudulently. This accords with the rule that *dolus "semper abesse oportet in iudicia empti, quod bonae fidei sit."*[61] Not only was the seller liable for making express misrepresentations, but also for fraudulently concealing a latent defect:[62] "*Dolum malum a se abesse praestare venditor debet, qui non tantum in eo est qui fallendi causa obscure loquitur, sed etiam qui insidiose obscure dissimulat*".[63] Accordingly, the *actio empti* was available to the purchaser where the vendor expressly assured the purchaser during the conclusion of the contract that the object of the sale was free of defects, or possessed certain qualities, as well as in the case where the vendor fraudulently, i.e. *dolo malo*, failed to disclose a defect known to him.[64] Moreover, a vendor was deemed to have acted fraudulently if he had made untrue statements regarding the subject-matter of the sale in "reckless ignorance as to their truth or falsehood."[65] Also, where the circumstances of the sale were such that the buyer had no other possibility to inform himself as to the subject-matter of the sale, but to rely upon the statements of the vendor, the vendor was bound to inform him fully of all the circumstances relating to the subject-matter within his knowledge.[66] Even if the vendor, in such a case, innocently failed to disclose information material to the sale,

[57] Apart from the Alexandrian grain merchant, *Cicero* also uses the example of the owner of a house who knows exclusively of certain defects in his home, and, nevertheless, sells the house without informing the buyer thereof for a price far higher than he would have been able to get otherwise; see CICERO: *De Officiis* 3, XIII.
[58] SCHERMAIER: op. cit., p. 91.
[59] MOYLE: **The Contract of Sale** pp. 57-58.
[60] ZIMMERMANN: **The Law of Obligations** pp. 308-30.
[61] Dig. 19. 1. 6. 9.: fraud must always be absent in the action on sale where regard is had to good faith.
[62] MOYLE: op. cit., pp. 58-59.
[63] Dig. 18. 1. 43. 2.: Translation in MACKINTOSH: **The Roman Law of Sale** p. 93: "The seller must always warrant his innocence of fraud – a term which includes not only ambiguous statements intended to mislead, but also studied and equivocal concealment."
[64] SCHERMAIER: op. cit., pp. 86-87; ZIMMERMANN: **The Law of Obligations** pp. 309.
[65] MOYLE: op. cit., p. 59.
[66] Ibid., p. 60.

the buyer would have similar rights against the vendor as in the case where the vendor was guilty of an absolutely fraudulent misrepresentation:[67]

> "*Quid tamen si ignoravit quidem [servum] furem esse, adseveravait autem bonae frugi et fidum et caro vendidit? videamus an ex empto teneatur. et putem teneri. Atqui ignoravit: sed non debuit facile quae ignorabat adseverare ... non debuit facilis esse ad temerariam indicationem.*"[68]

The effect of these different forms of fraud varied with the particular circumstances of the case.[69] Fraud alone was never enough to vitiate the contract, except if it went to the root of the contract, i.e. if the mistake in the mind of one of the contracting parties as a result of the misrepresentation or failure to disclose had been essential or fundamental in his decision to contract and therefore excluded consent: "fraud in itself [did] not exclude consent, but merely [supplied] an erroneous motive for entering into the contract."[70] Thus, if the party against whom the fraud had been committed, would not have made the contract had he known the truth, he would be entitled to avoid the contract. He could do so by merely resisting the action if the other party sued him, or he could institute the *actio ex empto* for restitution of the goods, or *ex vendito* for restitution of the money, whichever the case may be.[71] This was the position under Civil Law.[72]

However, the Civil Law did not fulfil all the needs of merchants doing business in the Roman markets, particularly the need for a remedy where losses were suffered as a result of latent defects in slaves and beasts of burden, which were impossible to detect until some time after the sale.[73] As a result, the *Aediles*, i.e. the magistrates in charge of the Roman markets, created certain remedies by edict, the so-called aedilitian remedies, to deal with defects in slaves and livestock sold on these markets.[74] By reason of these aedilitian remedies, namely the *actio redhibitoria*[75] and

---

[67] Ibid.

[68] Dig. 19. 1. 13. 3.; Translation in MACKINTOSH: op. cit., p. 171: "But what if the seller, without knowing that the slave was a thief, certifies him as well behaved and honest, and sells him dear? Can he be reached by the action on purchase? I am inclined to think he can. But it may be urged, he did not know; the answer is, he should not lightly have asserted what he did not know. ...[He] should not have been so ready to make rash assertions."

[69] MOYLE: op. cit., p. 61.

[70] Ibid.

[71] Ibid., citing and quoting Dig. 19. 1. 11. 5.: "*Si quis virginem se emere putasset, cum mulier venisset, et sciens errare eum venditor passus sit, redhibitionem quidem ex hac causa non esse, verum tamen ex empto competere actionem ad resolvendam emptionem, et pretio restituo mulier reddatur.*" (Translation in MACKINTOSH: op. cit., p. 159: "If one believed he was buying a virgin, whereas the woman on sale was a mother, and the seller knowing his mistake lets him carry out the transaction, though it does not ground the action for return, yet an action on purchase is competent to have the sale cancelled, the woman taken back, and the price restored.")

[72] MOYLE: op. cit., p. 189.

[73] Ibid., p. 192.

[74] WHITTAKER and ZIMMERMANN: op. cit., p. 17; also MOYLE: op. cit., 192-194.

the *actio quanti minoris*[76], the vendor was bound to inform the purchaser of any flaws in the slave or animal, whether he was aware of them or not.[77] The defect should have been in existence at the time when the contract was made.[78] The vendor was, therefore, not liable for defects that arose after the contract had been made. That constituted a risk which the purchaser had to take.[79] The defect also had to be unknown to the purchaser.[80] Moreover, the purchaser would be presumed to be aware of the defect if circumstances existed from which the reasonable man could be expected to infer it.[81] Further to this, the defect must have been invisible, or such that if his attention were not drawn to it, he could not have perceived it.[82]

The aedilitian remedies were available where the slaves or cattle[83] that had been the object of the sale, had one of the defects referred to in the aedilitian edict and that defect had not been disclosed by the vendor, or where the slaves or cattle did not

---

[75] Action for redhibition.

[76] Action for reduction of the price.

[77] MOYLE: op. cit., p. 193.

[78] Dig. 21. 1. 54.: "*Actioni redhibitoriae non est locus, si mancipium bonis condicionibus emptum fugerit, quod ante non fugerat.*" (There is no room for an action of redhibition, if a slave, who had been bought on good conditions and who had never fled before, took flight.); MOYLE: op. cit., p. 197; POTHIER: ***Traité du Contrat de Vente*** § 212.

[79] MOYLE: op. cit., p. 197.

[80] Ibid., p. 197; POTHIER: ***Traité du Contrat de Vente*** § 210; CICERO: *De Off.* 3, XVI, where *Cicero* recites the dispute between M. Marius Gratidianus and C. Sergio Orata. The former resold to the latter a house subject to an encumbrance, of which he, i.e. C. Sergio Orata, necessarily knew. C. Sergio Orata's action, based on the letter of the law that "*quod vitii venditor non dixisset sciens, id oportere praestari*", i.e. a seller has to make good the defect which he, though knowing of it, did not disclose, failed, for, it being in accordance with equity, no disclosure was needed where the buyer had been aware of the defect; Dig. 21. 1. 48. 4.: "*In aedilicíis actionibus exceptionem opponi aequum est, si emptor sciret de fuga aut vinculis aut ceteris rebus similibus, ut venditor absolvatur.*" (In the aedilitian actions it is in accordance with equity to bring an exception, if the buyer had knowledge of [a slave's earlier] flight or imprisonment or other similar circumstances, with the consequence that the action against the seller will not be allowed.)

[81] MOYLE: op. cit., p. 197; Dig. 21. 1. 48. 4.: "*Ei, qui servum vinctum vendiderit, aedilicium edictum remitti aequum est: multo enim amplius est id facere, quam pronuntiare, in vinculis fuisse.*" (It is in accordance with equity not to apply the aedilitian edict on him who sold a slave in chains: this act speaks much louder than a mere announcement that the slave had been in jail.)

[82] MOYLE: op. cit., p. 198, citing and quoting Dig. 18. 1. 15. 1.: "*Ignorantia emptori prodest, quae non in supinum hominem cadit*"; (Translation in MACKINTOSH: op. cit., p. 37: "It is only such ignorance as does not argue carelessness that will avail the purchaser.") Dig. 21. 1. 1. 6: "*Si intellegatur vitium morbusve mancipii (ut plerumque signis quibusdam solent demonstrare vitia), potest dici edictum cessare: hoc enim tantum intuendum est, ne emptor decipiatur.*" (If a defect or illness is visible on the slave (defects are mostly revealed through certain symptoms) one may say that the Edict is not applicable: one should only take care that the buyer is not misled.); Dig. 21. 1. 14. 10: "*...ad eos enim morbos vitiaque pertinere edictum aedilium probandum est, quae quis ignoravit vel ignorare potuit.*" (...the correct approach is that the Aedilian Edict applies to diceases and defects of which one does not know, or of which could not know.)

[83] The aedilitian remedies were at first only applicable to the sale of slaves and cattle on the marketplace.

possess a quality promised by the vendor, or where the vendor acted fraudulently.[84] The purchaser could rescind the contract or claim a return in the purchase price proportionate to the defects discovered by respectively instituting the *actio redhibitoria* or the *actio quanti minoris* within a fixed period after the sale was concluded.[85] The remedy envisaged by the *actio redhibitoria* entailed not only the return of the object of sale against repayment of the purchase price, but both parties had to be restored to the same position as if the sale had not been concluded. The vendor could be liable against the purchaser e.g. where the slave caused damage to his property, or the purchaser against the vendor where he acquired an inheritance through the slave. With the remedy of the *actio quanti minoris*, the purchaser could claim from the vendor the difference between what the object of sale was really worth, and what it would have been worth had it been free of defects or possessed the promised qualities. This led to a return of part of the purchase price.[86] The aedilitian remedies were available against an innocent vendor, whereas the so-called *vendor sciens* was liable for consequential loss also: there were even cases in which an assurance was imputed and the seller consequently held liable despite his ignorance of the defect.[87]

The aedilitian remedies were constantly extended and in the time of Labeo they were applicable to the sales of all things whatsoever,[88] and later even engrafted upon other transactions closely analogous to sale.[89] The reason for the reception of the aedilitian remedies into the *ius civile* seems to be twofold: Roman economic life became more complex and the simple rules of *caveat emptor* marking the civil law were not sufficient to deal with this growth.[90] It became customary for the parties to a contract of sale to protect themselves by including an express warranty to contracts of sale through stipulation, even outside the market place.[91] This warranty soon was promoted from the status of a mere *accidentalia*, to part of the *naturalia* of the contract.[92] However, this system remained inconvenient and cumbersome in the everyday conduct of commerce in the Roman market places.[93] Secondly, the aedilitian remedies provided a reasonably satisfactory set of model rules to accommodate the need for extended protection of the purchaser:

---

[84] ZIMMERMANN: **The Law of Obligations** pp. 317-318.
[85] MOYLE: op. cit., pp. 193-194.
[86] ZIMMERMANN: **The Law of Obligations** pp. 317-318.
[87] SCHERMAIER: op. cit., pp. 86-87.
[88] MOYLE: op. cit., p. 194, citing and quoting Dig. 21. 1. 1. pr.: "*Labeo scribit edictum aedilium curulium de venditionibus rerum esse, tam earum, quae soli sint, quam earum, quae mobiles aut se moventes.*" (Labeo writes that the aedilitian edict in respect of the sale of things is relevant to immovable things, as well as movable things and things moving out of their on accord.)
[89] MOYLE: op. cit., p. 195.
[90] Ibid., p. 191; ZIMMERMANN: **The Law of Obligations** p. 321.
[91] MOYLE: op. cit., p. 192; ZIMMERMANN: **The Law of Obligations** p. 321.
[92] ZIMMERMANN: **The Law of Obligations** p. 321.
[93] MOYLE: op. cit., p. 192.

> "These rules were well balanced, particularly in so far as they imposed an 'objective' liability on the vendor (that is, he was liable irrespective of whether he was at fault or whether he had made special assertions), but they did not allow the purchaser to claim his full damages (*quod interest*)... All in all, then, warranty for latent defects was taken to be implicit in the contract of sale, even in cases where the seller had not known about the defects himself. This warranty, implied by law, was based on a generalization of the aedilitian remedies and was effected by means of a more refined interpretation of what was owed, in good faith, under the *actio empti*."[94]

The reception of the aedilitian remedies into the *ius civile* was facilitated by the principle of ***bona fides***, which has been very appropriately described as one of the most fertile agents in the development of Roman contract law.[95] The result was that the harsh rules relating to the principle of *caveat emptor* were largely abandoned,[96] in favour of the aedilitian rules, which were read into the *oportere ex fide bona* clause of the *actio emptio et venditio*.[97] Thus, by receiving the aedilitian rules into the *ius civile*, a system of "graduated liability" [98] was established where no relief had been previously available.[99]

Apart from the liability for latent defects entering the *ius civile* on the back of the *bona fides* principle, the *iudicia bonae fidei* also led to other institutions becoming part of the *ius civile* such as enabling the judge to consider error (mistake) and *metus* (duress) in deciding whether or not to allow an *actio empti* or *venditi*.[100]

2.1.3 The role of *bona fides* in the writings of the medieval and natural lawyers

The modern theory of contract grew from the recognition by Roman lawyers that a promise can create an obligation in law[101] and the subsequent replacement of the Roman *numerus clausus* of contracts concluded *nudo consensu* with the idea that all informal agreements are binding.[102] During the Middle Ages the stipulation, being the cornerstone of actional law, i.e. law based on actions relating to the *numerus clausus* of Roman contracts, faded into insignificance.[103] Accordingly, it was the

---

[94] ZIMMERMANN: **The Law of Obligations** p. 321; see also ZIMMERMANN: "*Good Faith and Equity*" in **Southern Cross** pp. 248-249.

[95] WHITTAKER and ZIMMERMANN: op. cit., p. 17; ZIMMERMANN: **The Law of Obligations** p. 320.

[96] WHITTAKER and ZIMMERMANN: op. cit., p. 17.

[97] ZIMMERMANN: **The Law of Obligations** p. 321; on the phrase *oportere ex fide bona*, cf. p. 18 *supra*.

[98] Ibid., where the author cites *Iulianus*, who stressed the difference between the vendor sciens and the vendor ignorans, pointing out that the former was liable for *omnia detrimenta, quae ex ea emptione emptor traxerit*, whereas the latter was liable only for *quanti minoris*.

[99] Ibid., p. 321.

[100] WHITTAKER and ZIMMERMANN: op. cit., p. 17.

[101] NEHF, James: op. cit., p. 117.

[102] ZIMMERMANN: "*Good Faith and Equity*" in **Southern Cross** p. 219.

[103] Ibid., pp. 219 and 546.

consensual contracts of Roman law, based on *bona fides*, which gave birth to the modern theory of contract.[104] Consequently, all contracts were to be considered *bonae fidei*, leading *Cornelis Willem Decker*, an advocate in Amsterdam in the late eighteenth century, to state that

> "...we may also conveniently dispense with the division of contracts into *stricti juris* and *bonae fidei*... for according to our customs all contracts are considered to be *bonae fidei*, which necessarily follows, if we hold that with us all contracts are constituted by consent."[105]

During the tenth and eleventh centuries, the jurisprudence on the European continent was greatly influenced by ecclesiastical law.[106] In consequence of pledging their faith to the church, parties to a contract were expected to honour their contractual obligations.[107] Later, during this period, promissors started to circumvent the ecclesiasts and pledged their faith directly to their contractual counterparts. A contractual promise was, as a consequence, only regarded as of value upon the willingness of the promissor to sacrifice his faith at the instance of a breach on his part.[108] The concept of good faith in canon law was therefore intimately connected with the "...moral underpinnings of promissory obligation".[109]

The medieval jurists who wrote about Roman and Canon law employed the term *bona fides* in three types of conduct which were to be expected from contracting parties: firstly, the importance of keeping one's word; secondly, that neither party should be allowed to obtain an unfair advantage above the other by misleading him or driving a hard bargain; and, thirdly, that the parties should conform to the duties expected from an honest person even if these duties were not expressly undertaken.[110]

Medieval jurists based the obligation to keep one's word on "faith", "equity" and the *ius gentium*, which was binding upon all peoples.[111] One of the texts which were used to explain this obligation in terms of good faith and equity, stemmed from *Ulpianus*, who wrote about a praetorian edict:

[104] Ibid., p. 219; SCHERMAIER: op. cit., pp. 91-92.
[105] ZIMMERMANN: "*Good Faith and Equity*" in **Southern Cross** p. 220.
[106] NEHF, James: op. cit., p. 117.
[107] Ibid., p. 117.
[108] Ibid., p. 118.
[109] NEHF, James: op. cit., p. 118; also POWELL, R.: **Good Faith in Contracts** p. 8.
[110] GORDLEY: *Good Faith in the Medieval* Ius Commune **Good Faith in European Contract Law** p. 94.
[111] Ibid., p. 95.

> "*Huius edicti aequitas naturalis est, quid enim tam congruum fidei humanae, quaam ea quae inter eos placuerunt servare*"[112]

Both the civil lawyers and the canonists, relying on very general texts such as that in the previous paragraph, agreed that agreements must be kept.[113] The problem confronting the medieval jurists, however, was to reconcile this principle with the distinction in Roman contract law between contracts *consensu et re* as well as between nominate and innominate contracts.[114] Whereas the civilians never convincingly solved this problem, the Canon lawyers ignored the Roman distinctions and kept to the Biblical maxim that "God does not distinguish between mere speech and an oath."[115]

With regard to the second point, medieval jurists argued that good faith also meant that contractual parties should not be allowed to mislead or take advantage of each other, i.e. good faith required that there should be no *dolus* or deceit.[116] In this regard a distinction was drawn between "causal" and "incidental" fraud. "Causal fraud" referred to the situation where a person was led into a contract which he would not have concluded otherwise. In such a case, the "victim" of the contract was allowed to escape entirely from the contract.[117] In turn, "incidental fraud" referred to the case where a person was led to contract on less favourable terms. In this case, the "victim" could demand a reduction of the price if it be shown that the other party in fact deceived him deliberately.[118] Where the victim of "incidental fraud" could not show that the deceit was deliberate, but that the consideration was not just, he was a victim of *dolus ex re ipsa*, i.e. "a fraud that appears from the transaction itself". The medieval jurists derived the phrase "*dolus ex re ipsa*" from a Roman text suggesting that in the case of a *stipulatio*, i.e. a contract *stricti iuris*, the *exceptio doli* might find application if there were no *dolus*, but "the transaction itself had deceit within it".[119] The remedy in this instance was either a return of the object of sale, or payment of the just price.[120] However, in the case of *dolus ex re*

---

[112] Dig. 2. 14. 1.; This edict is based on natural equity, for what else can be so in conformity with human faith, than to observe that which is to be agreed between men.

[113] GORDLEY: op. cit., p. 98-99.

[114] Ibid., p. 98-99.

[115] Ibid., citing the *Decretum*, *Causa* 22, *Quaestio* 5, c. 12.

[116] Ibid., p. 100.

[117] Ibid., p. 101.

[118] GORDLEY: op. cit., p. 101.

[119] Dig. 45, 1, 36: "*Si quis, cum aliter eum convenisset obligari, aliter per machinationem obligatus est, erit quidem suptilitate iuris obstrictus, sed doli exceptione uti potest: quia enim per dolum obligatus est, competit ei exceptio. Idem est si nullus dolus intercessit stipulantis, sed res ipsa in se dolum habet: cum enim qui petat ex ea stipulatione, hoc ipso dolo facit, quod petit.*"

[120] It is argued however, that the medieval jurists were not advancing a theory for relief for an unjust price. As it was known that this type of *dolus* was not *dolus* in the ordinary sense, it merely served to acknowledge the fact that the effect of *dolus ex re ipsa* was the same as that of an intentional "incidental fraud". See GORDLEY: op. cit., p. 102.

ipsa, the medieval jurists did not propose a theory to explain why an unintentional fraud should be remedied.[121]

Turning to the final function, good faith obliged the parties to a contract to do whatever else could be expected of an honest person engaged in a particular type of transaction:[122]

> "... *nihil magis bonae fidei congruit quam id praestari, quod inter contrahentes actum est. Quod si nihil convenit, tunc ea praestabuntur quae naturaliter insunt huius iudicii potestate.*"[123]

This obligation is what modern jurists would refer to as the implied terms of the contract, i.e. the terms that are to be read into the contract in order to deal with the matters on which the parties are silent. Accordingly the parties to a contract were not only obliged to avoid deceit, but were also bound by terms which they might not even have contemplated, but which were dictated by the requirement of good faith.[124]

The medieval jurists were of the opinion that good faith was to be taken into account in all contracts, but made no attempt to formulate a clear definition of *bona fides*[125] that could assist in its application in the above-mentioned situations. It was the last great medieval lawyer, *Baldus de Ubaldis*[126], who, borrowing from *Aristotle* and *Thomas Aquinas*, clarified the concept of good faith to a great extent.[127] He offered three definitions of *bona fides*.[128] According to the definitions of *Baldus*, *bona fides* is first of all a principle of fairness in legal relations and which is of general

[121] GORDLEY: op. cit., p. 102.
[122] Ibid., p. 103.
[123] Dig. 19. 1. 11, cited and quoted by GORDLEY: op. cit., p. 102, and translated: "... nothing is more in accord with good faith than to do what was agreed by the contracting parties. If nothing was agreed, one should perform what naturally is included according to the decision of the judge."
[124] GORDLEY: op. cit., p. 103.
[125] The medieval jurists furthermore employed keywords like *natura*, *aequum* and *substantia* instead of *bona fides*. This was necessary to fit the Roman texts which they studied, into their own schema or system, for example it was said that the implied terms, in the absence of express provisions, were part of the *nature* of the contract.
[126] *Baldus* was born at Perugia in 1327, and died at Pavia in 1406. He was professor of law at Bologna, Perugia, Pisa, Florence, Padua and Pavia. His most famous pupil must certainly have been *Piere de Beaufort*, who later became *Pope Gregory* XI; see SHERMAN: **Roman Law in the Modern World** § 219.
[127] GORDLEY, op. cit., pp. 94 and 114.
[128] See HORN, Norbert: ***Aequitas in den Lehren des Baldus*** p. 163 where he cites and discusses the three definitions in *Baldus'* commentaries on the *Decretals*, at X 1. 29. 3. n. 6 and 7, namely: "(a) *voco bonam fidem id est bonam mentis qualitatem et conscientiam quae etiam in contractibus stricti iuris requiritur ut D 45. 1. 36...*; (b) *Secundo dicit(ur) bona fides id est legalitas que potissime requiritur in his qui plurimum negocianturd. Et in his non differt pactum nudum a stipulatione ut C 4. 18. 1, Nov 4. 3. 1. Unde campsores qui tenent mensam authoritate publica, non habent beneficium excussionis.*; (c) *tertio modo dicitur bona fides quedam adjectio sive qualitas contractus quae designate ius excellentiam ut Inst. 4. 6. 28.*"

application in all contracts irrespective of their nature.[129] Secondly, *Baldus* thought that *bona fides* was the equivalent of *legalitas*, which was a *sine qua non* for commercial transactions.[130] By *legalitas*, *Baldus* referred to the legality of contractual obligations.[131] Accordingly, *bona fides* in this context was a principle of contractual fidelity in legal transactions and formed the foundation of the binding nature of contracts, again, irrespective of whether a contract would be *bonae fidei* or *stricti iuris*.[132] *Baldus'* third definition concerned *bona fides* as a particular characteristic of contracts of that nature.[133] The central and critical requirement of good faith, apart from keeping one's promise and refraining from deceit, according to *Baldus*, was that no-one should be enriched at another's expense.[134] This requirement of "equality in exchange" delimited the principle of *bona fides* in that the duty to keep one's promise was only valid insofar as there had been a valid *causa*, i.e. an exchange of things of equivalent value.[135] By stressing the importance of equality in exchange in the context of good faith and equity, *Baldus* accounted for the theory of *dolus ex re ipsa* and provided a source of implied obligations to which the parties to a contract had not expressly agreed.[136]

There was a general tendency in the writings of the late Scholastics and the northern Natural lawyers not to base their conclusions on the wording of particular Roman texts, and references in their writings to *bona fides* were scarce.[137] Nevertheless, the greatest French jurist of the eighteenth century, *Robert Joseph Pothier*[138], spent twelve years writing the *Pandectae Justinianae in novum ordinem digestae*, in which he, as the title of the work suggests, arranged the Roman law scientifically.[139] *Pothier* was also the author of various treatises on the customary law of France, which was later to form the backbone of the French Civil Code.[140] In his treatise on the law of obligations, *Pothier* too attached importance to the equality that should reign in the contract. Indeed, one of the defects that might occur in the contract was inequality.[141] In the tradition of *Baldus* and *Pothier's* predecessor, *Jean Domat*, *Pothier* wrote that "equity must reign in all agreements",

---

[129] HORN, Norbert: op. cit., p. 163.
[130] Ibid.
[131] Ibid., p. 164.
[132] Ibid.
[133] As opposed to contracts *stricti iuris*. HORN, Norbert: op. cit., p. 164.
[134] GORDLEY: op. cit., pp. 108 and 114.
[135] Ibid., p. 114.
[136] Ibid.
[137] Ibid., p. 115.
[138] *Pothier* was born at Orleans 1699, and died there in 1772. He was a judge of the Orleans presidial court from 1720 to 1770 and was appointed professor of law in that city in 1749; cf. SHERMAN: op. cit. § 250.
[139] SHERMAN: op. cit., § 250.
[140] Ibid.
[141] POTHIER: ***Traité des Obligations*** *Première Partie*, *Chap.* I, *Sect.* I, *Art.* III, § III, *n.* 33; Other defects which may occur in contracts according to *Pothier* apart from inequality were error, fraud, want of liberty, want of good consideration and want of real obligation.

and that "equity in matters of commerce consists in equality".[142] However, Aristotelian notions of "equality in exchange" faded into insignificance during the nineteenth century.[143]

Pothier, being a scholar of Roman law, based the rule against fraud – a term he applied to "every artifice made use of by one person for the purpose of deceiving another" – on good faith:[144]

> *"Lorsqu'une partie a été engagée à contracter par le dol de l'autre, le contrat n'est pas absolument et essentiellement nul, parce qu'un consentement, quoique supris, ne laisse pas d'être consentement ; mais ce contrat est vicieux, et la partie qui a èté surprise peut, dans le dix ans, en prenant des lettres de rescision, le faire rescinder, parce qu'il pèche contre la bonne foi qui doit règner dans les contrats.*[145]
> *Dans le for intérieur, on doit regarder comme contraire à cette bonne foi, tout ce que s'ècarte tant soit peu de la sincérité la plus exacte et la plus scrupuleuse: la seule dissimulation sur ce qui concerne la chose qui fait l'objet du marché, et que la partie avec qui je contracte aurait intérêt de savoir, est contraire à cette bonne foi ; car, puisqu'il nous est commandé d'aimer notre prochain autant que nous-mêmes, il ne peut nous être permis de lui rien cacher de ce que nous n'aurions pas voulu qu'on nous cachât, si nous eussions été à sa place...*
> *Dans le for extérieur, une partie ne serait pas écoutée à se plaindre de ces légères atteintes que celui avec qui il a contracté aurait données à la bonne foi; autrement il y aurait un trop grand nombre de conventions qui seraient dans le cas de la rescision, ce qui donnerait lieu à trop de procès, et causerait un dérangement dans le commerce. Il n'y a que ce qui blesse ouvertement la bonne foi qui soit, dans ce for, regardé comme un vrai dol, suffisant pour donner lieu à la rescision du contrat, tels que toutes les mauvaises manoeuvres et tous les mauvais artifices qu'une partie aurait employés pour engager l'autre à contracter ...*[146]
> *Il n'y a que le dol qui a donné lieu au contrat, qui puisse donner lieu à la rescision; c'est-à-dire, le dol par lequel l'une des parties a engagé l'autre à contracter, qui n'aurait pas contracté sans cela: tout autre dol*

[142] POTHIER: ***Traité des Obligations*** *Première Partie, Chap.* I, *Sect.* I, *Art.* III, § III, *n.* 33.
[143] GORDLEY: op. cit., p. 115.
[144] POTHIER: **Law of Obligations** s. 1, Art. III, § 2, 28.
[145] POTHIER: ***Traité des Obligations*** *Première Partie, Chap.* I, *Sect.* I, *Art.* III, § III, *n.* 29; Translation in POTHIER: **Law of Obligations** s. 1, Art. III, § 2, 29: "When a party has been induced to contract by the fraud of another the contract is not absolutely and essentially void, because a consent, though obtained by surprise, is still a consent; but the contract is vicious , and the party surprised may institute a process of its rescission within ten years."
[146] POTHIER: ***Traité des Obligations*** *Première Partie, Chap.* I, *Sect.* I, *Art.* III, § III, *n.* 30; Translation in POTHIER: **Law of Obligations** s. 1, Art. III, § 2, 30: "As a matter of conscience any deviation from the most exact and scrupulous sincerity is repugnant to the good faith that ought to prevail in contracts. Any dissimulation concerning the object of the contract, and what the opposite party has an interest in knowing, is contrary to that good faith: for, since we are commanded to love our neighbour as ourselves, we are not permitted to conceal from him any thing which we should be unwilling to have had concealed from ourselves under similar circumstances. But in civil tribunals a person cannot be allowed to complain of trifling deviations from good faith in the party with whom he has contracted. Nothing but what is plainly injurious to good faith ought to be there considered as a fraud sufficient to impeach a contract, such as the criminal manoeuvres and artifices employed by one party to induce the other to contract..."

> *qui intervient dans les contrats, donne seulement lieu à des dommages et intérêts pour la réparation du tort causé à la partie qui a été trompée.*"[147]

These paragraphs from *Pothier*'s famous *Traité des Obligations*, do not only confirm the medieval appreciation of *bona fides* as a principle aimed at the prevention of fraud, but also provide some clarity as to how the principle operated in contract law to fulfil that purpose. It appears that *Pothier* thought that a breach of good faith in a contract tainted by fraud, allowed the innocent party to rescind the contract. Also, not all circumstances were considered to be such as to lead to a breach of good faith if they were not disclosed: the undisclosed facts had to be material to the object of the contract and not a mere triviality. Moreover, *Pothier* stressed in all the paragraphs quoted above, that rescission would only be available where the contract had been induced by the concealment. Accordingly, where a party merely induced another to contract on terms more favourable for the former, the correct remedy would not be rescission, but damages.

It is still the opinion of some modern-day jurists that the concept of good faith is inherently not definable:

> "Some German jurists have warned that we should not expect to find a clear rule. We must be content with a list of *Fallgruppen*. Similarly, the American jurist Robert Summers had described 'good faith' as an 'excluder': a concept that cannot be defined but excludes heterogeneous instances of good faith. Those who hold this view might well point to the experience of the medieval jurists. Before *Baldus*, they never defined good faith in a way that helped to resolve cases. Instead, they described discrete situations in which good faith was required. They explained what good faith required in these situations with systems or schema which seem quite independent of any general conception of good faith. When *Baldus* tried to give 'good faith' a more definite meaning, he drew on Aristotelian philosophical ideas that are now quite out of fashion. Perhaps the medieval experience suggests that we will always need an expression like 'good faith' but we will never be able to define it. We should remain content with our list of *Fallgruppen*." [148]

However, even today it would seem that the various instances in which the principle of good faith operates fit into one of the categories of the medieval jurists, i.e. keeping one's promise, not deliberately deceiving the other party or driving an overly harsh bargain and keeping those obligations implied into the contract as a matter of fair interpretation.[149] Although a definite meaning of *bona fides* may not be attainable, the "legal institutions" it had formed and the legal rules and duties, "the finely nuanced considerations" for which it served as mould are

[147] POTHIER: ***Traité des Obligations*** *Première Partie*, *Chap.* I, *Sect.* I, *Art.* III, § III, *n.* 29; Translation in POTHIER: **Law of Obligations** s. 1, Art. III, § 2, 31: "It is only the fraud which induces the contract that can furnish ground for the impeachment of it; that is, the fraud by which one party induces another to contract who would not have contracted otherwise. Any other fraud only entitles the party to a reparation in damages for the injury sustained."
[148] GORDLEY: op. cit., p. 116.
[149] Ibid., p. 117.

very much a part of the civilian heritage of modern legal systems, particularly those on the European continent.[150]

2.1.4 *Bona Fides* in England

The law of promissory obligations in England was also influenced by the developments in canon law on the European continent, especially through the Court of Chancery. The first chancellors were schooled in canon law, and as men of the church applied ecclesiastical law in the Court of Chancery. In applying principles of fairness, the chancellors did not enforce contracts which were grossly unfair, or where one party to the contract took unfair advantage of his adversary. In the eighteenth century, Lord Mansfield was an important advocate of the good faith principle in his efforts to incorporate general equitable considerations into the English law of contract. Certainly one of the most important cases in this regard over which Lord Mansfield presided, was *Carter v Boehm*[151], in which he held:

> "The governing principle is applicable to all contracts and dealings. Good faith forbids either party from concealing what he privately knows, to draw the other into a bargain, from his ignorance to that fact, and his believing the contrary."[152]

Lord Mansfield's efforts, however profound, did not succeed whilst courts preferred increasingly to apply the principles of *caveat emptor*, and jealously protected the doctrine of freedom to contract.[153] However, the influence of the principle of *bona fides* on English law is discussed in greater detail in chapter 4 of this work.[154]

---

[150] SCHERMAIER: op. cit., p. 89.

[151] (1766) 3 Burr. 1907; cf. the discussion of this case at p. 96 ff. *infra*.

[152] Ibid., at p. 1910.

[153] NEHF, James: op. cit., p. 118; also see Lord Mustill in *Pan Atlantic Insurance Co. Ltd.. and Another v. Pine Top Insurance Co. Ltd.* [1994] 2 Lloyd's Rep. 427 at p. 444 and Lord Hobhouse of Woodborough in *Manifest Shipping Co. Ltd.. v. Uni-Polaris Insurance Co. Ltd.. and la Réunion Europèene* [2001] 1 Lloyd's Rep. 389 at p. 398.

[154] Cf. 4.3.1 Signs of Good Faith in Early English Contract Law.

2.2 HISTORY OF THE MARINE INSURANCE CONTRACT

Pothier defined the marine insurance contract as –

> "*...un contrat par lequel l'un des contractants se charge du risque des cas fortuits auxquels une chose est exposée, et s'oblige envers l'autre contractant de l'indemniser de la perte que lui causeraient ces cas fortuits, s'ils arrivaient, moyennant une somme que l'autre contractant lui donne ou s'oblige de lui donner pour le prix des risques dont il le charge.*"[155]

In the following paragraphs, the extraordinary history of the contract of marine insurance will be traced from its inception in Greek and Roman maritime loans and the use of risk clauses through to where it was considered a separate contract as defined by Pothier above. An understanding of the foundations of the contract is crucial in order to understand the role that *bona fides* played in the marine insurance contract.

2.2.1 Of travelling money and premiums

The marine insurance contract is the oldest form of insurance and has rightly been said to be the mother of modern insurance.[156] Although the modern form of marine insurance, by which one party (the insurer) undertakes to indemnify another (the assured) against loss, in consideration of a premium, cannot be said to have existed before the opening years of the fourteenth century,[157] it has been suggested that the origins of the insurance contract can be traced back as far as around 2000 B.C. in Babylonia.[158] It consisted of a contract to lend trading capital to travelling merchants. The moneylender provided the merchant with a loan in order to finance the purchase of goods and assumed the risk of the loss of the goods due to robbery in transit, charging the merchant a premium rate of interest on the loan.[159]

However, marine insurance is generally believed to have its earliest origins in the maritime loan or *pecunia traiecticia*,[160] a form of Bottomry loan, i.e. a loan or

---

[155] POTHIER: ***Traité d'Assurance*** Chap. I, Sect. I, n. 2, a contract by which one of the contracting parties takes upon himself the risk of fortuitous events to which a thing is exposed, and obliges himself as against the other contracting party to indemnify the loss caused by such fortuitous events, if they happened, for a sum that the other contractual party pays or promises to pay to him as a price for the risks which he is transferring; also see VAN DER LINDEN: ***Koopmans Handboek*** IV, *Boek* VI, *Afdeeling* § 1, calling *Pothier*'s definition *naauwkeurig*, i.e. precise.

[156] HARE: **Shipping Law & Admiralty Jurisdiction in South Africa** p. 650; NEHLSEN-VON STRYK: ***Die venezianische Seeversicherung im 15. Jahrhundert*** p. 3, citing the entry to "*Versicherung*" in MANES: ***Handwörterbuch d. Staatswissenschaften*** Vol. VIII, p. 624 where it states that marine insurance is the "*Mutter der modernen Versicherung.*"

[157] SANBOURN: **Origins of the Early English Maritime and Commercial Law** pp. 234-235.

[158] HARE: op. cit., p. 650.

[159] Ibid.; REINECKE and VAN DER MERWE: **General Principles of Insurance** p. 4.

[160] SANBOURN: op. cit., p. 235.

mortgage of a ship on the condition that if she be lost, the lender loses the money advanced on her; but that if she arrives safely, the moneylender not only receives his money back, but also a premium.[161] Around the fourth century B.C., in the time of Demosthenes, the Greeks laid the foundations for this form of maritime loan which was used until the thirteenth century.[162] Similarly, a moneylender would provide a merchant with capital for overseas trade, whilst the vessel or the goods served as hypothec.[163] As the capital was exposed to maritime risks, the moneylender agreed that the loan was only to be repaid upon safe arrival of the vessel and the goods, i.e. the subject of the hypothec, against payment of a premium rate[164] of interest.[165] The Greek maritime loan thus formed the basis of the *pecunia traiecticia* which was used by the Romans from the first century B.C.[166] The *pecunia traiecticia* was defined as money which is carried over sea, or goods bought with the money and carried over sea:[167] "*Traiecticia ea pecunia est quae trans mare vehitur: ceterum si eodem loci consumatur, non erit traecticia.*"[168] Thus, if the money was spent in the same place where it was borrowed, it would not be money *traiecticia.*[169]

Under the normal Roman contract of loan[170] the borrower remained liable for repayment, even though he might have lost what he had received.[171] The *pecunia traiecticia* deviated from the normal rules of *mutuum*, as the risk for the capital was on the lender.[172] Furthermore, unlike under the rules of *mutuum*, the lender remained entitled to the capital and to the merchandise thereby acquired.[173] The merchandise purchased with the money lent, or to be purchased with the proceeds of sale of these goods, or even other goods belonging to the borrower sailing on other ships, were in fact regarded as pledged to the lender.[174] Consequently, if the goods were to be lost in transit, the moneylender lost the object of liability and his claim for repayment was terminated.[175]

---

[161] MARTIN: **The History of Lloyd's and of Marine Insurance in Great Britain** pp. 2-3.

[162] SANBOURN: op. cit., p. 7.

[163] REINECKE and VAN DER MERWE: op. cit., p. 4; SANBOURN: op. cit., p. 7.

[164] Zimmermann mentions that the rate ranged between 22½ and 33 1/3 per cent depending on the distance to be covered by the ship. See ZIMMERMANN: **The Law of Obligations** p. 182; Trölsch suggests the rates were fixed between 24 and 26 per cent. See TRöLSCH: **Die Obliegenheiten in der Seeversicherung** p. 6.

[165] SANBOURN: op. cit., p. 7.

[166] REINECKE and VAN DER MERWE: op. cit., p. 4.

[167] SANBOURN: op. cit., p. 17.

[168] Dig. 22. 2. 1.

[169] SANBOURN: op. cit., p. 7.

[170] Known as *mutuum*.

[171] ZIMMERMANN: **The Law of Obligations** p. 154.

[172] Ibid., p. 181.

[173] Ibid., p. 183.

[174] SANBOURN: op. cit., p. 17.

[175] ZIMMERMANN: **The Law of Obligations** pp. 182-183.

In post-classical time, the *pecunia traiecticia* became known by the term *foenus nauticum*.[176] Up to the time of Justinian, the interest rate to be charged by moneylenders for the *foenus nauticum*, also called maritime interest, was unlimited as the higher interest rate on these loans was considered not merely to be compensation for the use of capital, but a *premium periculi*.[177] Naturally, where the borrower took the risk upon himself, the lender was not allowed to charge maritime interest.[178] As a result, the high interest rate was only to be paid for the days that the goods were being transported at sea, and not when it was in port, i.e. from the day fixed in the contract on which the ship would depart until its arrival at the port of destination.[179] The debtor was, furthermore, only to be released from liability if the goods were lost due to a typical risk of the sea[180] and not where a loss occurred due to other accidents or carelessness on the part of the merchant.[181] In A.D. 533, Justinian passed an Edict by which the legal maximum rate of interest was fixed at 6 per cent.[182] A special exemption was made in the case of *foenus nauticum*: the Edict fixed the rate of interest for the maritime loan on 12%, of which 6% was considered the risk premium.[183] It was thereby acknowledged that *foenus nauticum* did not involve a mere lending of money, but an adventure involving maritime risks.[184]

The *foenus nauticum*[185] continued to play an important role throughout the Middle Ages at the close of which it developed in two directions.[186] On the one hand it developed into what is still known as loan on bottomry. On the other hand, more importantly, it cleared the way for the Italian merchants to develop the first forms of premium insurance.[187] An important moment in the evolution of marine insurance was in 1227, when Pope Gregorius IX issued the "*Naviganti vel eundi ad nundinas*" decree, prohibiting the maritime loan due to the usurious character of the interest charged.[188] This resulted in merchants finding ingenious ways to finance the maritime adventure and spread the risk.[189] One method was the simulation of a

---

[176] Ibid.

[177] A risk premium; ibid.

[178] SANBOURN: op. cit., p. 17.

[179] Ibid

[180] E.g. *marina tempestas, naufragium* and *piratarum insidiae*.

[181] ZIMMERMANN: **The Law of Obligations** p. 182.

[182] MARTIN: **The History of Lloyd's** p. 3.

[183] HARE: op. cit., p. 651, fn. 6; MARTIN: op. cit., p. 3.

[184] MARTIN: op. cit., p. 3.

[185] Cf. MARTIN: op. cit., p. 4, who expressed doubt whether the form of maritime loan known as Bottomry, or *foenus nauticum*, was practised after the revival of commerce in the Middle Ages in Italy and other Mediterranean states. The reason for this doubt appears to be the fact that neither of the old maritime codes, i.e. the "*Rooles d'Oléron*" and the "*Consolato del Mare*", both dating from around the thirteenth century, makes mention of Bottomry.

[186] HARE: op. cit., p. 651; SANBOURN: op. cit., p. 18.

[187] SANBOURN: op. cit., p. 18.

[188] HARE: op. cit., p. 651.

[189] SANBOURN: op. cit., p. 239.

contract of sale between a financier (the creditor), and a merchant (the debtor), in which the financier, instead of forwarding money to the merchant, was to be the buyer of the merchandise and at the same time assumed the risk for the safe arrival of the goods at the payment of a premium added to the sale price. The payment of the price was deferred and made dependent upon the loss of the goods, whilst a clause was included to the effect that the contract was to expire upon safe arrival of the goods.[190] Another form of disguising a loan on which interest and a form of risk premium were payable, was a contract for sale, which included a term that delivery of the goods or payment of the purchase price were to be made at a different place from where the contract was concluded, or that payment was to be in another currency from that of the loan.[191] The risk in these contracts, therefore, attached to transportation of the goods, and the contract often included a risk clause referring to the safe arrival of the debtor, money or goods, instead of the safe arrival of a vessel.[192] Another method used by merchants was a contract called *commenda*, in which the *commendator* provided capital to his *commendatarius* for purposes of trading overseas. The *commendator* bore the maritime risk attaching to the capital. The *commendatarius*, as he was providing the labour, shared in the profit on successful completion of the venture.[193]

In order for marine insurance to develop as a separate and independent contract from the use of risk clauses in these contracts, the freeing of the undertaking to assume a maritime risk from some fictitious form of the contract of loan or sale had to take place and the assured had to become bound to pay the premium.[194] This process has been aptly described in the following terms:

> "In order for the premium and the risk to split apart from the principal contract and to give life to an independent contract, in which the one should be the equivalent of the other, this only need occur, that a third person intervene between the purchaser who intended to purchase goods conditioned on safe arrival, and the vendor who intended to cast upon the other party the risk of the sea and of nations, and assume the risk of the cargo in consideration of the payment of the difference which the current rate of trade and of exchange had plainly established."[195]

These first contracts in which maritime risks were undertaken in exchange for money by an independent party were concluded in Genoa and Pisa towards the end of the fourteenth century.[196] During the fourteenth century and thereafter the use

[190] Ibid.
[191] Ibid.
[192] REINECKE and VAN DER MERWE: op. cit., p. 5.
[193] REINECKE and VAN DER MERWE: op. cit., p. 5.
[194] HARE: op. cit., p. 651; SANBOURN: op. cit., p. 244.
[195] SANBOURN: op. cit., p. 18 citing and quoting in translation from BENSA, Enrico: ***Il Conratto di Assicurazione nel Medio Evo*** p. 32.
[196] HARE: op. cit., p. 651; DOVER: **A Handbook to Marine Insurance** pp. 1-34 REINECKE and VAN DER MERWE: op. cit., p. 4; Joubert, J.A. in *Mutual and Federal Ins v Oudtshoorn Municipality* 1985 (1) 419 at p. 427; VON ZIEGLER: *The 'Utmost Good Faith' in Marine*

of insurance flourished and spread to other important commercial cities in Europe such as Bruges and Barcelona.[197] Surprisingly, the clauses of these early marine insurance contracts remain the backbone of the modern law of marine insurance.[198] This can be demonstrated by reference to the risks covered in probably the oldest known marine insurance policy underwritten in 1385:

> "*E il rischio che gli assicuratori corrono in sulla detta roba, carica, o si dee caricare in sulla detta nave, si è dall or ache la detta nave farà vela – da Mutrone per andare in Aqua morta; si è di Dio, di mare, di gente, di fuoco, di gitto di mare; di ritenimento di signori o di Comuni, o d'olcun'altra persona, o di rappresaglia o d'arresto e d'ogni altro caso, pericolo, fortuna, impedimento o caso sinistro, che per verun mod one potesse intervenire o fusse intervenuto, e fussono fatti I casi come si volessero o di che condizione, salvo di stiva o di dogana.*"[199]

The form of these early policies was taken over in the larger part of Western Europe as well as in England as a result of the flourishing trade and the great influence of especially the Italian merchants.[200] The first evidence of a marine insurance contract concluded in Hamburg dates from 1588,[201] whereas the earliest English policy which has been discovered bears date 1613.[202] Insurance, it is "universally agreed" according to Park, was introduced by the "active and

---

Insurance Law on the Continent **Marine Insurance at the turn of the Millennium** p. 21; SANBOURN: op. cit., at p. 240 suggests on the authority of Bensa that insurance was already practised in the main commercial cities of Italy during the first 20 years of the fourteenth century. The author refers to the existence of account books of the Florentine merchants, Francesco del Bene and Company, dating from 1318-1320 which exhibit the "undeniable use of insurance". However, at p. 244 where the author discusses what he considers to be the oldest marine insurance policy in existence, dating from 1347, he acknowledges that the contract is "copying the form of the maritime loan" and that "… the debtor (the insurer) pretends to have received the sum insured and promises to pay it to the creditor (the insured) at a fixed date unless the ship or the merchandise shall arrive in safety." At p. 247 the author also says that this policy is "in the form of a fictitious maritime loan". Sanbourn appears to argue that these early contracts were in fact contracts of insurance, although disguised for fear of being found illegal by the church. Towards the close of the fourteenth century, however, the insurance contract was in general use and its form, accordingly, became less disguised; TRöLSCH: op. cit., p. 6 argues that the earliest marine insurance contract dates from 1385, and that those contracts of earlier dates mentioned by other authors, in fact were still simulated contracts of sale or loan. The deed dated 1385, according to Trölsch, was the first which was designated on its face an insurance contract.

[197] SANBOURN: op. cit., p. 243 and pp. 249-250.

[198] Ibid., p. 253.

[199] Ibid., quoting and translating from the original Italian: "And the risks which the insurers are content to bear concerning the said goods, shipped, or to be shipped upon the said vessel, from the hour when the said vessel shall set sail to go from Mutrone to Aigues Mortes; they are of God, the sea, nations, fire, and of jettison; of restraint of princes or of peoples or of any other person, of reprisals, of arrest and of every other case, peril, fortune, impediment or mishap, which in any way can happen, or may have happened, no matter how or under what condition the cases occur, excepting ballast and custom-house duties."

[200] SANBOURN: op. cit., p. 253.

[201] TRöLSCH: op. cit., p. 6.

[202] MARTIN: op. cit., at p. 46, where he quotes the text of the policy in full.

industrious" Lombards who came to England from Italy in the thirteenth century.[203] The author based his conclusion on a clause "to this day inserted in all policies of insurance 'that this writing or policy of assurance shall be of as much force and effect as any writing heretofore made in Lombard Street, etc'..."[204] Lombard Street was the place where "these Italians are known to have taken up their residence, and carried on their trade."[205] However, prior to the reign of Queen Elizabeth I, very few insurance policies were effected in England, and if at all, no disputes relating to them had been heard in the superior courts.[206] In fact, the first case relating to a matter of insurance was heard in England during the 30th year of her reign, in 1588.[207]

2.2.2 Early codifications and treatise

By 1369 the first Order in Genoa, regarded as the oldest piece of insurance legislation so far traced, mentioned the notion of "*assekuranz*", which means insurance. Interestingly, the Order is evidence of the interference by the church in commerce, since it prescribed heavy fines upon a litigant who would dare to raise the question of usury in order to bring the case before an ecclesiastical court, since "through impediments of this sort, instruments of exchange and other contract of merchants ... could not be ordered to be executed."[208] The second oldest regulation, amongst other things declaring void a policy made after the loss became known, came a few years later around 1383 and was also from Genoa.[209]

These early regulations were not very extensive and tended to regulate certain usages and customs of the merchants.[210] In 1435, the law of marine insurance was first codified in the Statutes of Barcelona.[211] After a revision of these statutes in 1484, they were published with the *Consolato del Mare* in the same book, which added to its importance and assisted its circulation in the rest of Europe.[212] The

[203] PARK, J.A.: **System of Marine Insurance** p. xxxv of the Introduction.

[204] Ibid.

[205] PARK, J.A.: op. cit., p. xxxv of the Introduction.

[206] Ibid.

[207] Ibid.

[208] SANBOURN: op. cit., p. 246, quoting from the Latin text of the Order.; GOUDSMIT: ***Geschiedenis van het Nederlandsche Zeerecht*** p. 201 mentions an act of King Fernando of Portugal, who reigned between 1367 and 1383, in which the he ordered the creation of a mutual insurance company it order to provide some form of guarantee for the ship owners of his country against the perils that they faced at sea.

[209] SANBOURN: op. cit., p. 256.

[210] Ibid., p. 258.

[211] Ibid., p. 259, where he mentions some of the subjects treated by the code: "It prohibits the insuring of foreign ships, establishes the proportion which the amount of the insurance may bear to the value of the cargo, defines the capacity of the parties, regulates insurance brokers, the contract's form, the payment of the premium, the procedure to enforce the contract, and states the rule governing the presumption of loss." Also cf. GOUDSMIT: op. cit., p. 203.

[212] SANBOURN: op. cit., p. 259.

Consulato del Mare had a great influence on the legal development in Europe and had been the model for all legislation of the later Middle Ages.[213]

The French codification of Louis XIV, the *Ordonnance de la Marine*, which was enacted in 1681, as well as the German *Hamburgische Assecuranz- und Haverei-Ordnung*[214] of 1731 also were influential documents dealing with marine insurance.[215] The *Ordonnance de la Marine* – embodying the substance of the *Consolato del Mare*, the Laws of Oléron and the Laws of Wisby – has been acclaimed as the most comprehensive of all Continental codifications of marine insurance law and practice, forming, in fact, the basis of the Hamburg codification of 1731.[216] Lord Mansfield, renowned for his command of the civil tradition, introduced much of the substance of the *Ordonnance* into English law during the eighteenth century.[217] Apart from the *Ordonnance*, there was also the "*Guidon*", an old tract dealing with maritime usages and customs in the French language, which was probably the most important source of French legislators and writers on the subject such as Emérigon.[218]

By the sixteenth century the two most influential works on marine insurance were Petrus de Santerna's *De Assecurationibus et Sponsionibus* (1554) and Benevenutus Straccha's *De Assecurationibus.* These two works were held in high regard throughout Western Europe as authorities on marine insurance.[219] Reception of the Italian Law Merchant including the law of marine insurance occurred throughout Europe and England during the same time.[220] Other important treatise on the law of marine insurance appeared later, such as *Franciscus Roccus' De Navibus et Naulo, item de Assecurationibus Notabilia* (1708), *Pothier*'s *Traité du Contrat d'Assurance* and *Emérigon*'s *Traité des Assurances et des Contrats á la grosse.*[221]

2.2.3 Early classification of marine insurance contracts

The jurists, who first described the marine insurance contract, were uncertain how to classify the contract of marine insurance within the civil law.[222] The Italian writers especially sought to classify the contract by reference to Roman law.[223] Attempts were made to describe it as *emptio et venditio*, *locatio et conductio*, *contractus*

---

[213] BEWES, W.A.: **The Romance of the Law Merchant** p. 81; SANBOURN: op. cit., p. 259 .

[214] The Underwriting and Average Regulations of the City of Hamburg.

[215] TRöLSCH: op. cit., p. 8.

[216] DOVER: op. cit., p. 23; SHERMAN: op. cit. § 251.

[217] SHERMAN: op. cit. § 251 and § 397.

[218] PARK, J.A.: op. cit., p. xxxii of the Introduction.

[219] Joubert, J.A. in *Mutual and Federal Ins v Oudtshoorn Municipality* 1985 (1) 419, at pp. 427-428.

[220] Ibid.

[221] DE JAGER: **The Roots and Future of the South African Law of Marine Insurance** pp. 15 and 29.

[222] Joubert, J.A. in *Mutual and Federal Ins v Oudtshoorn Municipality* 1985 (1) 419, at pp. 427-428.

[223] EMéRIGON: **Treatise** p. 6, (***Traité des Assurances*** Chap. I, *Sect.* II, § 1).

innominatus and *contractus fideiussionis.*[224] *Roccus* suggested that the accepted view was that marine insurance was a kind of contract of sale.[225] In this scheme, the insurer was considered the *vendor*, the assured the purchaser, the maritime risk the *merx* and the premium the *pretium.*[226] *Pothier*, did not classify the contract of insurance as *emptio et venditio*, but considered it to be of the same species as the contract of sale:

> "*C'est une espèce de contrat de vente: les assureurs sont les vendeurs, l'assuré est l'acheteur ; la chose vendue est la décharge des risques auxquels est exposée la chose assurée. Les assureurs vendent en quelque façon à l'assuré, et s'obligent de lui faire avoir et de lui procurer la décharge de ces risques, en prenant sur eux ces risques, et en s'obligeant d'en indemniser l'assuré. La prime que l'assuré paie ou s'oblige de payer aux assureurs, est le prix de cette vente.*"[227]
> (Emphasis in original text)

Further to this, *Pothier* considered the contract of insurance to share the synallagmatic character of the contract of sale, by which he meant that the parties to the insurance contract had reciprocal obligations:

> "*Le contrat d'assurance, comme les contrats de vente, est synallagmatique; car il produit des obligations réciproques. L'assureur s'oblige envers l'assuré de le garantir on de l'indemniser des fortunes de mer, et l'assuré s'oblige réciproquement envers l'assureur de lui payer la prime convenue.*"[228] (Emphasis in original text)

Another French jurist of great importance to write about marine insurance was *Balthazard Marie Emérigon*, the author of an extensive work on that subject, the *Traité des Assurances*. *Emérigon* wrote the treatise between 1780 and 1781 in his home

---

[224] EMéRIGON: **Treatise** p. 6, (***Traité*** *Chap.* I, *Sect.* II, § 1); ROCCUS: ***Tractaat over Assurantien ofte Verzekeringen*** *Art.* 3, *No.* 3-6; Joubert, J.A. in *Mutual and Federal Ins v Oudtshoorn Municipality* 1985 (1) 419, at pp. 427-428.

[225] ROCCUS: op. cit., Art. 3, *No.* 7.

[226] Joubert, J.A. in *Mutual and Federal Ins v Oudtshoorn Municipality* 1985 (1) 419, at pp. 427-428; *Roccus* explained it slightly different by suggesting that the insurer was selling his obligation to pay to the assured the value of the thing insured in the event that it will have perished. See ROCCUS: op. cit., *Art.* 3, *No.* 7.

[227] POTHIER: ***Traité d'Assurance*** *Chap.* I, *Sect.* I, *n.* 4: It is a kind of contract of sale : the insurers are the vendors, the assured is the buyer; the thing sold is the discharge of the risks to which the thing insured is exposed. The insurers sell in some manner to the assured, and oblige themselves to provide and procure the discharge of these risks, and to take on these risks and oblige themselves to indemnify the assured against them. The premium that the assured pays or promises to pay the insurers is the price for this sale.

[228] POTHIER: ***Traité d'Assurance*** *Chap.* I, *Sect.* I, *n.* 6; Translated by Samuel Meredith in EMéRIGON: **Treatise** p. 5: "The contract of insurance is synallagmatic, for it produces reciprocal obligations; the insurer enters into an obligation to the assured to guaranty and indemnify him against the perils of the sea, and the assured binds himself in turn to the insurer to pay him the premium agreed upon." The translator further explains the term "synallagmatic" as follows at note (b): "It describes contracts obligatory on one side as well as the other, as *sale*, and is opposed to contracts in which a single party binds himself towards another, as in the loan of money."

town, Marseilles.[229] It was published in 1783, one year before his death. He stated unambiguously that insurance, "...properly so called, is neither a sale, letting to hire, partnership, nor a wager, nor any thing of what certain writers have imagined it to be."[230] However, he too described the contract in terms reminding of the contract of sale: writing about the premium, *Emérigon* stated that "*periculi pretium est*"[231], i.e. that the premium constituted the "...price of the peril against which the insurer guarantees, in case of accident to the subject insured."[232] The contract of insurance possessed, in his scheme of things, a legitimate consideration and a determinate object and was clothed in a formal promise.[233] The contract became complete after the subject insured had been placed at risk, the risk being of the essence of the contract.[234] Accordingly, the risk formed a legal condition of the contract:

> "*Si ce risque réel ou putatif manque, le Contrat s'évanouit par défaut de matiere. Tout comme la vente, la stipulation, ou le legs d'une choſe n'existe pas, ne font d'aucune valeur, de même l'Assurance d'une chose non exposée aux risques de la mer, ne signifie rien. Quemadmodúm enim rei non existentis, nec valet emptio; et stipulatio non subsistit rerum quae non existant; neque legatum valet; quod in rerum naturâ non reperitur: itá quoque assecuratio, si in nave non habeantur merces, nullius momenti est.*"[235]

These two elements, the premium paid by the assured, and the risk assumed by the insurer, are two correlatives and together constitute the essence of the contract of marine insurance: "*Forma essentialis consistit in susceptione periculi, et determinato super eá pretio.*"[236]

Roccus and other early authors on marine insurance were of the opinion that insurance was a conditional contract.[237] *Emérigon* identified two reasons for this

[229] EMéRIGON: **Treatise** p. xxviii of the introduction by Samuel Meredith.

[230] EMéRIGON: **Treatise** p. 11 (***Traité*** *Chap.* I, *Sect.* II § 2).

[231] EMéRIGON: **Treatise** p. 51 (***Traité*** *Chap.* III, *Sect.* I, § 1), citing *i.a.* as authority POTHIER: ***Traité d'Assurance*** *Chap.* I, *Sect.* I, *n.* 8 and *Chap.* I, *Sect.* II, *n.* 81.

[232] EMéRIGON: **Treatise** at p. 51 (***Traité*** *Chap.* III, *Sect.* I, § 1 and § 2), where the author suggests that the word "premium" either comes from the word "*praemium*", which signifies price, or from the word "*primò*", because, he states, "...the premium was paid before all, and at the time of signing the policy." This latter explanation was also offered by POTHIER: ***Traité d'Assurance*** at *n.* 81: "*Elle est appelée prime, parce qu'elle se payait primò et avant tout...*" (emphasis in original text).

[233] EMéRIGON: **Treatise** p. 10 (***Traité*** *Chap.* I, *Sect.* II, §2).

[234] Ibid.

[235] EMéRIGON: ***Traité des Assurances*** *Chap.* I, *Sect.* II, §2, citing *Marquardus lib.* 2, c. 13, r. 23; translation by Samuel Meredith in EMéRIGON: **Treatise** p. 11: "If this risk, real or putative, be wanting, the contract disappears for want of a subject. Just as the sale, stipulation or bequest of a thing which does not exist is of no effect, so the insurance of a subject not exposed to the risks of the sea signifies nothing."

[236] EMéRIGON: **Treatise** p. 51 (***Traité*** *Chap.* III, *Sect.* I, § 3), citing and quoting Stypmannus. *part.* 4, *cap.* 7, *n.* 303, *pag.* 456; also POTHIER: ***Traité d'Assurance*** n. 81.

[237] ROCCUS: op. cit., *Art.* 13, *No.* 33, referring also to *Santerna, de assecur. part.* 3, *Num.* 24 and 25; EMéRIGON: **Treatise** p. 11 (***Traité*** *Chap.* I, *Sect.* III, § 1).

assertion: first, the contract of insurance would be null if, before the inception of the risk, the voyage was cancelled, i.e. "the contract is revoked by default in the risk".[238] Secondly, he suggested that the contract was conditional, since the insurers were not bound to pay, except if the loss or damage resulted from the perils of the sea, relying on a statement of *Pothier* to that effect.[239] However, the paragraph on which *Emérigon* relied, dealt with the consensual character of the contract. *Pothier* stated that the contract of insurance was consensual, since it became perfect by the consent of the parties to it. In this context, *Pothier* stated that although the obligation of the insurers to indemnify depended on the condition that the things insured perished or were damaged by perils of the sea, still –

> "*... le contrat ne laisse pas d'être parfait ; l'obligation est contractée, quoique conditionnellement, n'étant plus dès lors au pouvoir des assureurs de s'en désister, et de n'être pas obligés, si l'accident arrive.*"[240]

Also *Goldschmidt* stated that the insurance contract was not a conditional contract at all.[241] The condition under which the insurer promises to pay, belongs to the essence of this form of contract, and as such is a *conditio iuris.*[242]

Emérigon agreed with *Pothier* where he stated that insurance belonged to the class of aleatory contracts, i.e. contracts upon speculation. These are defined as contracts in which what is given by one contractual party to the other is the price of a risk of which he relieves that party[243]. Wrote *Pothier*:

> "*Il est évident que ce contrat est de la classe des contrats aléatoires,...; car la prime que l'assureur reçoit, n'est pas,...l'equivalent d'une autre chose qu'il donne ou s'oblige de donne à la place, puisqu'il n'aura rien à donner, si le vaisseau arrive à bon port, et n'essuie aucun accident ; et au contraire, si le vaisseu périt, l'indemnité qu'il sera tenu de donner à l'assureé, étant une chose beaucoup plus considérable que la prime qu'il a reçue de lui, n'en peut être regardée comme l'équivalent. La prime que l'assureur reçoit, n'est donc pas le prix d'une autre chose qu'il donne, mais le prix du resque dont il se charge par le contrat, ce qui est le vrai caractère des contrats aléatoires.*"[244] (Emphasis in original text)

---

[238] EMéRIGON: **Treatise** p. 12 (***Traité*** *Chap.* I, *Sect.* III, §1).
[239] EMéRIGON: **Treatise** p. 12 (***Traité*** *Chap.* I, *Sect.* III, § 1).
[240] POTHIER: ***Traité d'Assurance*** *Chap.* I, *Sect.* II, *n.* 5, translated by Samuel Meredith in EMéRIGON: **Treatise** at p. 12: "....the contract is complete: the obligation is assumed, though conditionally, it not being in the power of the insurers to free themselves from it and escape responsibility, should the accident occur."
[241] GOLDSCHMIDT: ***System des Handelsrechts*** § 158, *n.* 3.
[242] Ibid.
[243] POTHIER: ***Traité d'Assurance*** see the *Article Prélimniaire n.* 1.
[244] POTHIER: ***Traité d'Assurance*** *Chap.* I, *Sect.* I, *n.* 8 : ("This contract, unquestionably, belongs to the class of contracts upon speculation... ; because the premium that the insurer receives is not the equivalent to another thing that he gives or promises to give in its place, since he will have nothing to give, if the ship arrived safely and no accident whatsoever occurs; on the contrary, if the vessel perishes, the indemnity that he will be obliged to pay to the assured, being a thing much more valuable than the premium that he has received from him, cannot be regarded as the equivalent. The premium that the insurer receives, therefore, is not the price of another

Emérigon, in language that may very well be called poetical, described the speculative nature of the marine insurance contract and the implication thereof on those who engage in that trade, as follows:

> *"C'est ici une espece de jeu qui exige beaucoup de prudence de la part de ceux qui s'y adonnent. Il faut faire l'analyse des hasards, et posséder la science du calcul des probabilités, prévoir les écueils de la mer, et ceux de la mauvaise foi, ne pas perdre de vue les cas insolites et extraordinaires, combiner le tout, le comparer avec le taux des Primes, et juger quel sera le résultat de l'ensemble.*
> *Pareilles spéculations sont l'ouvrage du génie. Mais si la théorie, dirigée par l'expérience, n'est que trop souvent fautive, quel sera le sort des Négocians, qui alléchés par l'appas du gain, signent dans toutes les Polices qu'on leur présente, sans considérer le précipice où la fortune aveugle et leur témérité peuvent les entraîner?"*[245]

Goldschmidt doubted that anything was added by classifying the insurance contract as *aleatory*, or as he called it, "*gewagtes Geschäft*".[246] This term, according to him, was legally meaningless, at least "*gemeinrechtlich*", since no special legal principles existed in the common law for such contracts.[247]

thing that he gives, but the price of the risk he takes on himself by reason of the contract, which is the true character of a contract upon speculation.")

[245] EMéRIGON: **Treatise** p. 12 (***Traité*** *Chap.* I, *Sect.* III, § 2), translated by Samuel Meredith in EMéRIGON: **Treatise** p. 12: "It is a species of play demanding great prudence on the part of those who meddle with it. Perils must be analyzed and chances accurately calculated; the hidden dangers of the sea foreseen, as well as those of bad faith, and rare and extraordinary emergencies taken into view. All these must we combine, and measure with the rates of premium, to enable us to judge of the final result. Speculations like these belong to the province of genius. But if theory, under the guide of experience, is but too often at fault, what must be the fate of merchants, who, enticed by the allurements of gain, place their signatures to every policy presented to them, regardless of the precipice to which blind fortune and their own rashness may lead them? "

[246] GOLDSCHMIDT: op. cit. § 158 *n*. 1.

[247] Ibid.

2.3 THE HISTORY OF GOOD FAITH IN MARINE INSURANCE LAW

One of the oldest examples of marine insurance policies which was concluded in Florence in 1393, stated that the contract should be performed – "*secundum bonam fidem et consuetudinem mercatorum.*"[248]

It would appear as though it has been accepted over centuries that, on general principles, the contract of marine insurance is subject to *bona fides*, and that any infringement on that principle including concealment, nullifies the contract and releases the other party from his obligations.[249] Appeal Judge Jansen in the South African case of *Mutual and Federal Insurance v Oudtshoorn Municipality*[250] quoted article 22 of the *Ordonnantie, Statuyt ende Policie op't feyt van de Contracten van de Assurantien ende Verseeckeringen*, enacted on 20 January 1570[251] by King Philip II of the Netherlands in support of the assertion that *bona fides* was the appropriate principle applicable to insurance contracts –

> "*Ende alsoo dese Contracten van verseeckeringen oft asseurantien, gehouden ende geestimeert worden, voor Contracten van goeder trauen, daerinne egheen fraulde oft bedrogh en behoorde te interwenieren oft geschieden...*"[252]

According to this ordinance, therefore, insurance contracts were contracts of good faith in which there was no room for fraud.[253] Also the *Ordonnance de la Marine* which was enacted in 1681 in France, included a rule to the effect that the insurer was to rely on the good faith of the assured.[254]

The duty to disclose was also not unfamiliar to the jurists of the time and was i.a. discussed by Benevenutus Straccha in *De Assecurationibus*[255]. Both the insurer and

---

248 RITTER: ***Das Recht der Seeversicherung*** p. 271.

249 DE JONGE.: ***De Mededeelingsplicht van den Verzekerde in Theorie en practijk*** p. 14.

250 1985 (1) 419.

251 Interestingly, this ordinance is sometimes referred to as being of 20 January 1570, and sometimes as of 20 January 1571. The reason for this is that since the thirteenth century, it was the custom in some countries, including Holland and Flanders, to have the New Year start on Easter. Thus, if Easter fell on 14 April in *A.D.* 1571, the consequence would be that the New Year, i.e. 1571, only began 14 April 1571. The result is that 20 January 1571 *A.D.* would be referred to as 20 January 1570 on the document containing the ordinance. This was the position until 16 June 1575, when King Philip ruled that the year should start on 1 January. See: GOUDSMIT: op. cit., pp. 251-252.

252 1985 (1) 419 at p. 432C; GOUDSMIT: op. cit., p. 265; DE JONGE.: op. cit., p. 15; ("And since these contracts of assurance are held and considered to be contracts of good faith, no fraud should enter or occur in it...").

253 GOUDSMIT: op. cit., pp. 265-266; DE JONGE.: op. cit., p. 15.

254 VON ZIEGLER: *The 'Utmost Good Faith' in Marine Insurance Law on the Continent* **Marine Insurance at the turn of the Millennium** p. 23.

255 Joubert, J.A. refers to various authorities in *Mutual and Federal Ins v Oudtshoorn Municipality* 1985 (1) 419, at p. 432F-G.

assured were to disclose prior to the conclusion of the contract of insurance those facts material to the *riscum* or *periculum*, and the assessment of the premium, of which the parties had actual or constructive knowledge. Breach of the duty of disclosure was considered to be a fraud or *mala fides*, entitling the aggrieved party to avoid the contract.[256]

2.3.1 *Stricti iuris* or *bonae fidei*

Emérigon [257] spent a whole section[258] in his treatise on the question of *bona fides* in marine insurance contracts, setting out by explaining the Roman law distinction between contracts *bonae fidei* and contracts *stricti juris*.[259] As Roman law did not know insurance, the marine insurance contract, of course, had not been classified as one or the other.[260] *Emérigon*, however, argued that marine insurance exhibited characteristics of both and therefore could be assigned to either category depending on the circumstances of the case.[261]

The old authors, such as *Roccus*[262], *Santerna*[263] and *Caeseregis*[264], appear to have been in agreement that since the marine insurance contract was the result of stipulations of two contracting parties – the words used by the parties in the policy exhibited the intention of the parties and it was, therefore, not permitted to depart from these words – it naturally belonged to the class of contracts *stricti iuris*.[265] Accordingly, the words of the policy were to be construed literally and according to their proper meaning.[266] As a result, *Pothier* laid down a firm rule that insurers were not bound by the risks once there had been a variance from the contents of the policy, unless it was consented to or the result of necessity:

> "*Les assureurs ne sont pas tenus des risques, lorsqu'on s'est écarté de ce qui est porté par la police, si ce n'est de leur consentement, ou en cas de nécessité.*"[267]

Park, too, was of the opinion that the policy was the foundation upon which the whole contract depended[268]:

---

[256] For the position in contract law in general, see POTHIER: ***Traité des Obligations*** *Première Partie, Chap.* I, *Sect.* III, *Art.* II, § 29 and § 30.
[257] See *supra* p. 40.
[258] See the fifth section of the first chapter of the Treatise.
[259] EMéRIGON: **Treatise** p. 14 (***Traité*** *Chap.* I, *Sect.* IV).
[260] EMéRIGON: **Treatise** p. 16 (***Traité*** *Chap.* I, *Sect.* V, § 1).
[261] Ibid.
[262] ROCCUS: op. cit., *Art.* 18, *No.* 53-54.
[263] *De Assecur. part.* 3, *n.* 38.
[264] *disc.* 1, *n.*107.
[265] EMéRIGON: **Treatise** p. 16, (***Traité*** *Chap.* I, *Sect.* V, § 1), citing Caesaregis, *disc.* 1, *n.* 1.: "*In materiâ assecurationis principaliter inhaerendum est verbis apocae (policy) assecurationis; quinimò haec pro lege habenda sunt, nec ab his recedere debemus, quia contrahentium voluntas melius haberi non potest.*"
[266] EMéRIGON: **Treatise** p. 16 (***Traité*** *Chap.* I, *Sect.* V, § 1); ROCCUS: op. cit., *Art.* 61, *No.* 217: "*En de woorden, in een police van Assurantie vervat, moeten eygentlyk en stiptelyk verstaan warden....*"
[267] POTHIER: ***Traité d'Assurance*** *Chap.* I, *Sect.* II, *n.* 68; EMéRIGON: **Treatise** at pp. 16-17.

> "Although policies of assurance are not specialities, but esteemed merely as parol contracts, yet they have always been held as sacred agreements, and of the first credit: so much so, that when once they are underwritten, they can never be altered by any authority whatever; because it would open a door to an infinite variety of frauds, and introduce uncertainty into a species of contract, of which certainty and precision are the most essential requisites."[269]

Emérigon, however, clearly and unambiguously stated that the contract of marine insurance was also *bonae fidei*:

> "*Les memes Auteurs* [i.e. *Roccus, Santerna et Caesaregis*] *dissent que la bonne foi doit régner dans le Contrat d'Assurance, et qu'on doit en écarter les subtilités du droit, pour s'en tenir à l'équité, qui est l'ame du commerce. Iste contractus assecurationis est bonae fidei; et ideo repuiritur in illo bona fides, non dolus, non fraus, sed solum aequitas, quae est anima commercii; et praticandus non est cum juris apicibus et regoribus.*"[270]

Van der Keessel,[271] author of two extensive works on Roman-Dutch insurance law, namely the *Praelectiones Iuris Hodierni ad Hugonis Grotii ad Iurisprudentiam Hollandicam* and the *Theses Selecti Iuris Zelandici*,[272] was of the same opinion, holding the contract of marine insurance out as a nominate contract of good faith whereby, in consideration of a certain price or premium, the losses which may arise from unforeseen danger to the property of another are undertaken to be made good.[273] He defined the contract thus:

> "*Assecuratio est contractus nominatus, consensualis, bonae fidei, quo, pro certo pretio, suscipitur praestatio damni, quod ex incerto periculi accidere rei alienate potest.*"[274]

Also *Van der Linden*[275], another important Roman-Dutch author stated in his *Regtsgeleerd, Practicaal en Koopmans Handboek* that the contract of insurance was one governed by good faith:

> "*Over't algemeen moet men in die behandeling van all geschillen, uit Assurantiën voortspruitende, in't oog houden, dat het Contract van Assurantie eene handeling is, waar in de goede trouw heerschen moet, en waar in, noch aan de zijde van den Assuradeur, noch van den Geassureerden, niets gedoogd kan worden,*

---

268 PARK, J.A.: op. cit., p. vii of the Preface.
269 PARK, J.A.: op. cit., p. 1.
270 EMéRIGON: ***Traité*** *Chap.* I, *Sect.* V, § 1, citing Caesaregis, *disc.* 1, *n.* 2; translation by Samuel Meredith in EMéRIGON: **Treatise** p. 17: "According to the same authors, good faith is to govern in the contract of insurance. The subtleties of law are to be made to yield to that equity, which is the soul of commerce."
271 *Dionysius Godefridus van der Keessel*, 1738-1816.
272 DE JAGER: op. cit., p. 26.
273 WILLE & MILLIN: **Mercantile Law of South Africa** p. 223.
274 VAN DER KEESSEL: ***Theses Selectae*** 712.
275 1756-1835.

> *het welk naar bedriegrije zwemen zoude: in zoo verre, dat, die in deeze overeenkoming listiglijk handelt, gehouden is in alle kosten, schaden en winstderving, buiten de strafe van de* Hooge *Overheid*."[276]

According to *Pothier*, good faith reigned in insurance contracts, in the same way as in all other contracts:

> "*La bonne foi qui doit régner dans le contrat d'assurance, de meme que dans tous les autres,oblige chacun des contractants de ne rien dissimuler à l'autre de ce qu'il sait sur les choses qui font la matière du contrat: car cette dissimulation est un dol...* "[277]

Also the great *Grotius*[278] wrote that insurance contracts were subject to good faith:

> "*Verzeeckering mag geschieden in zulcker voege als de handelaers willen... op zulcke voorwaerden als haer gelieft, mids niet strijdende jegens de goede trouwe.*"[279]

Goldschmidt[280] too, the German jurist who is known particularly for his ***magnum opus*** on German commercial law, the *System des Handelsrechts*, considered that insurance is a contract *bonae fidei.*[281]

In South Africa it has been suggested that the duty of disclosure may have its roots in the aedilitian remedies:

> "At the same time it must be understood that this part of our law is based upon principles well known to the civil law. It was by extending the principles of the Aedilitian Edict and of the law of *dolus malus* that the European jurists and judges have elaborated the law of marine and other insurances. At the root of the aedilitian *actio redhibitorea* lies the principle that a contract of sale can be avoided if the subject-matter contains a latent defect

---

[276] VAN DER LINDEN: ***Koopmans Handboek*** *Boek* 4, *Afdeeling* 6, § 10; (In general, in their dealing with all disputes resulting out of policies of assurance, men must keep in mind that the contract of assurance is an act in which good faith must reign, and in which, neither on the part of the insurer, nor on that of the assured, nothing that might border on fraud could be tolerated: insofar that those acting cunningly in these agreements, are held to be liable for all costs, damages and loss of profit in addition to liability in criminal proceedings.)

[277] POTHIER: ***Traité d'Assurance*** *Chap.* III, *Sect.* III, *n.* 191: "The good faith that should reign in this contract, as in all others, binds each of the parties to dissimulate nothing from the other of what he knows in connection with the subject-matter of the contract: for such dissimulation is a fraud *(*dol*)*..."

[278] *Hugo Grotius* was born at Delft in 1583, and died at Rostock in 1645; see SHERMAN: op. cit. § 266.

[279] GROTIUS: ***Inleidinge*** *Boek* III, *Deel* 2, § 6; Translation in LEE, R.W.: **Grotius: The Jurisprudence of Holland** pp. 421 and 423: "The contract of insurance may be made in any way the parties please... on such conditions as they please, provide there is nothing contrary to good faith."

[280] *Levin Goldschmidt* was born at Danzig in 1829 and died at Wilhelmshöhe in 1897; see the entry at pp. 1747-1749, vol. 1 of the ***Handwörterbuch zur deutschen Rechtsgeschichte***.

[281] GOLDSCHMIDT : ***System des Handelsrechts*** § 158 *n.* 6.

> unknown to the purchaser, which would have affected his judgement in buying it had he known of its existence.[282]
> ... In the sale of slaves, animals, etc., the Civil Law exacted *uberrima fides* and the contract could be set aside both on account of concealment of faults and of misrepresentation (Voet 21.1.3).[283]

It is important to note at this point, that this statement does not reflect a proper account of the Civil Law. Voet did not employ the phrase *uberrima fides* in his treatment of the *actio redhibitoria* and the *action quanti minoris*. Voet merely acknowledged that these actions lay for both concealment and misrepresentation.[284]

> "The concealment of a material fact was often as culpable as misrepresentation. *'Dolum malum a se abesse praestare venditor debet, qui non tantum in eo est, qui fallendi causa obscure loquitur, sed etiam qui insidose obscure dissimulat' (D.18.1.43.2).*[285] *'Si sciens reticuit et emptorem decepit, omnia detrimenta, quae ex ea emptione emptor traxerit, praestaturum ei' (D. 19.1.13. pr.).*[286]
> If, however, the defect is so plain that no reasonable person could have been deceived, there is no such concealment of a material fact as will justify a cancellation. *'Praecipue eas (aedilitias actions) excludit scientia emtoris, sive ille verbis apertis aut rebus ipsis et factis a venditore monitus fuerit, secundum antedicta, sive aliunde cognoverit ante venditionem, rem vitio latente laborare' (D. 21.1.48.3* and *4; Voet, 21.1.9).*[287]
> It must, moreover, be the concealment of some material fact, not of a mere trifling defect. *'Sed et morbum vitiumque gravius subesse oportet, quod usum ministeriumque rei impediat' (Voet, 21.1.8).*[288]
> These principles were elaborated and eventually produced the ... rules as regards contracts of insurance and those of a similar nature."[289]

This would of course accord with the earlier classification of the insurance contract as a kind of contract of sale.

---

[282] WESSELS, J.W.: **Law of Contract in South Africa** Vol. 1 at par. 1039; quoted with approval by Joubert, J.A. in *Mutual and Federal Ins v Oudtshoorn Municipality* 1985 (1) 419, at p. 432I.
[283] WESSELS, J.W.: op. cit., Vol. 1 at par. 1040.
[284] VOET 21. 1. 3: Translation in GANE, P.: **The Selective Voet** Vol. 3 at p. 645: "They are indeed specially available as a result of reticence as to disease, defect or race; but nevertheless also as a result of a statement or promise, as when a seller has declared that certain good qualities or excellence or craftsmanship are present, but it is not found to be so; or on the other hand has stated that certain defects are absent, for instance that a slave is not a gambler or is not a thief, when all the same those defects are present."
[285] "The seller must always warrant his innocence of fraud – a term which includes not only ambiguous statements intended to mislead, but also studied and equivocal concealment."
[286] "If he knows it and says nothing, and so deceives the buyer, he is responsible to him for all loss resulting from the purchase." WESSELS, J.W.: op. cit., Vol. 1 at par. 1041.
[287] "(These aedilitian actions) are especially excluded by knowledge on the part of the purchaser, whether he was warned by the vendor in plain words or by the things and facts themselves, as already said, or whether he knew from other sources, before the sale, that the thing was subject to a latent defect."
[288] Translation in GANE, P.: op. cit., Vol. 3 at p. 653: "Then again a disease or defect of a somewhat serious kind ought to exist, such as interferes with the use and service of the thing."
[289] WESSELS, J.W.: op. cit., Vol. 1 at par. 1042.

In the light of these texts, it seems incontrovertible that the major authors who discussed the contract of marine insurance up until and particularly around the seventeenth and eighteenth centuries agreed that the marine insurance contract was *bonae fidei*, and that *bona fides* had to reign in the contract. But what did they mean by *bona fides*? In the following paragraphs the duties which the parties to the marine insurance policy were bound to perform as a consequence of the general principle of *bona fides*, and the remedies available for breach of these duties, will be discussed.

2.3.2 Duties flowing from *bona fides*

Grotius wrote that any party to the contract of marine insurance acting dishonestly, would be held liable accordingly:

> "*Wie in deze overkominge listelick handelt, is ghehouden in alle kosten, schaden ende winstderving, boven de straffe van de hooge overheid.*"[290]

Van der Linden, as seen above, based this duty not to act fraudulently on good faith.[291] *Emérigon* explained the duties of the parties to the contract as a result of it being subject to *bona fides* as follows:

> "*Si l'une des parties a usé de dol et d'artifice, la moindre peine qu'elle doive encourir, c'est que l'Assurance soit déclarée nulle à son égard. On est coupable de dol, non-seulement lorsque, pour se procurer des Assureurs, ou pour les inviter à se contenter d'une prime moindre, l'on affirme, ou l'on fait entendre des faits contraires à la vérité, mais encore lorsque l'on dissimule de circonstances graves qu'il leur eût importé de connoître avant que de souscrire la police. Dolus malus non tantùm in eo est, qui fallendi causâ obscurè loquitur; sed etiam qui insidiosè obscurè dissimulat.*[292]
> *Il est rare que les Assureurs se rendent coupables de fraude. Obligés de s'en tenir aux faits qu'on leur affirme, et aux pieces qu'on leur exhibe, ils ne sont que trop souvent victimes de leur bonne foi. Le guidon de la Mer, ch. 2, art 15, les compare à des pupilles.*
> *Mais ils doivent prouver d'une maniere concluante, le dol dont ils se plaignent.*
> *Autant que la nature du Contrat le permet, le sort des Assureurs et des Assurés doit être le même à l'actif et au passif. Celui qui veut se faire assurer, doit manifester tous les faits dont il importe aux Assureurs d'être instruits. Les regles que Ciceron établit d'une maniere admirable au sujet du Vaisseau qui, suivi de plusieurs autres, arrive le premier avec un chargement de blé dans le Port d'une Ville affamée, (lib.* 3, *de officiis, cap.* 12 *ff) retrouvent leur application au Contrat d'Assurance.*"[293]

---

[290] GROTIUS: ***Inleidinge*** *Boek* 3, *Deel* 24, § 20; "If any party to this contract acts dishonestly he is liable for all costs, damages and loss of profit in addition to his liability to criminal proceedings." Translation in LEE, R.W.: op. cit., p. 421.

[291] VAN DER LINDEN: ***Koopmans Handboek*** *Boek* IV, *Afdeeling* VI, § 10; see the text to footnote 276 *supra*.

[292] The author draws here from L. 43, § 2, ff. *de contrah empt.;* L. 43, § 2, ff. *de dolo malo*; also Dig. 18. 1. 43. 2 ("Not only is he tainted by fraud, who uses obscure language to mislead, but also conceals…").

[293] EMéRIGON: ***Traité*** *Chap.* I, *Sect.* V, § 2; translation by Samuel Meredith in EMéRIGON: **Treatise** pp. 17-18. "If one of the parties has been guilty of fraud and artifice, the least penalty he should incur is that the insurance with respect to him be declared void. One is guilty of fraud,

Pothier, as mentioned above, also considered good faith to forbid both the insurer and assured to hold back information that related to the subject-matter of the contract.[294] Accordingly, both parties had to disclose everything that might have an effect on the risk against which the insurance had been made:

> *"Les risques qui sont à courir sur les effets assurés, étant une des principales choses qui font la matière du contrat d'assurance, chacun des contractants ne doit rien dissimuler à l'autre de tout ce qu'il sait sur ce qui peut augmenter ou diminuer ces risques. Par exemple, en temps de guerre, les assureurs qui ont connaissance du prochain retour de la paix, ne doivent pas le cahcer à celui qui fait assurer, pour tirer de lui une prime plus considérable que celle qu'il voudrait donner, s'il avait cette connaissance."*[295]

Pothier, furthermore, drew a distinction between the keeping back of information, or *dissimulation* as it is referred to in older authorities, and a false declaration, or misrepresentation. In *Pothier*'s legal scheme, the obligation not to keep back information, which is known by a contractual party in relation to the subject-matter of a contract, is imposed by good faith. As such, the obligation forms part of the natural law, or what *Pothier* referred to as the *for de la conscience* or the *for intérieur*.[296] In turn, the obligation not to lead the other into error by the misrepresentation of matters which are of the substance of the contract, concerns the positive law, or *for extérieur*.[297]

---

not only when to procure himself insurers, or to induce them to rest content with a less premium, he avers or insinuates facts contrary to the truth, but also when he conceals important circumstances which it concerns them to know before underwriting the policy.
It is rarely that fraud is found on the part of the insurers. They are obliged to be governed by the assertions made and the documents exhibited to them, and too often fall victims to their own honesty. The Guidon finds a resemblance between their condition and that of wards. It is incumbent on them, however, to prove conclusively the fraud of which they complain.
So far as the nature of the contract will allow, the chance of the insurers and of the assured must be the same, whether the one shall be entitled to claim and the other bound to pay. A person about to effect insurance must reveal all the facts which it imports the insurers to know. The rules so admirably laid down by Cicero, as to the vessel which, followed by others, arrives first with a cargo of corn at the port of a famished town, are applicable to the contract of insurance."

[294] See the text to footnote 277 *supra*.

[295] POTHIER: ***Traité d'Assurance*** *Chap.* III, *Sect.* III, *n.* 191: The risks that attach to the subject-matter insured, being one of the principal things that form the substance of the contract of insurance, each contracting party must not conceal to the other anything that he knows which can increase or reduce these risks. For example, in time of war, the insurers who have knowledge of the return of peace, may not conceal this from him who made the insurance, in order to draw from him a higher premium than that, which he would be prepared to pay, if he had that knowledge.

[296] POTHIER: ***Traité d'Assurance*** *Chap.* III, *Sect.* III, *n.* 196: *"L'obligation que la bonne foi impose aux parties de ne rien dissimuler de ce qu'elles savant sur les choses qui sont de la substance du contrat, ne concerne ordinairement que le for de la conscience."*

[297] Ibid.: *"Il en est autrement de l'obligation qu'elle impose à chacune des parties, de ne pas induire l'autre en erreur, par de fausses declarations, sur les choses qui sont de la substance du contrat: celle-ci concerne le for extérieur."*; Samuel Meredith explains Pothier's use of *for intérieur* and *for extérieur* beautifully in a note in EMéRIGON: **Treatise** p. 633, n. (d): "The first indicates the natural law; it applies to

Emérigon, careful to show that despite this distinction, the effect in law of both the keeping back of information and of a misrepresentation is to make the policy void, explained *Pothier*'s categorisation of the obligations flowing from good faith as follows:

> "*La fausse déclarations est positive par elle-même. Il est facile de la prouver. Voilà pourquoi elle fournit dans le for extériur un moyen aisé d'attaquer le Contrat. La dissimulation ne laissant par elle-même aucune trace réelle et physique, la chose ne concerne ordinairement que le for de la conscience. Mais il n'est pas moins vrai que la dissimulation des faits ne soit un dol véritable. Si elle est prouvée, on ne doit pas hésiter de casser l'Assurance, qui est esentiellement un Contrat de bonne foi, duquel l'équité veut qu'on écarte toute feinte et toute surprise...*
> *En un mot, il n'y a point de différence sur ce point entre le for intérieur et le for extérieur. Tout dol qui n'est pas prouvé, doit être réprimé ; mais tout dol qui set prouvé, doit être réprimé ; et je condamne très-fort la doctrine scandaleuse du Jesuite Lessius, en son Traité de justitiâ et jure, lib. 2, cap. 28, n. 27, pag. 355, qui soutient qu'un Assureur, pour profiter d'une prime avantageuse, peut dissimuler les faits dont il est instruit en son particulier. Les faits, dit-il, à moi seul connus, qui diminuent le péril, n'en diminuent pas la croyance commune. Adverte si ordinariè multùm detur pro assecuratione, ob magna periculi, quae plerùmque vel à tempestate, vel à pirates impendent, quamvis ego praesciam ex astrologiâ, vel aliundè, non fore tempestatem; aut ex literis amici, non fore piratas, aut fore securum comitatum, possum nihilominùs pretium ordinarium assecurationis accipere; quia illa obligatio passim tanti aaestimatur, eò quòd periculi ordinariè occurrentia sint magna. Occultae enim illae causae, mihi duntaxat notae, quae periculum minuunt, communem aestimationem.*
> *D'apres ce principe, le commerce des Assurances ne seroit qu'un brigandage. Mais les Négocians honnêtes en agissent bien autrement. Ils n'abusent amais de l'ignorance de l'Assuré ; et lorsqu'il s'agit de se faire assurer eux-mêmes, ils n'omettent aucune circonstance des risques auxquels leurs Assureurs doivent s'exposer.*"[298]

---

all the relations and conjunctures of life, it discriminates with wonderful acuteness and precision, is never at fault, and having no positive sanction but what legislation and general reason have given it, commends itself with great and conclusive force to almost every intelligence. The second serves to designate the civil law, whose worst blame is that it falls short of the model it imitates, - whose first excellence, that it aims at conformity with a good pattern. It is, however, but the code of natural justice imperfectly translated into human language."

[298] EMéRIGON: ***Traité des Assurances*** *Chap.* XV, *Sect.* III, § 3; translation by Samuel Meredith in EMéRIGON: **Treatise** pp. 633-634: "A false declaration is positive in its nature. It is ready of proof. Hence it furnishes in the *for extérieur* an easy means of attacking the contract. On the other hand, dissimulation not necessarily leaving any real and physical trace behind it, it ordinarily concerns only the tribunal of conscience. But it is not the less true that the dissimulation of facts is a veritable fraud. If proved, it is to avoid the insurance… .
In effect there is no difference on this point between the *for intérieur* and the *for extérieur.* All fraud not proved, remains unpunished to the eyes of men; but every fraud which is proved is to be repressed; and I condemn severely the shameful doctrine of the Jesuit, Lesius, that an insurer, in order to profit by an advantageous premium, may dissimulate the facts within his own private knowledge. Facts, says he, known to myself alone, which diminish the peril, do not diminish the general estimate of it… .
On this principle the business of insurances would be hardly more than a system of robbery. But honourable merchants act far differently. They never abuse the ignorance of the assured; and when effecting insurance for themselves, they omit no circumstance of the risks to which their insurers are about to expose themselves." (*Emérigon* made these statements in the part of his

The first legislation that dealt with the duties flowing from the observance of good faith in insurance contracts in great detail was the *Hamburger Assekuranz- und Havarie-Ordnung* of 1731.[299] The *Ordonnance de la Marine* of 1681 did include a duty to include various facts in the policy, e.g. the name of the vessel, the name of the port where the vessel was to depart, the time the policy was to commence and terminate, etc, but it did not circumscribe the duty in as much detail as the *Hamburger Assekuranz- und Havarie-Ordnung*.[300] The latter also required that, in order that the policy be completed correctly, it should be clearly indicated at what time the vessel departed from the port at which the risk was to commence.[301] The regulation, however, contained further articles relating to the duty to disclose, which it is necessary to quote in full:

> "(*Tit.* IV, *Art.* 12) *Ein jeder kann sich zu aller Zeit, wann und wie es ihm gefällig ist, versichern lassen. Er ist aber gehalten seine von dem Schiffe habende Nachricht dem Assekuradeur getreulich zu eröffnen und in der Police anzuzeigen, ob und wie lange das Schiff von dem Orte, wo es seine Ladung Eingenomen, bereits abgegangen, oder ob noch daselbst, oder am welchen orte sonst es liege. Geschiehet in der Police keine Erwähnung davon, so wird es so genommen, daß, zufolge der jüngsten Nachricht und Wissenschaft, die der Assekurirte zur Zeit der Versicherung davon gehabt und erhalten, oder wenigstens haben können, das Schiff noch wirklich an dem Orte der Ladung gelegen. Wäre aber das Schiff der Zeit bereits abgegangen, oder schon über die gewöhnliche Zeit unterwegs, und derjenige, der versichern läßt, hätte darum gewußt und solches nicht angezeigt, so ist die Assekuranz von keinen Würden, der Assekuradeur aber die volle Prämie zu behalten befugt.*[302]
>
> (*Tit.* IV, *Art.* 13) *Wenn einer, der die Versicherung thun läßt, die Wissenschaft und Nachricht, welche er von seinem Correspondenten hat, sie möge beschaffen sein, wie sie wolle, und eintreffen oder nicht, aufrichtig und redlich in der Police angezeigt; so hat die Versicherung ihre Richtigkeit, und sind die Assekuradeurs in allen Fällen daran verbunden, in Entstehung dessen aber zu nichts gehalten.*"[303]

---

treatise dealing with the making of insurance on a vessel which was already either lost or arrived at the time the policy was signed, for which see p. 53 *infra*.)

[299] DE JONGE.: ***De Mededeelingsplicht van den Verzekerde in Theorie en Practijk*** p. 13

[300] *Ordonnance de la Marine*, *Liv.* III, *Tit.* VI, *art.* 3; PARDESSUS: ***Collection de Lois Maritimes*** Vol. 4, p. 370 ; also see VALIN: ***Commentaire sur L'Ordonnance de la Marine*** p. 58, and the discussion at pp. 447-462.

[301] *Tit.* I, *Art.* 4: "*Zu richtiger Ausfüllung der Policen wird erfordert, daß deutlich darin angezeigt werde die Zeit, wann das Schiff von dem Orte, wo die Gefahr anfängt, abgegangen.*" See: NOLTE: ***Benecke's System*** Vol. 2, pp. 11-12.

[302] DE JONGE.: op. cit., p. 13; (Anyone can at all times make an insurance, how and when he find it convenient. He is, however, obliged faithfully to disclose to the underwriter any information received of the ship and to indicate in the policy if and for how long the ship has left the place where it loaded its cargo, or whether it is still lying in the same or at any other place. If no mention is made of it in the policy, it will be taken that, according to the latest information and knowledge that the assured had and received at the time of the insurance, or leastwise could have had, the ship was still lying at the place of loading. If the ship already sailed or had been *en route* for longer than the usual time, and the assured knew about it and did not disclose it, the insurance is invalid, although the insurer is entitled to retain the premium.)

[303] DE JONGE.: op. cit., p. 13; (If someone who makes an insurance, honestly and reasonably included in the policy the knowledge and information that he has from his correspondents, no

The *Hamburger Assekuranz- und Havarie-Ordnung* of 1731 also contained a provision dealing with the disclosure with regard to the cargo that was to be carried by a vessel:

> "(*Tit.* IV, *Art.* 10) *Alles dasjenige, was von den im Kriege Begriffenen Mächten als Contrebande geachtet, erklärt und offenbar dafür bekannt gemacht wird, soll in Kriegs-Zeiten, bei Strafe der Nullität des Contractes, in der Policen namentlich erwähnt, wenigstens überhaupt, daß Contrebande Waaren in dem Schiffe geladen, angezeigt werden.*"[304]

The *Hollandsche Consultatien, Advysen en Advertissementen* of 6 April 1622 stated:

> "*Een Asseuradeur ten tijde van 't passeren van die Police van Asseurantie... niet geweten habbende dat de geasseureerde goederen waren Contrabande goederen... en dat de geaseureerde zulks wel heeft geweten... is den Asseuradeur niet gehouden aan den geasseureerde te vergoeden de Confiscatie... die uit zoodanigen oorzaak daar op volgt.*"[305]

However, apart from the *Hamburger Assekuranz- und Havarie-Ordnung* of 1731 which was the first legislative instrument that dealt extensively with the matter of disclosure, there were several other municipal regulations that governed the law relating to marine insurance. Some of them also touched upon the issue of good faith and the duties thereof, e.g. disclosure. One of the earliest municipal laws, a *Keur* of 31 January 1598, stems from Amsterdam. In article 3 thereof, it is provided that the policy shall be null in the event that the assured culpably failed to disclose the name of the vessel, the name of the Captain, as well as the place of loading and of discharge.[306] Similar provisions are to be found in other municipal laws in Holland[307], notably the *Rotterdam*sche *Keur* of 1721 that provided in article LXXXIII that "*alles hetgeen by deze Ordonnantie geboden is daar in te expresseren.*"[308]

---

matter how it is obtained and whether it proves to be true or not, the insurance will be in order and the underwriters are bound to it in all cases, but not held liable in case of non-disclosure." The German word "*Entstehung*" is used in this context in the place of the word "*Unterlassung*": see NOLTE: op. cit., Vol. 2, p. 12.

[304] DE JONGE.: op. cit., p. 14; (Everything declared and publicised as contraband by powers engaged in war, shall, in times of war, be listed in the policy, at the very least, it shall be disclosed that contraband was loaded onto the ship, failure of which shall lead to the contract being a nullity.)

[305] *Derde Deel* CLXXV; DE JONGE.: op. cit., p. 14; (An insurer not knowing that the insured goods were contraband at the time the policy of insurance had been executed whilst the assured did know of the fact ... the insurer is not bound to reimburse the assured for the confiscation that follows from such a cause.)

[306] GOUDSMIT: op. cit., pp. 312-313; DE JONGE.: op. cit., p. 15.

[307] GOUDSMIT: op. cit.,, particularly this author's discussion of article 2 of the Amsterdam *Keur* of 10 March 1744 at p. 336, as well as of article 20 of the *Rotterdamsche Keur* of 1635 and articles LXXVIII and LXXIX of the *Rotterdamsche Keur* of 1721; also DE JONGE.: op. cit., p. 15.

[308] GOUDSMIT: op. cit., p. 395; (everything commanded by this Ordinance is to be expressed in it [i.e. the policy]).

2.3.3 Extent of the duties to disclose and not to misrepresent

In dealing with misrepresentation occurring in the description of the vessel, *Emérigon* said that the assured should take care to disclose the true character of the ship.[309] However, this statement was not without a qualification: if the insurers knew for certain on which ship they were underwriting a policy, it would not matter if she was falsely described: "*falsa demonstration non nocet*", the false description does not harm.[310] Still, –

> *"...s'il ne conste pas que les Assureurs aient connu le navire énoncé dans la police, et si la fausse qualifaction qu'on lui a donnée, a été de nature à diminuer l'idée du risque dont ils se chargeoient, ils sont recevables à se plaindre de cette surprise, et à requérir la cassation de l'Assurance."*[311]

Therefore, where an insurer underwrote a policy on a ship of a particular description, he could rescind the contract if it appeared that the vessel in fact did not conform to the description given by the assured. The reason for this was that the insurer signed the policy on the ship of that particular description in good faith. If she turned out to be of some other description which would expose her to more dangers than a vessel of the assured's description, such a misrepresentation would strike at the substance of the insurer's intention, and, as a consequence would avoid the contract.[312] Accordingly, if the false description diminished the underwriter's estimation of the risk, the policy would be void.[313] However, if the description were false, but did not diminish the estimation of the risk , i.e. if it were "indifferent to the object of the peril", the insurer would have no reason to complain and the policy would remain valid.[314] An example of such a case involved insurance on the cargo aboard the *pinque* "*St. François*". She was subsequently taken. The insurers refused to pay on the policy, producing proof that the vessel "was masted *à vible,* and that she was a polacre", i.e. a kind of vessel used to navigate the Mediterranean with square sails on a great mast, and lateens[315] on a second smaller mast. The insurers were held to the policy and ordered to pay the loss, "...because the risk upon the St. François, a polacre, had been in every sense the same as upon the St.

---

[309] EMéRIGON: **Treatise** p. 128 (***Traité*** *Chap.* VI, *Sect.* III, § 1), citing Casaregis, *disc.* 1, *n.* 30 as authority.

[310] Ibid.

[311] EMéRIGON: ***Traité*** *Chap.* VI, *Sect.* III, § 1; translation in EMéRIGON: **Treatise** p. 129: "...if it is not shown that the insurers knew the vessel announced in the policy, and if the false description given it is of a nature to lessen the estimation of the risk taken, they are entitled to complain of this surprise, and to demand the rescinding of the insurance."

[312] EMéRIGON: **Treatise** p. 129 (***Traité*** *Chap.* VI, *Sect.* III, § 1).

[313] EMéRIGON: **Treatise** p. 131 (***Traité*** *Chap.* VI, *Sect.* III, § 3).

[314] Ibid.

[315] Lateens are triangular sails at an angle of 45 degrees to the mast, common in the Mediterranean, as a result of which it has its name. In French it is known as "*voile latine*", i.e. Latin sails. See: **Concise Oxford Dictionary**

François, a pinque; the intrinsic form of the masting not altering at all the nature or goodness of the vessel."[316]

Another matter related to the "*Junon de Bayonne*", a French cruiser which made six prizes in 1746. One of these six prizes, the "*Port Marchand*", during the engagement that preceded her taking, had her main mast as well as the mast next aft of the main mast shattered. The Commander, Captain *Vigoureux*, repaired the damages and having put a crew on each ship, returned with two of the prizes to Bayonne. He insured the other four prizes including the "*Port Marchand*", in Marseilles, not mentioning the state that she was in. Shortly afterwards, news was received that she, together with the other three prizes, had been retaken by the English. The insurers defended the claim, i.a. on the basis that the policy did not exhibit the weak condition of the "*Port Marchand*". The insurers were ordered to pay on the policy, "...on the ground that they must have presumed that vessels captured by force of arms had been maltreated."[317]

Another case to which the author referred in the context of goods that could not be insured,[318] and which explained something of the extent of the duty to disclose, involved insurance upon a cargo of silk onboard the "*St. Joseph*".[319] It happened that the silk was considered as contraband by the Spanish. Nevertheless, *Emérigon* found that the cargo could be insured in France: only effects considered to be contraband by the French could not be insured in France. Important to note though, is that neither the insurers, nor *Emérigon* in his treatise, suggested that this was a circumstance that should have been disclosed by the assured.

From a reading of *Emérigon* and the cases that he mentioned, two remarks can be made regarding the extent of the duties flowing from good faith. First of all, the duties to disclose and not to misrepresent related to facts that were essential to the subject-matter of the contract of marine insurance, i.e. the maritime risk insured against. Second, only non-disclosure or misrepresentation of such facts that would distort the perception of the risk were considered to be a breach of these duties and against good faith.

2.3.4 Excursus: Insurance on *good or bad news*

Van Bynkershoek,[320] one of the most eminent Dutch jurists and Romanists of the early eighteenth century and famous for his work on maritime law, made it

[316] EMéRIGON: ***Traité*** *Chap.* VI, *Sect.* III, § 3; translation by Samuel Meredith in EMéRIGON: **Treatise** p. 131.
[317] EMéRIGON: **Treatise** pp. 138-139, also p. 190 (***Traité*** *Chap.* VI, *Sect.* IV, § 4 and *Chap.* VIII, *Sect.* IX, § 3).
[318] EMéRIGON: **Treatise** p. 171 (***Traité*** *Chap.* VIII, *Sect.* V, § 2).
[319] Cf. p. 65 *infra*.
[320] *Cornelius van Bynkershoek* was born at Middelburg in Zeeland, 1673, and died 1743.

abundantly clear that in order for the contract of marine insurance to be valid, the risk must be uncertain and unknown to both insurer and assured:

> "*Ut ratae sint assecuraiones, necesse est, ignorari statum, in quo sunt res, de quibus agitur. De Grotius de Jure Belli L. II. C. 12. §.23. it scripsit: Contractus avertendi periculi, quem asseurationem vocant, omnino nullus erit, si contrahentium alter rem, de qua agitur, aut salvam, quo destinabatur, pervinisse, aut periisse sciverit.*"[321]

Accordingly, the contract of insurance was void if one of the parties knew that the risk was not uncertain. *Van der Linden* added that even where one of the parties to the policy *could have known* that the risk was not uncertain anymore, the policy would be void.[322] This matter was also dealt with in one of the earliest codes dealing with insurance matters, i.e. the *Hamburger Assekuranz- und Havarie-Ordnung* of 1731:

> "*Ist ein Schiff zur Zeit da die Assekuranz geschieht bereits vergangen oder verloren, und kann der Assekurirte allenfalls eidlich erhärten, daß er von dem Schaden und Verlust des Schiffes, zu der Zeit, da er die Versicherung thun lassen, oder solche zu thun befohlen, nicht gewußt, so hat die Assekuranz, wann sie eher geschlossen worden, als der Assekurirte Nachricht von dem Schaden erhalten, oder falls derselbe außerhalb Landes sich befindet, ehe solche Nachricht von ihm hieher geschrieben und allhier kund werden können, an beiden Seiten ihre Richtigkeit, und müssen die Assekuradeurs den Schaden ihrer Verpflichtung gemäß, bezahlen.*"[323]

A *Placaet* of King Philip of 1563[324] went further and declared that the policy was to be null merely by reason of the fact that the ship or things insured were perished at the time the insurance was made. This was not a correct statement of the usages of the time, nor was it in conformity with the Statutes of Barcelona.[325] Accordingly, the position was rectified in a subsequent *Placaet* of 1570, which declared that a policy should only be void in the above-mentioned circumstances when, at the

---

[321] VAN BYNKERSHOEK: ***Quast. Jur. Priv.*** *Lib.* 4, *Cap.* 26, *n.* 6; VAN DER LINDEN: op. cit., *Boek* IV, *Afdeeling* VI, § IV stated: "*Dit gevaar moet onzeker zijn, en aan de wederzijdsche contractanten onbekend. Hierom is Assurantie volstrekt van geene waarde, indien één van hun geweten heeft, dat het geassureerde goed, of ter plaatse zijner bestemming behouden was aangekomen, of verongelukt.*"; (The risk must be uncertain, and not known to the respective contracting parties. Therefore, the contract of insurance is absolutely void, if one of them knew that the thing insured either had arrived at its destination intact, or had perished.)

[322] VAN DER LINDEN: op. cit., *Boek* 4, *Afdeeling* 6, § 4.

[323] *Tit.* V, *Art.* 9; DE JONGE.: op. cit., pp. 13-14; (Is a ship perished or lost at the time the assurance is concluded, and if the assured can substantiate if need be, that he did not know of the damage and loss of the ship at the time he concluded the insurance or ordered such, the insurance remains intact for both parties, if it was concluded before the assured received notice of the loss, or if he was out of the country before such notice could be dispatched by him and became known here, and the insurers must pay the claim in accordance with their obligation.)

[324] *Cap.* III. *Van der Versekeringen ofte Asseurantien*, *Art.* 4, in VERWER: ***Nederlants See-Rechten*** p. 129.

[325] See p. 38 *supra*; GOUDSMIT: op. cit., p. 246.

moment when the policy was signed, the assured had knowledge of the loss of the vessel or things insured.[326]

The owner of a vessel or merchandise or someone having an interest thereupon (in those days when information was not as readily available as in our age that are more or less defined by the immediate availability of information) might have wished, upon hearing a rumour of loss at sea of the ship, to obtain cover, or where the cover ran out and there was still no news about her safe arrival, to extend the cover. Under these circumstances, the parties normally concluded the policy *on good or bad news*. The clause *on good or bad news*, in fact, appears to have been inserted in most insurance policies of the time.[327] In England, ships that had been missing for some time were insured *lost or not lost*, a practice *Park* condemned as "very hazardous". His reason was that "if the ship should be lost at the time of the insurance, still the underwriter, provided there be no fraud is liable".[328] The effect was indeed that the insurer promised to pay the loss, even though news of the disaster should reach the parties a moment after the signing of the policy,[329] and that the assured promised to pay the premium even though the news of the safe arrival of his ship should reach them immediately after the policy had been signed.[330] "The contract is reciprocal: it turns on a benefit to the insurer if the news is good; it turns on a benefit to the assured if bad."[331] Another effect of the clause was that the presumption *juris et de jure* did not operate.[332] As between the insurer and the assured, however, the fate of the vessel must have been uncertain upon signing the policy: "...the two parties must have acted in good faith: otherwise the clause on good or bad news would be null, and the contract also would be so."[333]

[326] GOUDSMIT: op. cit., p. 246.
[327] EMéRIGON: **Treatise** p. 642 (***Traité*** *Chap.* XV, *Sect.* V), states that the agreement *on good or bad news* was in the printed form at Rouen and at Bordeaux and, although not so at Marseilles, was seldom omitted in policies concluded there, and at p. 643, that at that present day (being the late eighteenth century) it was the custom to insert this clause in all policies. VAN DER LINDEN: op. cit., *Boek* 4, *Afdeeling* 6, § 4, makes mention of marine insurance contracts on "*goede en kwade tijdinge*".
[328] PARK, J.A.: op. cit., p. 28, where he also says that the words "*lost or not lost*" were "*peculiar to English policies, not being inserted in the policies of foreign nations.*"
[329] The implication is of course that, under these circumstances, the risk already materialised before the insurance was entered into.
[330] EMéRIGON: **Treatise** p. 643 (***Traité*** *Chap.* XV, *Sect.* V).
[331] Ibid.
[332] Ibid., pp. 637 and 642 (***Traité*** *Chap.* XV, *Sect.* IV and *Chap.* XV, *Sect.* V); this was a presumption of fraud that operated against either party to the policy where, through the proximity of the places, it might have been possible for either the insurer to know of the safe arrival of the vessel, or for the assured of her loss. The different regulations of the time laid down different measures by means of which it could be ascertained whether the news of arrival or loss might have been known. So, the Règlement of Barcelona stated that news travelled at one league to the hour, whereas the *Ordonnance de la Marine* prescribed a league and a half to the hour.
[333] Ibid., p. 643 (***Traité*** *Chap.* XV, *Sect.* V).

In cases of insurance on good or bad news, *Emérigon* pointed out on the authority of *Pothier*, that the law worked with a fiction.[334] According to *Pothier*, the rules of the natural law required that a contract for marine insurance would be null if the subject-matter of the policy was no longer in existence upon conclusion of the contract. This would be the case even where both parties were ignorant of the fact. This was the consequence according to the natural law in a contract of sale, when the *merx* no longer existed at the time of the contract although the parties were ignorant of that fact, and the natural law required the same in the case of insurance policies. But *Pothier* explained that the position in marine insurance law was slightly different:

> "*Mais le droit civil a ajouté sur ce point au droit naturel. Quoique les effets n'existassent plus, et fussent déjà péris lors du contrat par lequel on les a assures; si la partie n'en a su nip u savoir la perte lors du contrat, ces effets, par une fiction de droit, en consideration de la bonne foi de la parite qui a fait assurer, sont supposés avoir été encore existent au temps du contrat, et avoir pu lui server de matière, et n'être péris que lors de la nouvelle qu'on a eue de leur perte.*"[335]

Grotius dealt with this matter in the following way:

> "*Verzeeckering van goederen, die ten tijde van die verzeeckering buiten kennisse des ghene die de zelve laet verzeeckeren, waren vergaen, gerooft ofte bedorven, zijn krachtig: maer waren de goederen zoo lang te vooren vergaen, dat hy die laet verzeeckeren, daer van de wete konde hebben, 't zy ter zee ofte te lande, reeckenende drie mijlen voor een uir, zoo wird de kenisse ghehouden voor bewezen, 't en waer de verzeeckering ware geschied op goede ende quade tijding: in welcken gevalle den verzeeckerde, hem aenbiedende by eede te zuiveren, den verzeeckeraer zal zijn gehouden de verzeeckering te voldoen, ofte de kennisse van die verzeeckerde te bewijzen ...*"[336]

---

[334] Ibid., p. 643 (***Traité*** *Chap.* XV, *Sect.* II).

[335] POTHIER: ***Traité d'Assurance*** *Chap.* I., *Sect.* II., *n.* 12, translation by Samuel Meredith in EMéRIGON: **Treatise** p. 625: "The civil law has added on this point to the natural law. When the parties have contracted in good faith, and the insurer has not known nor could have known at the time of the contact, that the ship was arrived safe, and that the risks with which he charges himself by the contract had ceased, the civil law sustains the contract, in supposing, by a fiction of law, that the ship is arrived, and the risks ceased only from the day of news had of it. So, although the effects should have no longer existed, but were already perished at the time of the contract, if the party has not then known or could not have known the loss, these effects by fiction of law, in consideration of the good faith of the party, are supposed to have been still existing at the time of the contract, - to have served for its subject, and to have perished only at the time news was received of the loss." Cf. also EMéRIGON: **Treatise** at p. 643 (***Traité*** *Chap.* XV, *Sect.* II).

[336] GROTIUS: **Inleidinge** *Boek* 3, *Deel* 24, § 5; Translation in LEE, R.W.: op. cit., p. 421: "Insurance of goods which at the time of the insurance were perished, robbed, or spoilt without knowledge of the insured, is effectual: but if the goods had perished so long before that the insured could have knowledge of the fact, whether it were on sea or on land, counting three miles as one hour, then knowledge is held to be proved, unless the insurance were made on good or bad tidings: in this case the insured offering to clear himself by oath the insurer will be bound to make good the insurance or to prove that the insured had knowledge of the loss..."

Accordingly, good faith prohibited a party to the insurance policy from taking advantage of the ignorance of facts of which he was privately knowledgeable to the effect that the risk had already materialised, – i.e. where the ship was already lost – or where the risk was not eminent anymore – i.e. where the ship safely arrived. *Grotius* said that such knowledge not only disturbed the equality that should exist in all reciprocal contracts, but was contrary to the proper nature of the contract of insurance, which turned on an uncertain danger.[337]

Emérigon mentioned various examples of cases in France during the course of the eighteenth century, where the courts had to decide whether an assured or insurer acted against good faith in signing a policy of marine insurance, in the knowledge that the vessel had perished or had arrived. One[338] of these matters involved the pink[339] "*St. François*", which i.a. was to carry from Morvedre to Sette a cargo of wool in which a French merchant from Valentia, called *Duclos*, had an interest. On the 6th of August 1762, the vessel was taken by an English privateer. On the next day, *Duclos*, who had not yet had word of the incident, wrote the following to one *Chaudon* in Marseilles: "If on receipt you have no advice of the arrival at Sette of the pinque St. Francois, *Captain Olive*, I pray you to insure at once 60,000 livres on wool shipped for my account." While the letter was on its way to Marseilles, *Captain Olive* managed to escape with his crew and made a statement in front of the vice-consul of France at Vinneros on the 13th of August. On the 18th, *Chaudon*, having received the letter, approached a broker who opened the policy on the next day, i.e. the 19th of August, including a clause "*notwithstanding good or bad news*". On that same evening, the Spanish courier arrived with several letters advising of the capture of the "*St. François*". Among the letters was another letter from *Duclos*, in which he wrote to *Chaudon*: "I confirm my respects of the 7th of this month; particularly the request for insurance for 60,000 liv. … I wish the more that you should have effected the said insurance in whole, because of a rumour here that captain Olive has been taken… . We can say nothing of it yet, until we know positively what it relates to. Meanwhile, I shall be impatient to learn from you the completion of the insurance."[340] At eight o'clock the following morning, the broker attended to the underwriter *Aillaud*, who signed the policy for 3,000 liv., without affixing a new date. Upon leaving *Aillaud*'s house, the broker learned of the letters that arrived the evening before, telling of the capture. The broker hurried back to *Aillaud*'s house, where they altered the policy, leaving the signature, to assure for 100 liv. only. Subsequently, proceedings were instituted against *Aillaud* and the broker. Although *Aillaud* was held to be an honest man, it was said that he had condemned himself, and that "if the policy was good for 100 livres, it must be so for 3000 livres." The Admiralty in Marseilles accordingly ordered

[337] GROTIUS: ***De Jure Belli ac Pacis*** *lib.* 2, *cap.* 12, § 22.
[338] EMéRIGON: **Treatise** p. 628 (***Traité*** *Chap.* XV, *Sect.* III, § 2).
[339] A pink, also *pingue* or *pin(c)ke*, was a sailing-ship, especially with a narrow stern, originally small and flat-bottomed, according to **The Concise Oxford Dictionary**.
[340] EMéRIGON: **Treatise** p. 628 (***Traité*** *Chap.* XV, *Sect.* III, § 2).

Aillaud to pay the 3000 livres. Subsequently, on appeal the *parlement* of Aix, reversed the sentence. *Emérigon* reports the reasons for that decision:

> *"Il étoit prouvé ... que le 20, à 8 heures du matin, la nouvelle de la perte étoit publique dans Marseille ; et qu'à la même époque, le sieur Chaudon avoit déja reçu la derniere lettre de Duclos. Mais le sieur Chaudon n'avoit pas eu le moyen d'aviser le Courtier (qui étoit alors en tournée) pour qu'il cessât de chercher des signatures. Dans ces circonstances, le Parlement crut que l'équité répugnoit à la demande de l'Assuré. On n'eut garde cependant de condamner l'Assuré à la peine de double prime, parce qu'il n'étoit coupable d'aucune fraude.*
> *Pour la bonne regle, il semble que le Courtier auroit dû être reprimandé, soit pour avoir altéré l'acte par lui reçu, soit pour n'avoir pas renouvellé, ou fait renouveller la date de la police."*[341]

Accordingly, the policy was void not for fraud, neither for non-disclosure on the part of the assured, but because it was against equity to keep the policy intact, where the assured came to know before, and the insurer after, the policy was effected that there existed no basis for the insurance. This appears to be the actual reason for the decision: that equity or good faith dictates that the contractual parties, i.e. the assured and insurer, should be equals as far as their knowledge of facts relating to the basis of the contract is concerned. Accordingly, in this case, it was against good faith and equity to allow the assured to have the advantage of the fact that the insurer did not know of the loss, although the assured did not act fraudulently.

Another matter involved the ship "*La Belle Esclave*" which left Marseilles in 1754 for the Levant.[342] Subsequently, the commander of the "*Le Commerce*", Captain Teissel, reported at the Health Office at Marseilles that on the 9th of March between Sicily and Sardinia, he was boarded by an English privateer. The Captain stated that the privateer towed a French ship of about twelve or fourteen guns, that had left Marseilles a few days before. On the very last of day of March, the supercargo of Captain Teissel's ship made the following statement: "...the prize made by the English privateer was *out of Toulon*, so the sailors of the privateer say. She is a ship of fourteen or sixteen guns, painted black and yellow, with a bright figure-head. She was in ballast. I can give you no other information." (Emphasis in original text) This was an accurate description of the "*Belle Esclave*", except for

---

[341] EMéRIGON: ***Traité*** *Chap.* XV, *Sect.* III, § 2, translation by Samuel Meredith in EMéRIGON: **Treatise** p. 630: "It was shown ... [t]hat, on the 20th, at eight o'clock in the morning, the news of the loss was publicly known at Marseilles; and that, at the same moment, Chaudon has already received the last letter from Duclos. But Chaudon had no opportunity of instructing the broker (who was then on his walk) to cease soliciting signatures. Under these circumstances the parlement thought that equity was against the claim of the assured. They avoided condemning the assured to the penalty of *double premium*, because he was not guilty of any fraud. In strictness, the broker should have been reprimanded, both for having altered the instrument received by him, and for not having renewed, or caused to be renewed, the date in the policy." (Emphasis in translation, but not in the original French text.)

[342] The "Levant" is the Eastern part of the Mediterranean with its islands and surrounding countries, *vide* **The Concise Oxford Dictionary**.

the place of departure. On the same day, one Mr. Gouffre caused her to be insured for 1000 livres. Upon a subsequent action on the policy, the insurers were ordered to pay on the policy. The statement of Captain Teissel was held to contain nothing positive, whereas the letter written by the supercargo was not publicly known when the insurance was made.[343]

Emérigon mentions another matter[344] on which he was personally consulted in 1781 involving an insurance underwritten in Marseilles on a cargo heading for that city. In fact, upon underwriting the policy, the cargo had already been in port for 6 days. The policy was "*on good or bad news*", and the insurer contended that he was entitled to the premium. Apparently many merchants were of the opinion that the insurer should succeed. *Emérigon* did not agree and gave the following reasons for his decision:

> *"1°. le risque des merchandises d'un Navire déja arrive dans le Port de sa destination, ne fit jamais par lui-même la matiere d'une Assurance maritime.*
> *2°. La publicité du retour du Navire dans le lieu même où l'Assurance a été faite, suffit pour render nulle cette Assurance, suivant les regles ci-dessus rappellées.*
> *3°. L'article 40, h. t., en permettant de faire des Assurances sur bonnes ou mauvaises nouvelles, suppose qu'il y ait une distance entre l'endroit de l'arrivée du Vaisseau, et le lieu où la plice a été passée. Cela résulte de l'article qui précede.*
> *4°. Il répugneroit que dans pareilles circonstances, on laissât subsister un Contrat, duquel toute apparence de fraude doit être soigneusement écartée.*
> *Je fais que beaucoup de Négocians ne sont pas de cet avis; et l'on m'a attesté qu'en pareil cas, la prime avoit été payée. Je persiste cependant dans mon opinion. Notre Port est un asyle assuré pour les Navires qu'il renferme: Statio benè fida carinis. Ils ne peuvent y entrer, sans que le Capitaine ait fait sa déclaration assermentée au Bureau de la Santé. Pareilles déclarations sont aussitôt rendues publiques, et un Assureur a très-mauvaise grace de vouloir profiter de l'erreur supine d'un Citoyen mal avisé: L'abitante in una citta si deve presumere che sappia ciò che in quella notoriamente succede. Casaregis, il cambista instruito, cap. 1, n. 21. La présumption dont cet Auteur parle, est admissible contre l'Assureur qui voudroit profiter d'une prime gratuite, et nullement contre l'Assuré, dont l'ignorance réelle n'est pas equivoque: en pareil cas, le premier, certat de lucro captando; et le second, de damno vitando."*[345] (Emphasis in original text)

---

[343] EMéRIGON: **Treatise** pp. 631-632 (***Traité*** *Chap.* XV, *Sect.* III, § 2).

[344] EMéRIGON: **Treatise** p. 635 (***Traité*** *Chap.* XV, *Sect.* III, § 7).

[345] EMéRIGON: **Treatise** *Chap.* XV, *Sect.* III, § 7; translation by Samuel Meredith in EMéRIGON: **Treatise** p. 636: "The risk on goods of a vessel already arrived in the *port* of its destination, has never made by itself the subject of a marine insurance. The publicity of the vessel's return in the very place where the insurance has been made, suffices to render this insurance null, according to the rules before stated. The *Ordonnance*, in permitting insurances to be made on good or bad news, supposes that there is a distance between *the place of arrival of the ship, and the place where the policy has been passed.* It would be a contradiction in such circumstances, to enforce a contract, from which every suspicion of fraud ought to be carefully removed. ...I am aware that many merchants do not agree with me; and I have been informed, that, in a like case, the premium has been paid. Still I hold to my opinion. Our port is an assured asylum for the vessels it contains: *Statio benè fida carinis.* They cannot enter there without the captain has made his declaration on oath at the Health Office. These declarations are immediately made public, and an insurer could only with a very bad grace be willing to profit by the supineness of a

These decisions appear to have been dictated by the rule in Roman law – to which *Emérigon* referred in the second sentence of the previous paragraph – that a person is not to be presumed ignorant of what is known to all the inhabitants of the town where he dwells, nor of what is manifested in public advertisements. In this regard, Emérigon approved of the usage of Marseilles according to which it was for the insurers to prove that the news of the loss had been known in the city when the insurance was made, not that the assured knew of it.[346] However, ignorance of facts is presumed, according to the author, unless proof to the contrary suggests otherwise.[347] Accordingly, no one could be blamed for being deceived if he was merely ignorant of facts known to others.[348] Both parties to the insurance contract are presumed to have acted in good faith, until the contrary is proven.[349] The central notion appears to be that the parties should be put on an equal footing as far as information relating to the risk is concerned:

> "*S'il n'y a point de fraude, et que l'une des Parties ne soit pas plus instruite que l'autre, la moindre incertitude de l'événement heureux ou malheureux, suffit pour valider l'Assurance...*
> *Malgré le bruit public de la perte ou de l'arivée du Navire, l'Assurance seroit légitime, si ce bruit n'avoit aucun caractere de certitude, et qu'il fût également connu des Parties contractantes.*"[350] (Emphasis in original text)

It becomes, therefore, abundantly clear from the texts of the old authorities starting with the likes of *Santerna* and *Roccus*, right through to *Grotius*, *Van Bynkershoek*, *Pothier* and *Emérigon* that *bona fides* or good faith had been part and parcel of the marine insurance contract right from the start. This is confirmed by reference to the language used in the oldest policies available as well as by the provisions in the first regulations and acts dealing with marine insurance.

As in all other contracts, good faith, first of all, dictated that there should be no fraud or deceit in contracts of insurance. In the context of marine insurance, the function of good faith to deter fraud meant that both insurer and assured should not misrepresent any facts relating to the substance of the contract, i.e. the risk attaching to the subject-matter to be insured. Further to this, good faith required

citizen illy informed. *L'abitante in una citta*, says Casaregis, *si deve presumere che sappia ciò che in quella notoriamente succede.* The presumption of which this author speaks, applies to the case of an insurer who desires to profit by a gratuitous premium, and not to the assured, whose actual ignorance is not disputed: in such a case, the first, *certat de lucro captando*; and the second, de *damno vitando.*"

[346] Ibid., p. 634 (***Traité*** *Chap.* XV, *Sect.* III, § 4).

[347] Ibid. p. 634 (***Traité*** *Chap.* XV, *Sect.* III, § 5); also see ROCCUS: op. cit., *Art.* 51, *No.* 175.

[348] EMéRIGON: **Treatise** at p. 634 (***Traité*** *Chap.* XV, *Sect.* III, § 4).

[349] Ibid p. 635 (***Traité*** *Chap.* XV, *Sect.* III, § 5).

[350] EMéRIGON: ***Traité*** *Chap.* XV, *Sect.* III, § 6; translation by Samuel Meredith in EMéRIGON: **Treatise** p. 635: "If there is no fraud, and one of the parties is not better informed than the other, the least uncertainty of the event, fortunate or unfortunate, suffices to render the insurance valid.... Notwithstanding *public rumour* of the loss or arrival of the vessel, the insurance would be lawful, if this rumour had no character of certainty, and it was equally known by both parties."

the parties not to conceal any such fact relating to the risk. But this rule against concealment was also related to another function of good faith, namely to assure that insurer and assured concluded the policy on an equal informational footing. As we have seen, *Emérigon* suggested that the insurer and the assured should have an "equal chance"[351] in concluding the policy and *Grotius* thought that the keeping back of knowledge disturbed the equality that should exist in all reciprocal contracts.[352] The implication of such a requirement would be that neither the assured, nor the insurer should be allowed to take advantage of an informational advantage over the other. Indeed, for this proposition *Emérigon* called on the authority of *Cicero*, who had been an important proponent of the ethical functions of *bona fides*.[353] But, what were the consequences if the good faith had been disturbed in the contract of marine insurance? This question is the subject of the following paragraphs.

2.3.5 Remedies

Roccus stated that the insurer would not become liable where the assured had intentionally caused a false representation as to the value of the things insured to be entered into the policy, since such an assured knowingly acted in bad faith and a false representation annulled the contract of insurance.[354] In such a case, the insurer was not liable to return the premium; in fact, an insurer who had been the victim of fraud had a valid claim for payment of the premium.[355]

We have seen above[356] that *Pothier* considered good faith to dictate that both parties to the insurance contract must not *dissimulate*, i.e. keep back information material to the subject-matter which formed the substance of the contract of which one party knew and the other was ignorant. *Pothier* mentioned the example of the insurer who knew, in time of war, that peace was soon to return, but, in order to underwrite at a higher premium, kept this knowledge to himself and did not disclose the fact to the assured.[357] What would be the remedy in such a case? *Pothier* answered as follows:

> *"Cette espèce de dissimulation n'oblige guère que dans le for de la conscience; et dans ce for, elle oblige les assureurs qui ont dissimulé la connaissance qu'ils avaient, à restituer ce qu'ils ont reçu de plus que ce qui aurait dû être le prix de l'assurance, si toutes les parties eussent eu cette connaissance.*
> *Cette obligation a lieu, même en cas de perte du vaisseau ; et ils ne peuvent pas dire, pour s'en dispenser, qu'ils sont déjà assez malheureux de payer la somme assurée : l'iniquité du prix de l'assurance est quelque chose d'indépendant de l'événement. Quoique le vaisseau soit péri, il n'en est pas moins vrai qu'il*

[351] Cf. p. 50 *supra*.
[352] Cf. p. 60 *supra*.
[353] Cf. p. 18 *supra*.
[354] ROCCUS: op. cit., *Art.* 10, *No.* 27.
[355] Ibid., *Art.* 11, *No.* 29.
[356] See footnote 295 *supra*.
[357] POTHIER: ***Traité d'Assurance*** *Chap.* III, *Sect.* III, *n.* 191.

> *a été assuré à un prix excessif, et par conséquent l'obligation de restituer ce qu'il y a d'excessif, ne subsiste pas moins.*"[358]

Emérigon wrote that the policy should be void with respect to any party to it who acted fraudulently and with artifice, by stating facts that were not true or by concealing facts which it concerned the other party to know, in order to procure the policy or to induce him to accept a lesser premium.[359] The author also dealt briefly with the remedies for non-disclosure and misrepresentation in his chapter on the premium.[360] On the authority of *Valin* he stated that every circumstance that tended to increase the risk should be declared by the assured and that the declaration must by truthful, "on pain of nullity."[361] No other remedy would be justified; in fact, it would be "tyranny" if the policy would be sustained and the insurer forced to accept a higher premium:[362]

> "*...il faut ou anéantir le Contrat, ou le laisser subsister tel qu'il est.*
> *Si le Navire périt, et que les Assureurs prouvent qu'on leur a dissimulé quelque circonstance essentielle, le Contrat doit être cassé. Il n'est plus temps après le temps du risque, et que la perte est arrivée, de leur offrir le prix du risque.*"[363]
> (Emphasis in original text)

But the insurer will not be allowed to avoid the policy or to claim a higher premium if it surfaces that he has made a bad bargain. *Emérigon* mentioned the case of a cargo of silks that had been insured upon the ship "*St. Joseph*" for four per cent with certain insurers. Another group of insurers also underwrote for four per cent, however, excluding the risk of confiscation by the Spaniards. The "*St. Joseph*" was indeed confiscated by the Spaniards. The first insurers, who did not complain of deceit, were held to pay the loss.[364]

---

[358] Ibid., *Chap.* III, *Sect.* III *n.* 192: That kind of concealment almost exclusively is a matter for the natural law ; and in that law, it obliges the insurers who concealed the knowledge that they had, to restore that which they received over and above what would have been the price of the assurance, if all parties had that knowledge.
That obligation exists even where the ship has been lost; and they cannot avoid this by saying that they are unlucky enough as it is by paying the sum insured: the inequity of the price of the insurance is something that is independent of the event. Although the ship is lost, it is not less true that it had been assured at an excessive price, and as a consequence the obligation to return that which is excessive does not cease to exist.

[359] EMéRIGON: ***Traité*** *Chap.* I, *Sect.* V, § 2; cf. footnote 293 *supra*.

[360] Ibid. *Chap.* III.

[361] EMéRIGON: **Treatise** p. 58 (***Traité*** *Chap.* III, *Sect.* III).

[362] Ibid.

[363] Ibid., citing POTHIER: ***Traité d'Assurance*** at *Chap.* III, *Sect.* III, *n.* 196; translation by Samuel Meredith in EMéRIGON: **Treatise** at p. 58: "...either the contract must be avoided, or it must have effect as it is. If the ship is lost, and the insurers prove a concealment of some material circumstance, the contract must be broken. It is no longer time, says Pothier, after the period of the risk and the loss have both arrived, to offer them the price of the risk."

[364] EMéRIGON: **Treatise** p. 59, and at p. 171 (***Traité*** *Chap.* III, *Sect.* III and *Chap.* VIII, *Sect.* V, § 2); cf. VALIN : ***Commentaire sur L'Ordonnance de la Marine*** *art.* 49 : "*Cependant, ajoute-t-*

Roman-Dutch authors such as *Grotius* and *Van der Linden* were of the opinion that anyone acting dishonestly in contracts of marine insurance would be liable for all costs, damages and loss of profit, in addition to criminal liability.[365]

Where it could be proved that an assured attempted to claim from an insurer an amount in excess of the value of the thing insured, the assured could not claim on the policy. Thus, wrote *Van der Linden*, where the sum insured exceeded the interest in the vessel, the consequence was that the insured sum would have to be adjusted to correspond with that interest; in fact, the assured's action on the policy would fail if it was instituted fraudulently:

> "*Dat de geassureerde somme de waarde van het interest in het schip te boven gaat, waar van het gevolg is, dat die sommme tot de echte waarde van dat interest gebragt moet worden; ja, zelfs de actie van den Geassureerden vervalt, indien zulks opzettelijk en met bedrog door hem gedaan was.*"[366]

Pothier stated in similar terms that :

> "*Enfin une troisième espèce d'exception, est lorsque les assureurs opposent que la somme assurée qui leur est demandée, excède la valeur des effets que le demandeur avait sur le navire ; ou du moins qu'elle excède la valeur de ce qui en restait à assurer ; si par une préc'dente police on avait déjà fait assurer une somme sur lesdits effets.*
> *Les assureurs, pour établir cette exception, sont admis à faire la preuve contraire de ce qui résulte des pièces signifiées par le demandeur pour établir la quantité et la valeur des marchandises de son chargement.*
> *Les assureurs sont admis à la preuve contrarire de l'estimation, même lrsqu'elle est portée par la police. C'est ce qui résulte de l'art. 8, où il est dit : 'Si l'assurance est faite sur le corps et quille du vaisseau, ses*

---

il, il y a une chose qui fait de la peine ; savoir, l'erreur ou la méprise des Assureurs qui n'avoient stipulé qu'une Prime de 4 pour cent, pour indemnité de tous risques ; tandis que, dans le même temps, d'autres Assureurs, en exigeant une pareille Prime, avoient eu la précaution de se faire tenir quittes de toute confiscation de la part des Espagnols. Pourquoi une si grande inégalité de condition entre ces divers Assureurs ? Il semble que les premiers auroient été dans le cas de demander au moins une augmentation de Prime très-considérable. Mais d'un autre côté, peut-on rien ajouter aux clauses d'une Police d'Assurance ? Il faut donc dire qu'il a été bien jugé en rigueur de droit, et que les premiers Assureurs sont seulement à plaindre de n'avoir pas mieux veillé à leurs intérêts."; translated by Samuel Meredith in EMéRIGON: **Treatise** p. 59: "But there is one thing which excites regret, viz. the error or want of foresight on the part of the insurers, who had agreed only for a premium of four per cent. for indemnity against all risks, while, at the same moment, other insurers, in demanding the like premium, prudently excluded the risk of confiscation by the Spaniard. Why such an inequality of condition between these different underwriters? Apparently the first would have been in case to demand at least a very considerable increase of premium; but , on the other side, nothing may be added to the clauses of a policy of insurance. We must admit therefore, that the case was well judged in rigour of law, and that the first insurers are only to be pitied for not having better watched over their interests."

[365] GROTIUS: ***Inleidinge*** *Boek* 3, *Deel* 24, § 20; VAN DER LINDEN: op. cit., *Boek* 4, *Afdeeling* 6, § 10; cf. footnotes 290 and 276 *supra*.

[366] VAN DER LINDEN: op. cit. *Boek* 4, *Afdeeling* 6, § 10.

agrès.... l'estimation en sera faite par la police ; sauf à l'assureur, en cas de fraude, de faire procéder à une nouvelle estimation."[367]

(Emphasis in original text)

In the case of insurance on good or bad news, we have seen in the previous paragraphs that the insurance would be invalid where it was shown that either the assured or the insurer in fact had exclusive knowledge of the loss or safe arrival of the vessel or goods insured.[368]

The important authors were, therefore, of one mind that in all cases where it could be established that one of the parties to the policy had a misconception of the risk insured against as a result of the other exploiting an informational advantage either by concealing or misrepresenting facts essential to that risk, the marine insurance policy would be invalid. Different language was used, e.g. the policy would be "void"[369], or "invalid"[370], or "null".[371] It would seem that it was generally accepted that where the assured acted fraudulently, the insurer was entitled to retain the premium.[372] None of the authors excluded the possibility of the remedy of damages. Nevertheless, only the Roman-Dutch lawyers expressly mentioned damages as a remedy in the event that the marine insurance policy had been obtained by dishonest means.[373] Where the claim of an assured on the policy had been tainted by fraud the assured's action must fail, again with the implication that the policy remained intact and the insurer could retain the premium. However, the texts mentioned in this regard[374] seem to relate rather to a claim based on an overvaluation in the policy. Similarly, if there had been an overvaluation in the

---

[367] POTHIER: ***Traité d'Assurance*** at *Chap.* III. *Sect.* 1. § VI *n.* 156; (Finally a third kind of exception is when the insurers prupose that the sum insured and demanded from them exceeds the value of the things that the claimant had on the vessel; or at least that it exceeds the value of that which remained to be insured; if by way of a previous policy an insurance was taken out on the said things.

The insurers, to establish this exception, are allowed to bring in proof contradicting that which results from the documents provided by the claimant to establish the quantity and the value of his cargo.

The insurers are allowed to provide proof to refute the valuation, even where it is part of the policy. That results from article 8 where it reads: 'If the insurance was made on the hull and keel of the ship, its tackle... the valuation thereof shall be in the policy; except, where the insurer, in case of fraud, shall be entitled to proceed to make a new valuation.)

[368] Cf. *supra* at p. 53 ff.

[369] Cf. Emérigon, footnote 293 *supra*; also *Van der Linden*, footnote 321 *supra*.

[370] Cf. the Hamburg *Ordnung* of 1731, *Tit.* IV, *Art.* 12, footnote 302 *supra*.

[371] Cf. the Hamburg *Ordnung* of 1731, (*Tit.* IV *Art.* 10), footnote 304 *supra*; also the Amsterdam *Keur* of 1598, p. 54 *supra*; as well as *Roccus*, footnote 355 *supra*; and *Emérigon* and *Valin*, p. 65 *supra*, text to footnote 361.

[372] Cf. *Roccus*, text to footnote 355 *supra*; the Hamburg *Ordnung* of 1731, *Tit.* IV, *Art.* 12, footnote 302 *supra*.

[373] GROTIUS: ***Inleidinge*** *Boek* 3, *Deel* 24, § 20; VAN DER LINDEN: op. cit., *Boek* 4, *Afdeeling* 6, § 10; cf. footnotes 290, 276 as well as the text to footnotes 365 *supra*.

[374] Cf. text to footnote 366 *supra*.

policy, the insurance would remain valid and the insurer would have the opportunity to adjust the value.[375] Nevertheless, the sanction in Roman-Dutch law for the presentation of a fraudulent claim was a refusal to allow a fraudulent assured to profit by the fraud. Furthermore, the fraudulent assured was liable for any loss or expenditure caused by the fraudulent conduct. These remedies were combined with rigorous criminal sanctions.[376] Finally, where the fraud had been on the part of the insurer and the risk insured against materialised, the insurer was bound not only to indemnify the assured in accordance to the policy, but also to return that part of the premium which represented the difference between the charged premium and the premium that should have been payable if the insurer did not act fraudulently.[377]

[375] Cf. *Van der Linden*, text to footnote 366 *supra*; *Pothier*, text to footnote 367 *supra*.
[376] Cf. Marais, J.A. in *Schoeman v Constantia Insurance Co. Ltd.* 2003 (6) SA 313, at p. 317.
[377] Cf. *Pothier*, text to footnote 358 *supra*.

3. Good Faith and the Marine Insurance Contract on the Continent

In the law of obligations of continental legal systems, the principle of good faith is a general concept and, indeed, the cornerstone of any valid contract.[378] It has always been and still is a general requirement of legal systems on the European continent that all contracts, and in particular marine insurance contracts, be entered into and performed in good faith.[379] In contrast, the phrase ***uberrima fides*** never existed in Roman law, or in the writings of the medieval jurists on which the foundations of continental systems rest. Moreover, the concept of utmost good faith was never part of the development of the marine insurance contract. In fact, the marine insurance contract is not ***uberrimae fidei*** at all – it is simply a contract ***bonae fidei*** like all other contracts, i.e. it is vitiated by fraud and it must be executed in good faith by the parties to it.[380]

In France[381] the duty of good faith is required both in the general contract law[382] and in the insurance legislation.[383] Section 1134 of the *Code Civil* requires that "*les conventions doivent être executés de bonne foi*", i.e. that contracts be performed in good faith. In French law, the principle of good faith operates at various stages: first, before conclusion of the contract, the parties will have to conduct their negotiations in good faith.[384] After the contract has been made, the principle of good faith will apply when contractual clauses need to be interpreted, as well as when the parties wish to exercise their contractual rights.[385] As far as the latter is concerned, the principle of good faith has manifested itself in two duties, namely the "duty of loyalty" and the "duty of cooperation", the latter relating to particular contracts such as insurance contracts.[386] Even though the marine insurance contract is said to be ***bonae fidei***, this does not imply that the parties to it will be subject to any greater duties of care in executing the policy than the parties to any other type of contract.[387] The contrary point of view often amounts to *petitio principii*: its proponents base the duty of the assured to disclose information

---

[378] HUYBRECHTS: *Marine Insurance Law: A San Andreas Fault between the Common Law and Civil Law* **The Modern Law of Marine Insurance** Volume Two, p. 343.
[379] VON ZIEGLER: *The 'Utmost Good Faith' in Marine Insurance Law on the Continent* **Marine Insurance at the turn of the Millennium** p. 23.
[380] DE SMET: ***Les Assurances Maritimes*** *Chap.* II, § 84.
[381] WILHELMSEN: *Duty of Disclosure, Duty of Good Faith, Alteration of Risk and Warranties* **Comité Maritime International Yearbook 2000** p. 373.
[382] Art. 1134 of the *Code Civil*
[383] *Wilhelmsen* suggests that the requirement is to be found in art. L172-19 of the *Code des Assurances*. However, this article merely describes the duty to disclose and does not mention the principle of good faith.
[384] MUSY: *The Good Faith Principle in Contract Law* p. 3.
[385] HUYBRECHTS: op. cit., p. 343.
[386] MUSY: op. cit., p. 3, particularly fn. 8.
[387] DE SMET: op. cit., *Chap.* II, § 84.

relevant to the risk on the principle of (utmost) good faith, whilst at the same time calling insurance policies contracts of (utmost) good faith because the assured shoulders an obligation to reveal all facts relevant to the risk to the insurer.[388]

In Germany[389], every marine insurance contract is in the first place subject to the compulsory general conditions of the Civil Code – i.e. the *Bürgerliches Gesetzbuch*, or *BGB* – in particular § 242 which provides –

> "***Leistung nach Treu und Glauben***
> *Der Schuldner ist verpflichtet, die Leistung so zu bewirken, wie Treu und Glauben mit Rücksicht auf die Verkehrssitte es erfordern.*"[390]

Ever since the earliest marine insurance policies required the contract to be judged upon *secundum bonam fidem et consuetudinem mercatorum*, according to *Ritter*, judges, law makers and lawyers engaged in a tireless effort, using an almost fantastic variety of expressions, to spread the gospel of (utmost) good faith in insurance law from which originally the obligation of paying mutual consideration and the duties of disclosure had been derived and in terms of which these well-defined duties are viewed and dealt with today.[391] This observation, coming from a German commentator, necessarily holds true for German marine insurance law too. Clearly influenced by the same concept in English marine insurance law, and the opinions of English authors like *Arnould*, *Ritter* concludes that the insurance contract is a "*contractus uberrima fidei*".[392]

Marine insurance in Germany is covered in particular by the *Allgemeine Deutsche See-Versicherungs-Bedingungen* (*ADS*).[393] Although the *ADS* are in principle not legal provisions, but standard business conditions, they have the same effect as the former since the German jurisprudence acknowledges their special character, in that all interested parties participated in the drafting thereof, and as they almost acquired the character of commercial usage through long standing application since 1919.[394] The duty of good faith is required in § 13 of the *ADS* – "*Alle Beteiligten*

---

[388] Ibid, where the author suggests that good faith, in fact, has nothing to do with this, since the obligation to disclose those facts liable to influence the insurer's opinion of the risk is a condition for the formation of the contract of insurance.
[389] KOSTKA: *Marine Transport Insurance in Germany: The General German Cargo Conditions in Comparison to the Institute Cargo Clauses and Recent German Court Decisions* **Marine Insurance at the Turn of the Millennium** p. 361; WILHELMSEN: op. cit., p. 373.
[390] Translation in DIETL & LORENZ: (The debtor must perform his obligation in accordance with the requirements of good faith, taking into account the prevailing practice (or prevailing custom).) Also cf. EBKE, Werner F. and STEINHAUER, Bettina M.: *The Doctrine of Good Faith in German Contract Law* **Good Faith and Fault in Contract Law** at p. 171.
[391] RITTER: ***Das Recht der Seeversicherung*** § 13, *Anm.* 3.
[392] Ibid.
[393] I.e. the German Standard Insurance Conditions; VON ZIEGLER: op. cit., p. 25.
[394] KOSTKA: op. cit., p. 362.

haben Treu und Glauben im höchsten Maße zu betätigen."[395] The duty of good faith in this paragraph covers the marine insurance contract throughout its entire existence, i.e. from its inception until the contract comes to an end. It is therefore not limited to the performance of the contract, as appears to be the case under § 242 of the *BGB*. This may explain why the draftsmen of the *ADS* decided to use terminology resembling "utmost" good faith instead of good faith of § 242 of the *BGB*. A more viable though simple explanation may be that the draftsmen wished to obtain some form of uniformity with the English Marine Insurance Act of 1906, which provides in section 17 as follows: –

> "A contract of marine insurance is a contract based upon the utmost good faith, and, if the utmost good faith be not observed by either party, the contract may be avoided by the other party."[396]

Nevertheless in some respects, as will appear from the following paragraphs, the requirement of "utmost" good faith in the *ADS* is arguably still reflecting the spirit of the Civilian principle of *bona fides*, rather than that which is understood by utmost good faith under English law.

---

[395] (All parties concerned shall act in the utmost good faith.)

[396] Cf. SCHLEGELBERGER: op. cit., p. 58, where the author cites section 17 of the M.I.A. 1906 before setting out to discuss § 13 of the *ADS*.

3.1 DISCLOSURE AND MISREPRESENTATION ON THE CONTINENT

The provisions of the French *Code des Assurances*, which deal with disclosure and misrepresentation, were preceded by article 348 of the French Code of Commerce of 1807. Through development of the rule that the insurer should rely on the good faith of the assured, the concept of *reticence* was introduced in article 348, which provided:

> *"Toute réticence, toute fausse déclaration de la part de l'assuré, toute différence entre le contrat d'assurance et le connaissement, qui diminueracent l'opinion du risque ou en changeraient le sujet, annulent l'assurance.*
> *L'assurance est nulle même dans le cas où la réticence, la fausse déclaration où la différence n'auraient pas influé sur le dommage où la perte de l'objet assuré."* [397]

This principle and its application by the courts gave rise to much criticism, and the rule was subsequently modified in the 1966/67 reform of the maritime and marine insurance law in France. The effect of these reforms was that the assured who acted in good faith, were to be treated differently from the assured who acted in bad faith,[398] the main rule being stated in *art.* L 172-19.3° and 4° of the *Code des Assurances* where the assured is required to "*[d]éclarer exactement, lors de la conclusion du contrat, toutes les circonstances connues de lui qui sont de nature à faire apprécier par l'assureur le risque qu'il prend à sa charge...*",[399] as well as to "*[d]éclarer à l'assureur, dans la mesure où il les connaît, les aggravations de risques survenues au cours du contrat.*"[400] The code, therefore, provides for a duty to disclose both before and after conclusion of the contract of marine insurance. The facts subject to the duty of disclosure are those known by the assured and not the insurer, which are significant to the insurer with regard to the risk. Therefore, the assured will not be sanctioned for non-disclosure of facts not known by him.[401] Insofar as a non-disclosure or misrepresentation reduced his perception of the risk, the underwriter may be entitled to annul the contract. Thus, although neither of the two provisions expressly states the principle of good faith, it becomes indeed an important consideration in the question regarding the correct remedy for non-disclosure, provided for in *art.* L 172-2.:

---

397 Cited in English translation by VON ZIEGLER: op. cit., p. 24: "Any non-disclosure, any misrepresentation on the part of the insured, any discrepancy between the insurance contract and the Bill of Lading which would reduce the insurer's opinion of the risk or would alter its object, renders the insurance contract null and void.
The insurance is null even if the non-disclosure, the misrepresentation or the discrepancy would have had no influence on the occurrence of the damage or the loss of the thing insured."

398 VON ZIEGLER: op. cit., p. 24.

399 *Art.* 172. 19. 3°; (...truthfully declare, at the time of conclusion of the contract, all circumstances known to him that are liable to have an impact on the insurer's assessment of the risk that it covers...)

400 *Art.* 172. 19. 4°; (...disclose to the insurer, to the extent of his knowledge thereof, the increase of risk occurring during the pending contract.)

401 WILHELMSEN: op. cit., p. 358.

> "*Toute omission ou toute déclaration inexacte de l'assuré de nature à diminuer sensiblement l'opinion de l'assureur sur le risque, qu'elle ait ou non influé sur le dommage ou sur la perte de l'objet assuré, annule l'assurance à la demande de l'assureur.*
> *Toutefois, si l'assuré rapporte la preuve de sa bonne foi, l'assureur est, sauf stipulation plus favorable à l'égard de l'assuré, garant du risque proportionnellement à la prime perçue par rapport à celle qu'il aurait dû percevoir, sauf les cas où il établit qu'il n'aurait pas couvert les risques s'il les avait connus.*
> *La prime demeure acquise à l'assureur en cas de fraude de l'assuré.*"[402]

The remedy depends on whether the assured acted in good faith. If the assured cannot show his good faith, the contract is annulled, but the insurer must return the premium.[403] On the other hand, if the insurer can positively show that the assured was acting in bad faith (fraud), the contract will be annulled and the insurer may retain the premium.[404] However, if the assured proves his good faith, the contract will remain valid and the assured will retain the cover under the policy, but taking into account the principle of proportionality, i.e. any indemnity under the policy will be calculated in proportion to the premium actually paid compared with the premium that should have been paid on a proper assessment of the risk.[405] Nevertheless, the insurer may annul the contract if he can show that he would not have accepted the risk whatsoever, despite the good faith of the assured. In this case, the premium will have to be returned.[406] The French code, therefore, also differentiates between different forms of materiality: the contract may be avoided where the non-disclosed fact affects the acceptance of the risk, even where the non-disclosure happens in good faith, whereas the "rule of proportionality" will apply where the non-disclosed fact is merely material to the fixing of the premium.[407]

As was stated above, marine insurance law in Germany is covered fully by the *ADS*. The *ADS* contain in §19-21 the provisions relating to disclosure and misrepresentation and materiality.

The duty of disclosure is described in § 19 of the *ADS*:

---

[402] (Any omission or false statement by the insured, that is liable substantially to decrease the insurer's assessment of the risk, whether or not it has had an effect on the damage or loss of the insured property, shall nullify the insurance at the insurer's request.
However, save for the cases where the insurer proves that it would not have covered the risks if it had known of them, if the insured proves his good faith, the insurer shall cover the risk in proportion to the premium paid compared to that it should have been paid, unless there is a more favourable provision in favour of the insured.
The insurer shall be entitled to the premium in the event of the insured's fraud.)
[403] VON ZIEGLER: op. cit., p. 24.
[404] Ibid; WILHELMSEN: op. cit., p. 363.
[405] VON ZIEGLER: op. cit., pp. 24-25; WILHELMSEN: op. cit., p. 360.
[406] *Article* L 172-2 of the *Code des Assurances*; VON ZIEGLER: op. cit., p. 24.
[407] VON ZIEGLER: op. cit., p. 25.

> (1) *"Der Versicherungsnehmer hat bei der Schließung des Vertrages alle ihm bekannten Umstände, die für die Übernahme der Gefahr erheblich sind, anzuzeigen; es sei denn, daß die Umstände allgemein bekannt sind. Er hat insbesondere Nachrichten, die ihm zugegangen sind und für die Übernahme der Gefahr erheblich sind, dem Versicherer mitzuteilen, und zwar auch dann, wenn er die Nachricht für unbegründet oder für unzuverlässig hält.*
>
> (2) *Umstände, von denen der Versicherungsnehmer vor der Annahme eines auf die Schließung des Vertrages gerichteten Antrages Kenntnis erlangt, sind so schnell, wie es im ordnungsgemäßen Geschäftsgang tunlich ist, jedenfalls aber in derselben oder in ähnlicher Weise anzuzeigen, in welcher der Antrag übermittelt ist."*[408]

The circumstances that need to be disclosed must be material. For purposes of the *ADS*, a circumstance will be material if it has an influence on the insurer's decision to conclude the insurance contract, or on the terms on which the insurer is prepared to underwrite the policy.[409] There is a measure of uncertainty regarding the question whether the test for materiality concerns the actual underwriter, or whether it is an objective test.[410] Nevertheless, circumstances which are generally known[411] or of which the insurer is knowledgeable, are not subject to the duty to disclose.[412] Moreover, the circumstances must be known by the assured, i.e. it will not suffice if the assured knew of certain circumstances, which are no longer present in his mind at the time the policy is underwritten.[413] The assured's opinion of the circumstances is irrelevant. Accordingly, even if he doubts its accuracy or does not hold it to be material, the circumstances will have to be disclosed.[414]

The remedies for non-disclosure and misrepresentation are provided for in § 20 of the *ADS* :

> (1) *"Ist den Bestimmungen des § 19 zuwider die Anzeige eines erheblichen Umstandes unterblieben oder ist über einen erheblichen Umstand eine unrichtige Anzeige gemacht worden, so ist der Versicherer, soweit nicht ein anderes bestimmt ist, von der Verpflichtung zur Leistung frei. Das*

---

[408] German general rule of marine insurance: Translation by Erdewin Pinckernelle: "(1) Before the conclusion of the insurance contract the Assured shall disclose to the Underwriters every circumstance known to him and material for the decision to give cover, unless the circumstances are common knowledge. In particular, he shall pass on to Underwriters any information received which is material for the cover, no matter whether or not he holds them to be unfounded or unreliable.

(2) Such circumstances as may come to the knowledge of the Assured before the acceptance of his proposal by Underwriters must be imparted to him as speedily as is feasible in the ordinary course of business, but must at any rate be transmitted in the same or a similar way as was the proposal."

[409] SCHLEGELBERGER: op. cit., § 19, n. 2.

[410] Ibid., § 19, n. 3, suggests that the test for materiality is subjective, whereas RITTER: op. cit., § 19, note 31 suggests that the test is indeed objective, although the author admits that the assured may object that a particular circumstance, had it been disclosed, would not have prevented the insurer concluding the insurance contract in the way he did.

[411] RITTER: op. cit., § 13, *Anm.* 29 and 33; SCHLEGELBERGER: op. cit., § 19, n. 4.

[412] SCHLEGELBERGER: op. cit., § 19, n. 8.

[413] RITTER: op. cit., § 13, *Anm.* 39; SCHLEGELBERGER: op. cit., § 19, n. 7.

[414] SCHLEGELBERGER: op. cit., § 19, n. 11.

gleiche gilt, wenn die Anzeige eines erheblichen Umstandes deshalb unterblieben ist, weil der Versicherungsnehmer den Umstand infolge grober Fahrlässigkeit nicht kannte.

(2) *Die Verpflichtung des Versicherers bleibt bestehen, wenn der Versicherer den nicht angezeigten Umstand oder die Unrichtigkeit kannte. Das gleiche gilt, wenn die Anzeige ohne Verschulden des Versicherungsnehmers unterblieben ist.*

(3) *Bleibt die Verpflichtung des Versicherers gemäß Abs.2 Satz 2 bestehen, so gebührt dem Versicherer eine, der höheren Gefahr entsprechende höhere Prämie (Zuschlagprämie).*"[415]

The three sub-paragraphs of § 20 deal with five possible scenarios in the context of the duty of disclosure: (a) the assured has knowledge of the material circumstances; (b) the insurer also knew of the circumstances; (c) the assured had knowledge of the material circumstances and failed to disclose it without fault; (d) the assured did not know of the circumstances and was at fault; (e) the assured did not know of the circumstances and was not at fault.[416] In case of (a) or (d) the insurer will be discharged from liability, i.e. the insurer will be able to escape liability where the assured knew of the facts and did not disclose it due to mistake, or where the assured did not know of the facts due to gross negligence.[417] It appears from sub-paragraph (2) that there would be no breach of the duty of disclosure where the assured had no knowledge of the circumstances and the breach occurred in good faith.[418] In order to be discharged from liability, the insurer will have to show that the assured did have the necessary knowledge, or that his ignorance was due to gross negligence.[419] In scenario (c), where the insured was innocent in not knowing the facts, the contract will remain in force, but the premium will be adjusted.[420] Sub-paragraph (3) provides for a form of proportionality which applies to the premium rate, and not to the indemnity as under French law.[421] Some German commentators are of the opinion that where the premium is already so high that it is considered adequate for the increased risk, an additional premium will not be due.[422] Others suggest that the only measure is whether the risk would appear to be increased if the non-disclosed circumstance is taken into consideration.[423]

---

[415] **German general rules of marine insurance**: Translation by Erdewin Pinckernelle: "(1) Unless otherwise provided a failure to disclose a material circumstance, or a misrepresentation of the same, in contravention of section 19 shall discharge Underwriters from liability. The same applies to a failure to disclose a material circumstance because the Assured was not aware of it and his ignorance was due to gross negligence.

(2) Underwriters remain liable if they were aware of the concealed circumstances or of the misrepresentation. The same applies if the disclosure was not made, but the Assured was not at fault.

(3) Where Underwriters remain liable within the meaning of the last sentence of paragraph (2) of this section they are entitled to a higher premium rate (i.e. an additional premium) in accordance with the greater risk."

[416] SCHLEGELBERGER: op. cit., § 20, I, n. 1.

[417] VON ZIEGLER: op. cit., p. 25.

[418] WILHELMSEN: op. cit., p. 358.

[419] SCHLEGELBERGER: op. cit., § 20, I, n. 2.

[420] VON ZIEGLER: op. cit., p. 25.

[421] WILHELMSEN: op. cit., pp. 359-360.

Whereas the remedy for non-disclosure will depend on whether the assured was at fault or not, the insurer will be able to escape liability under the contract where the assured misrepresented a fact, irrespective of whether he was at fault or not.[424]

As regards materiality, the *ADS* provides in § 21 that –

> *"Als erheblich gelten insbesondere Umstände, die der Versicherungsnehmer unrichtig angegeben hat, wenn er die Richtigkeit der Anzeige zugesichert hat und Umstände, die der Versicherungsnehmer absichtlich verschwiegen hat oder absichtlich unrichtig angegeben, sowie im Zweifel auch Umstände, nach denen der Versicherer ausdrücklich gefragt hat."*[425]

Thus, § 21 creates an absolute presumption of materiality in three cases, i.e. where the assured warranted the correctness of a circumstance, or where he purposely concealed or misrepresented a circumstance with the aim that the insurer should not know of it or should not know the truth.[426] In all three cases the assured cannot aver that the circumstance was not material.[427] The objective materiality is established by the presumption; however, on a subjective level, the assured may object that the fact was not material to the particular insurer, that the fact was notorious or that the particular insurer knew of the fact.[428] As will be seen later on, this explanation comes close to the requirements in English marine insurance law of objective materiality from the point of view of the prudent underwriter, and subjective inducement of the actual underwriter.

---

[422] Cf. SCHLEGELBERGER: op. cit., § 20, I, n. 5.
[423] Cf. RITTER: op. cit., § 20, *Anm.* 21.
[424] VON ZIEGLER: op. cit., p. 25.
[425] **German general rules of marine insurance**: Translation by Erdewin Pinckernelle: "Circumstances are deemed to be material particularly if they were misrepresented by the assured, and he had declared his statement to be correct; furthermore such circumstances as were wilfully concealed or wilfully misrepresented; finally, as a rule, circumstances expressly inquired into by the Underwriters."
[426] SCHLEGELBERGER: op. cit., § 21, n. 1 and 2.
[427] Ibid., § 21, n. 3.
[428] Ibid.

3.2 POST-CONTRACTUAL DUTY OF GOOD FAITH

In France, one aspect of the continuing duty of good faith, namely the duty to disclose an alteration of risk, is provided for in *art.* L 172-3 of the *Code des Assurances*:

> "*Toute modification en cours de contrat, soit de ce qui a été convenu lors de sa formation, soit de l'objet assuré, d'où résulte une aggravation sensible du risque, entraîne la résiliation de l'assurance si elle n'a pas été déclarée à l'assureur dans les trois jours où l'assuré en a eu connaissance, jours fériés non compris, à moins que celui-ci n'apporte la preuve de sa bonne foi, auquel cas il est fait application des dispositions du deuxième alinéa de l'article L. 172-2.*
> *Si cette aggravation n'est pas le fait de l'assuré, l'assurance continue, moyennant augmentation de la prime correspondant à l'aggravation survenue.*
> *Si l'aggravation est le fait de l'assuré, l'assureur peut, soit résilier le contrat dans les trois jours à partir du moment où il en a eu connaissance, la prime lui étant acquise, soit exiger une augmentation de prime correspondant à l'aggravation survenue.*"[429]

Once it comes to the knowledge of the assured that the risk is affected or altered after the contract is concluded, whether it was caused by the assured or not, the duty to disclose will be activated.[430] If the insurer accepts the alteration, the policy will be valid, although the insurer may be entitled to additional premium.[431] Where the alteration was due to the assured, the insurer will have a right to cancel.[432]

The remedy for breaching the duty to disclose an alteration depends on the good faith of the assured. If the assured can show his good faith, i.e. where he cannot be blamed for his failure to notify the insurer of the alteration of risk, the insurer will be kept to the policy but will be entitled to reduce his liability for indemnity proportionally to the premium paid, and the premium that should have been paid had the alteration been taken into account.[433] Where the assured cannot prove his good faith, the non-disclosure of the alteration will result in an automatic termination of the contract three days after the alteration came to the knowledge of

[429] (Any modification of pending contract either of what has been agreed upon at the moment of its formation or of the insured property, from which results a substantial increase of the risk, shall entail the termination of the insurance if it has not been notified to the insurer within three days of the insured having had knowledge thereof, exclusive of public holidays, unless the insured proves its good faith, in which case the provisions of the second paragraph of article L 172-2 shall apply.
If such increase is not attributable to the insured, the insurance shall continue in consideration of an increase in premium corresponding to the increase of risk.
If the increase is attributable to the insured, the insurer may either terminate the contract within three days as from the moment it has had knowledge thereof besides the premium to which it is entitled or demand that the premium corresponding to the increase of risk be increased.)

[430] WILHELMSEN: op. cit., p. 377.

[431] Ibid., p. 378.

[432] Ibid., p. 378.

[433] Cf. the discussion of article L 172-2 *supra* at p. 74; WILHELMSEN: op. cit., pp. 380-381.

the assured.[434] There need not be a causal link between the alteration of risk and the casualty.[435]

In Germany, the position is slightly different. It is provided in § 23 of the *ADS* that the assured must not increase the risk:

> (1) "*Nach dem Abschluß des Vertrages darf der Versicherungsnehmer nicht ohne Einwilligung des Versicherers die Gefahr ändern, insbesondere erhöhen, oder die Änderung durch einen Dritten gestatten.*
> (2) *Als eine Gefahränderung ist es insbesondere anzusehen:*
> 1. *wenn der Antritt oder die Vollendung der versicherten Reise erheblich verzögert wird;*
> 2. *wenn von dem angegebenen oder üblichen Reiseweg abgewichen wird, jedoch kommt eine nur unerhebliche Abweichung nicht in Betracht;*
> 3. *wenn das Schiff andere als die angegebenen Zwischenhäfen kommt jedoch nicht in Betracht, wenn sie zur Ordereinholung erfolgt und zu diesem Zwecke üblich ist.*
> (3) *Als eine Gefahränderung ist es auch anzusehen, wenn die Reise nach einem anderen als dem angegebenen Bestimmungsorte gerichtet wird.*"[436]

The legal consequences of an alteration of the risk are dealt with in § 24 and § 25 of the *ADS*. The former provides that if the provisions of § 23 are violated and loss or damage occur thereafter, the underwriters shall be discharged from liability. There are four exceptions to this rule, in which case the underwriters shall remain liable, i.e. if the alteration was made in the interest of the underwriters; if the alteration was caused by a peril insured against; if it was imperative for humanitarian reasons; or if the alteration of the risk could not have an influence upon the occurrence of loss or damage, or upon the measure of indemnity.[437] If the underwriter remains liable, § 25 provides that an additional premium may be charged:

---

[434] WILHELMSEN: op. cit., p. 381.

[435] Article 172.3 of the *Code des Assurances*; WILHELMSEN: op. cit., p. 381.

[436] **German general rules of marine insurance**: Translation by Erdewin Pinckernelle: ((1) After the insurance is contracted the Assured must not alter or, in particular, increase the risk without Underwriters' consent, nor must he suffer the risk to be altered by a third party.
(2) Especially there is an alteration of risk
1. where the beginning or the end of the insured voyage is considerably delayed;
2. where a deviation is made from the declared or customary course of the voyage, though a slight deviation shall be permissible;
3. where the vessel calls on ports other than declared, or calls on them in an order different from what was originally declared or customary; a call for orders being, however, permissible if in general usage for that purpose.
(3) A change of destination from the one declared shall also be deemed to be an alteration of risk.)

[437] **German general rules of marine insurance**: Translation by Erdewin Pinckernelle; cf. RITTER: op. cit., § 24, *Anm.* 11-31.

> "*Dem Versicherer gebührt eine Zuschlagsprämie, wenn die Gefahr, die er trägt, infolge einer Gefahr, die er nicht trägt, geändert und er durch die Änderung von der Verpflichtung zur Leistung nicht befreit wird.*"[438]

An additional premium is that part of the increased premium intended to be paid in consideration for the increased risk.[439] The insurer shall be entitled to an additional premium in all cases where the risk was increased by an event not covered by the policy and which was not caused or intended by the assured.[440] The insurer shall also be entitled to an additional premium where the alteration was caused by the assured, but the third exception in § 24 becomes applicable.[441]

The actual duty to disclose an alteration of the risk is stated in § 26 of the *ADS*:

> "*Der Versicherungsnehmer hat, sobald er von einer Gefahrerhöhung Kenntnis erlangt hat, dem Versicherer unverzüglich Anzeige zu machen, wenn der Versicherer nicht durch die Erhöhung von der Verpflichtung zur Leistung befreit wird.*" [442]

There are two conditions for the duty to be applied: first, the risk must have been increased, and second, the assured must have had knowledge of the increase of the risk.[443] Every circumstance as a result of which the risk has been increased must be disclosed, irrespective of whether the assured at some point consented to the increase of the risk.[444] Importantly, § 26 constitutes a legal duty. Consequently, if the insurer negligently or intentionally fails to disclose an increase of the risk, he will be in breach of the duty to disclose and liable for damages.[445]

In this short overview, it becomes clear that in both French and German law, the marine insurance contract is *bonae fidei*, in that it is vitiated by fraud and the insurer and assured must act in good faith in concluding the contract. In both systems, the rules of disclosure and the remedies for its breach both before and after inception of the policy are such as to promote equity in the contract, which is one of the traditional functions of *bona fides*. In this regard, the choice of wording in § 13 of

---

[438] **German general rules of marine insurance**: Translation by Erdewin Pinckernelle; (Provided Underwriters are not discharged from liability by an alteration of risk they are entitled to an additional premium unless the increase of risk was caused by a peril covered by them.)
[439] RITTER: op. cit., § 25, *Anm.* 2.
[440] Ibid., § 25 *Anm.* 6.
[441] Ibid., § 25, *Anm.* 7; SCHLEGELBERGER: op. cit., § 25, n. 2.
[442] **German general rules of marine insurance**: Translation by Erdewin Pinckernelle; (Any increase of risk must be disclosed to Underwriters by the Assured as soon as the latter becomes aware of it, unless the insurer be discharged form liability by the increase.)
[443] SCHLEGELBERGER: op. cit., § 26, n. 1 and 2.
[444] RITTER: op. cit., § 26, *Anm.* 10; SCHLEGELBERGER: op. cit., § 26, n. 1.
[445] RITTER: op. cit., § 26, *Anm.* 13; SCHLEGELBERGER: op. cit., § 26, n. 4; cf. § 276 of the German Civil Code (*BGB*); also WILHELMSEN: op. cit., pp. 377, 380.

the *ADS* was indeed an unfortunate allusion to the English concept of "utmost good faith".

4. THE HISTORY OF THE PRINCIPLE OF "UTMOST GOOD FAITH" IN MARINE INSURANCE

4.1 INTRODUCTION

It has been said that the modern doctrine of "utmost" good faith or *uberrima fides*, as it recently became known in Latin, is a "long established doctrine"[446] in insurance contract law that has its origins in Roman law and that it was developed in the continental civil law before it became part of the English common law.[447] According to this theory, the principle of *uberrima fides* in marine insurance law was subsequently "recognised" by Lord Mansfield in the landmark case of *Carter v Boehm*[448] in the eighteenth century.[449]

This theory, with respect, does not reflect an accurate account of the development of the principle in English law. It is trite that Roman law, the various continental civil law systems, which were largely based on Roman law principles, as well as the Law Merchant only knew *bona fides* as a principle in law. There is no equivalent expression of "utmost" good faith in the civil law.[450] No special categories of *bona fides* exist, i.e. *uberrima fides* certainly does not mean that there will be no liability for *bona fides* falling short of utmost good faith![451] It might be that *bona fides* requires different duties which will correspond with the exigencies of any particular contractual relationship. However, the applicable principle is still *bona fides.*[452] Two texts have been cited to show the apparent antiquity of *uberrima fides*. The first deals with partnership and requires good faith in partnership agreements: "*In societas contractibus fides exuberet*".[453] The second is from the Digest and is also concerned with partnerships, likening the relationship of partners to that of brothers: "*Societas ius quodammodo fraternitatis in se habeat*"[454]. Neither of these texts, however, speaks of "*uberrima fides*". In fact, the former requires good faith to abound.[455]

---

[446] RHIDIAN THOMAS, D. (editor): op. cit., p. 26.
[447] PARK, Semin: op. cit., p. 19.
[448] (1766) 3 Burr. 1905.
[449] PARK, Semin: op. cit., p. 19; c.f. . SCHNEIDER: ***Uberrima Fides*** at p. 58, who goes one step further to state that Lord Mansfield formulated the general principle before it was recognised in continental marine insurance law.
[450] MILLNER, M.A.: op. cit. at p 188. ; SPIRO, E.: *Uberrima Fides* 1961 *T.H.R.H.R.* 196, at p. 196.
[451] SPIRO, E.: op. cit., 196, at p. 197.
[452] Ibid., at pp. 196-197.
[453] Cod. 4. 37. 3.
[454] Dig. 17. 2. 63. *in princ.*
[455] SPIRO, E.: op. cit., at pp. 196-197.

As to it being "long established", the renowned Lord Justice Scrutton disposed of the following, in some respects, remarkable, account of the doctrine of utmost good faith in *Rozanes v Bowen*[456]:

> "It has been for centuries in England the law in connection with insurance of all sorts, marine, fire, life, guarantee and every kind of policy that, as the underwriter knows nothing and the man who comes to him to ask him to insure knows everything, it is the duty of the assured, the man who desires to have a policy, to make a full disclosure to the underwriters without being asked of all the material circumstances, because the underwriter knows nothing and the assured knows everything. That is expressed by saying that it is a contract of the utmost good faith – *uberrima fides* (*sic*)."[457]

This view is not only commonly shared by most English jurists, but convinced even European lawyers. Thus, the Dutch authority on insurance law, *Mees*[458], wrote, "*[v]an oudsher is zij een contractus uberrimae fidei genoemd*".[459]

Similar language was used by *Ritter*, the German authority on marine insurance.[460] Still, the earliest case cited by English Judges for authority for the principle only dates back to the second half of the eighteenth century.[461] It would, therefore, be fair to say that this *dictum* of Scrutton, L.J. reflects a fairly recent statement of the law "and not a rule of great antiquity."[462] As will be explained below, the doctrine of utmost good faith or *uberrima fides*, at least as Scrutton, L.J. perceived it to be and as we know it today, in fact, is not even an accurate reflection of English marine insurance law in the eighteenth century.[463]

---

456 (1928) 32 Ll.L.R. 98.
457 (1928) 32 Ll.L.R. 98, at p. 102.
458 DORHOUT MEES: ***Verzekeringsrecht***.
459 DORHOUT MEES: op. cit., p. 62; also c.f. SCHNEIDER: op. cit. pp. 68-69, who also appears to be arguing in favour of the antiquity of a principle over and above normal good faith.
460 C.f. fn. 392 *supra*.
461 *Carter v Boehm* (1766) 3 Burr. 1905; for a discussion of this case, see *infra* p. 96.
462 HASSON: *The doctrine of* uberrima fides *in insurance law – a critical evaluation* (1969) 32 M.L.R. 615, at p. 616.
463 HASSON: op. cit., at p. 615.

4.2 CALLING A SPADE A SHOVEL?

It was only in the nineteenth century that reference to the duty of "utmost" good faith is to be found, arguably to distinguish those contracts to which the duty of disclosure applied. Lord Hobhouse in *The Star Sea*[464] mentioned some of these references:

> "Storey used the expression 'greatest good faith', Wharton 'the most abundant good faith'; a Scottish law dictionary (Traynor) used 'the most full and copious' good faith; some English Judges referred to 'perfect' good faith (Mr. Justice Willes, *Britton v. Royal Insurance Co.*, (1866) 4 F. & F. 905) and Lord Cockburn, C.J. to 'full and perfect faith' (*Bates v. Hewitt*, at p. 607)."[465]

Absent from this account, is Park's observation, written during the closing stages of the eighteenth century and apparently on the authority of the likes of *Grotius*[466], *Puffendorff*[467] and *Bynkershoek*[468] in the following terms:

> "The learned judges of our courts of law, feeling that the very essence of insurance consists in a rigid attention to the purest good faith, and the strictest integrity, have constantly held, that it is vacated and annulled by any the least shadow of fraud or undue concealment."[469]

The term "utmost" good faith however, was the most frequently used and finally, entrenched in the Marine Insurance Act 1906, became the uniform signifier of the principle in common law.

Likewise, the Latin equivalent of *uberrima fides*, or *uberrimae fidei*, is not a term of age at all. Again, Lord Hobhouse gave an enlightening *excursus* in *The Star Sea.*[470] Although it has been suggested that the Latin phrase was inspired by a similar construction in Book IV of the *Codex* of Justinian in relation to partnerships,[471] it is common cause that Roman law did not know the phrase *uberrima fides*. Roman law, however, was more than familiar with the concepts of *bona fides* and *mala fides*. The phrase "*uberrima fides*" was first recorded in *Dalglish v. Jarvie*[472], a judgement by Lord

[464] [2001] 1 Lloyd's Rep. 389.
[465] [2001] 1 Lloyd's Rep. 389 at p. 398; in this regard, generally also c.f. HARE, J.: **Shipping Law & Admiralty Jurisdiction in South Africa** p. 691; for another suggestion as to the meaning of *uberrima fides*, c.f. SCHNEIDER: op. cit. at p. 110, stating that the phrase refers to those requirements shouldered by the assured over and above those required by the general principle of good faith.
[466] ***De Jure Belli***, *lib*. 2. *c*. 12. s. 23.
[467] ***De Jure Nat*** 1. 5. c. 9. s. 8.
[468] ***Quest. Jur. Priv.*** 1. 4. c. 26.
[469] PARK: **System of Marine Insurances** p. 195.
[470] *The Star Sea* [2001] 1 Lloyd's Rep. 389, at pp. 398-399.
[471] See fn. 453 *supra* as well as the text to that note.
[472] (1850) 2 Mac. & G. 231.

Commissioner Rolfe (later Lord Cranworth, L.C.) in connection with the duty of disclosure to the court in an *ex parte* application.[473] Thus spoke the Lord Commissioner:

> "... upon one point it seems to me proper to add thus much, namely, that the application for a special injunction is very much governed by the same principles which govern insurances, matters which are said to require the utmost degree of good faith, '*uberrima fides*.' In cases of insurance a party is required not only to state all matters within his knowledge, which he believes to be material to the question of the insurance, but all which in point of fact are so. If he conceals anything that he knows to be material, it is a fraud; but besides that, if he conceals anything that may influence the rate of premium which the underwriter may require, although he does not know that it would have that effect, such concealment entirely vitiates the policy."[474]

Since English law does not have a general duty of good faith, the use of the word "utmost" in this context has been said to be nothing more than a form of hyperbole.[475] In this respect, the following remark by an Anglo-American commentator might appear quite cynical at first, but, in fact, is very much revealing of the history of this nomenclature:

> "To give a legal rule a certain rubric is of course a very important way of determining the fate in the future of that particular rule. ...If we go further and translate our rule into a foreign language, its 'goodness' (or badness' as the case may be) is heavily underlined. Thus a rule requiring 'uberrima fides' from a contracting party is more impressive sounding than merely requiring the exercise of 'the utmost good faith'."[476]

If the rule in insurance law were that the proposer for insurance had to act in mere good faith and disclose all material facts, nothing would have changed. In fact, if English law had known the general principle of good faith, there would have been no need to regard insurance contracts as extraordinary in any sense whatsoever.[477] This appeared to have been understood by at least one English jurist of the eighteenth century, namely Lord Mansfield, as will be argued in the following paragraphs. However, the etymological foundations of the principle, which has been described as "alien, vague, useless... [and] without any meaning in law",[478] are to be found in the remarks by English judges referred to above[479] and commentators such as *Park*, who wrote the following:

---

[473] *The Star Sea* [2001] 1 Lloyd's Rep. 389, at pp. 398-399; *Mutual and Federal Insurance v Oudtshoorn Municipality* 1985 (1) SA 419, at pp. 431-432. However, c.f. . SCHNEIDER: ***Uberrima Fides*** p. 77, stating the first reference is to found in *Wolff v Horncastle* (1798) 1 Bos & Pul 316, at p. 322; 126 E.R. 924, at p. 928, *per* Buller J..
[474] 2 Mac. & G. 231, at pp. 243-244.
[475] POWELL: op. cit., p. 12.
[476] HASSON: op. cit., at p. 615.
[477] POWELL: op. cit., at pp. 12-13.
[478] Joubert, J.A. in *Mutual and Federal Insurance v Oudtshoorn Municipality* 1985 (1) SA 419, at pp. 433.
[479] Cf. the text to fn. 465 *supra*.

> "In every contract between man and man, openness and sincerity are indispensably necessary to give it its due operation: because, fraud and cunning once introduced, suspicion soon follows, and all confidence and good faith are at an end. No contract can be good, unless it be equal; that is, neither side must have an advantage by any means, of which the other is not aware. This being admitted of contract in general, it holds with double force in those of insurance; because the underwriter computes his risk entirely from the account given by the person insured, and therefore it is absolutely necessary to the justice and validity of the contract, that this account be exact and complete. Accordingly, the learned judges of our courts of law, feeling that the very essence of insurance consist in a rigid attention to the purest good faith, and the strictest integrity, have constantly held, that it is vacated and annulled by any the least shadow of fraud or undue concealment."[480]

Arguably, *Park* did not intend to establish a new principle or a new category of contract. His remarks to the effect that fraud and inequality would militate against good faith in contracts in general, accord in broad terms with the civilian understanding of *bona fides* explained above.[481] One might also argue that his reference to these principles holding "with double force" in insurance, was rather an attempt to explain the operation of good faith in insurance, than stating a requirement of something more than normal good faith. Be that as it may, the majority of English commentators and judges thereafter used similar language which led to the notion of "utmost good faith" and the categorising of marine insurance as *bonae fidei.*

[480] PARK: op. cit., p. 194.
[481] Cf. 2.1 INTRODUCTION TO *BONA FIDES*.

4.3 A METAMORPHOSES OF PRINCIPLE

4.3.1 Signs of Good Faith in Early English Contract Law

At first glance, it might appear as though the principle of good faith was not all that foreign to English law in earlier times. By the close of the thirteenth century justice was delivered by three great courts in England, i.e. the King's Bench, the Common Bench or Court of Common Pleas and the Exchequer.[482] These courts administered the law in accordance with statute, as well as in accordance with the "common law", a phrase deriving from the Latin reference to the general law ,namely "*jus commune*", which was frequently used by the canonists. The common law was that part of the law that was unenacted, non-statutory and common to the whole of England and to all Englishmen.[483] The Exchequer, being also a government office, together with the Chancery constituted what one might refer to in modern-day terms as the civil service. The Chancery was the King's secretarial department and at its head stood the Chancellor.[484] The first Chancellors in England were all ecclesiastics.[485] They came into contact with the administration of justice in more than one way: first, before one could commence an action in one of the courts of law, a writ was to be obtained. These writs were drawn up and issued by the clerks working under the auspices of the Chancellor. The Chancery also had limited powers to invent new writs in order to provide for cases that did not fit into the framework of any of the existing writs. This new writ was, of course, subject to the approval of the courts of law.[486]

However, the Chancery had a second "job description": apart from the courts of law, the King himself had limited powers to administer justice[487] by reason of a residuum of discretion and equity in him.[488] It often happened that a claimant could not obtain adequate relief in the normal course of justice. He would then petition to the King or to the King and his Council who, in turn, would refer the petition to the Chancellor to be dealt with accordingly.[489] The King's Council was a small group of officials, household officers, clerks and advisers who continually attended upon the King.[490] It was, in fact, the Council that exercised the reserve of justice in the King[491], but since its members had "...little taste for the niceties of legal discussion and small interest in the grievances of persons who were not

---

[482] MAITLAND: **Equity** p. 2.
[483] Ibid.
[484] Ibid.
[485] POWELL: op. cit., p. 9.
[486] MAITLAND: op. cit., p. 3.
[487] Ibid.
[488] PLUCKNETT: **A Concise History of the Common Law** p. 138.
[489] MAITLAND: op. cit., p. 3; POTTER: **An Historical Introduction to English Law and its Institutions** p. 141.
[490] PLUCKNETT: op. cit., p. 137.
[491] Ibid., p. 138.

directly related to them by ties of kinship or lordship..."[492], it was only too happy to rid itself of that responsibility and to allow the Chancellor to deal with an ever increasing number of petitions.[493] In the course of the fourteenth century, petitioners started to go straight to the Chancellor, instead of to the King. The Chancellor then sent for the petitioner's adversary in order to examine him. The adversary had to answer the charges of the petitioner on oath after which the Chancellor would decide on both questions of fact and law.[494] The Chancellors, being ecclesiasts,[495] were versed in the Canon law and applied the same basic principles in the Court of Chancery as was used by the Canon lawyers in the Ecclesiastical Courts.[496] The procedure that was followed in the Courts of Chancery, in fact, had been borrowed from the summary procedure of the ecclesiastical courts.[497]

In these petitions to the King and his Chancellor, reference was often made to good faith. The petitioner frequently made his plea, stating that "the debtor had performed against good faith and conscience" or praying the Chancellor to compel the debtor to do "what truth, good faith and conscience require".[498] In turn the Chancellor, dealing with this petition, laid stress on the duty of good faith and conscience in handling this petition.[499] There is debate as to whether this reliance on "good faith" is to be traced back through the Canon law to the Roman principle of ***bona fides***. Some authors appear to see a relation between the reference to "good faith" in petitions to the Chancellor and the use of the phrase ***ex fide bona*** in the Roman formula.[500] Again, other authors are careful to acknowledge any influence of Roman law.[501] The function of the words "good faith" in these petitions, however, apart from having been put in to catch the eye of the Chancellor, also

---

492 POTTER: op. cit., p. 141.
493 PLUCKNETT: op. cit., p. 139; POTTER: op. cit., p. 141.
494 MAITLAND: op. cit., p. 3.
495 This holds truth up to the time of Wolsey, who was the last of the ecclesiastical Chancellors; POTTER: op. cit., p. 143.
496 POWELL: op. cit., p. 9.
497 MAITLAND: op. cit., p. 3.
498 CHESIRE and FIFOOT: **The Law of Contract** p. 7; POWELL: op. cit., p. 9.
499 POWELL: op. cit., p. 9; PARK, Semin: op. cit., p. 19.
500 POTTER: op. cit., p. 574, where the author acknowledges that although the law schools and the lawyers they produced might have prevented the reception of Roman law through intent, but also through their ignorance of "any system but their own", still Roman law might have had an effect on the English legal system. This was especially so during the time up to Wolsey, when all the Chancellors were ecclesiasts or clerics and, therefore, trained in canon and civil law, "systems to which they would naturally turn for a reason if it could be found when it was necessary to abate the rigour of the common law". Cf. in general also POWELL: op. cit.
501 Cf. MAITLAND: op. cit., pp. 1-11. Although even Maitland cannot deny some Roman influence: see p. 8: "On the whole my notion is that with the idea of a law of nature in their minds they decided cases without much reference to any written authority, now making use of some analogy drawn from the common law, and now of some great maxim of jurisprudence which they have borrowed from the canonists or the civilians."

"put in his hands the key with which he could without qualms open his court to the petitioner."[502]

Apart from the Courts of Chancery and its main functionary, the Chancellor, there were also the local Courts of the Boroughs and of the Fairs.[503] These courts were primarily serving merchants, and later in the fifteenth century also other litigants who found no remedy in the common law courts.[504] Indeed, this was more often than not the case, not least because the common law only catered for a limited number of transactions and lacked a general remedy for the breach of contract; in fact, a general conception of contract had yet to be received into the medieval common law.[505] Finally, during the sixteenth century, the common law courts bridged the gap and established the action of *assumpsit*, an action for general breach of promise providing a general remedy for breach of contract.[506] It has been said that the action of *assumpsit* seems to have rested on the basis of the notion of good faith, and that in that way the principle of good faith became part of the English common law.[507] However, it is doubtful whether this would be historically accurate, since the Common Law Courts did not use the defendant's failure to observe good faith as the basis for the plaintiff's cause of action.[508]

4.3.2 The Law Merchant and the English Court of Admiralty

The medieval merchants conducted their business, travelling from one country to another to buy and sell their merchandise at the great fairs and seaport towns of Europe.[509] These fairs and port towns, for that reason, had a very cosmopolitan character. Similarly, this international character of commerce required that the legal principles by means of which justice was served at these merchant centres had to be universally applicable to a great extent.[510] In this manner, a body of international principles of commercial and maritime law came into existence, which may be called the law merchant.[511] The concept of marine insurance first appeared in relation to that part of the law merchant dealing with maritime law.[512] It reached the shores of England and particularly London with the coming of the "active and industrious" Lombards in the thirteenth century.[513] The Lombards – fleeing

502 POWELL: op. cit., p. 9.
503 CHESIRE and FIFOOT: op. cit., p. 7.
504 CHESIRE and FIFOOT: op. cit., p. 7.
505 Ibid; POWELL: op. cit., p. 9.
506 POWELL: op. cit., p. 9.
507 PARK, Semin: op. cit., p. 21.
508 POWELL: op. cit., p. 10.
509 POTTER: op. cit., p. 164.
510 Ibid; PLUCKNETT: op. cit., p. 222.
511 PLUCKNETT: op. cit., p. 222.
512 HOLDSWORTH: **A History of English law** Volume 5, p. 85.
513 PARK: op. cit., p. xxxv of the Introduction; LAY: **A Text Book of the History of Marine Insurance** pp. 13-15; MARTIN: **The History of Lloyd's and of Marine Insurance in Great Britain** p. 23; RöPLING: ***Die Geschichte der englischen Seeversicherung*** p. 20.

Northern Italy before the belligerent *Kaiser Friedrich* on one account[514], and on another, coming to England as the "Pope's merchants", selling pardons and transmitting the ecclesiastical revenues to Rome[515] – brought along not only their wealth, which soon put them in a profitable money-lending business, but also their expertise in the law merchant and marine insurance.[516]

The law merchant and particularly that part of it dealing with maritime law had its roots firmly in Roman law and natural justice and was further developed by the civilians as well as in the Admiralty Courts.[517] To this extent it exhibited a certain similarity with the early principles of the Chancery, considered above, which were also based on natural justice.[518] An example of this similarity and particularly interesting in the context of good faith, was the "favouritism and protection of the *bona fide* purchaser" in both the Law Merchant and Equity.[519]

The courts that administered the law merchant and particularly maritime law were mostly the courts of seaport towns.[520] This had been so in England as well, where, in the early Middle Ages, many seaport towns had jurisdiction in maritime cases.[521] These courts were as such recognized as tribunals of the law merchant.[522] However, the King's Council also dealt with maritime pleas in cases involving foreign merchants.[523] During the middle of the fourteenth century the Court of the Admiral was instituted by King Edward III. This Court enjoyed both a criminal and a civil jurisdiction, which it acquired in a similar manner as that of the Chancellor and the Courts of Chancery,[524] described above.[525] Accordingly, the King's Council would receive a petition from a foreign merchant, which it would, in turn, delegate to the Admiral.[526] This led to a hostile reaction from the various local courts, who jealously wished to protect their ancient rights.[527] Through petitions to the Crown, these courts initially succeeded in preventing the Admiral from interfering with their jurisdiction.[528] During the fifteenth century the position

---

514 MARTIN: op. cit., p. 19; LAY: op. cit., p. 14.
515 RöPLING: op. cit., p. 20.
516 LAY: op. cit., p. 15.
517 POTTER: op. cit., p. 574: Although Roman law was no longer the binding force anymore, it was still used to fill gaps in the substantive law.
518 Ibid., p. 189.
519 Ibid.
520 HOLDSWORTH: op. cit., Volume 1 p. 530.
521 Ibid., Volume 1 p. 531.
522 Ibid., Volume 1 p. 530, calling on the authority of the Red Book of Bristol.
523 POTTER: op. cit., p. 175.
524 Ibid., p. 176.
525 Cf. p. 89 *supra*.
526 POTTER: op. cit., p. 176.
527 HOLDSWORTH: op. cit., Volume 1, p. 531.
528 POTTER: op. cit., p. 176 mentions one petition to King Richard III: "The petition enrolled in 1390 (R.P. 14 Ric. II, p. 282) commences 'Prayer by your Commons from your Cities and Boroughs having ports on the sea,' and goes on to relate that the usurpation of jurisdiction by the

of the maritime courts weakened in the face of a Crown that was determined to assert itself and centralize the courts, and as a consequence these courts were steadily superseded by the Court of Admiralty.[529]

In the sixteenth century, the Tudor policy was to extend the jurisdiction of the Admiralty, and it accordingly grew in importance.[530] During the forty-third year of the reign of Queen Elizabeth, in 1601, a statutory commission was established "*for the hearinge and determynynge of causes arisinge, from pollicies of assurance.*"[531] The commission presiding over the court was to consist of "*the judge of the admiraltie for the time beinge, the recorder of London for the time beinge, two doctors of the civel lawe, and two common lawyers, and eighte grave and discrete merchantes or … any five of them...*"[532] The commission was to try disputes on marine insurance contracts which were registered in London[533], "*in a briefe and summarie course, as to theire discrecion shall seeme meete, withoute formalities of pleadinges or proceedinge.*"[534] The court managed to gain neither the favour of the mercantile community, nor of those for whose benefit it was intended.[535] Apart from the fact that the jurisdiction of the commission was too limited, it being confined to such causes only "as arose in London",[536] the constitution of the commission was too diverse and numerous and its procedure too time-consuming.[537] If this was not enough to pull the plug and sink this court, it was certainly done by the decision that an action upon a policy of insurance could not be barred at common law by saying that the plaintiff had instituted proceedings before the Elizabethan court of insurance.[538] The court subsequently fell into complete disuse.[539] It is interesting to note, however, that two doctors of the civil law were included in the commission, which would confirm the fact that the legal principles applying in contracts of marine insurance had its roots in the civil tradition.

Admiral has deprived them of profits derived from trying certain 'Pleas Contracts Covernances and Trespas' as well 'by land as sea,' which they have enjoyed as '*parcelle de lour Ferme*' time out of mind or under grant in a charter."

529 HOLDSWORTH: op. cit., Volume 1, p. 531; PLUCKNETT: op. cit., p. 222; POTTER: op. cit., pp. 175-180; HOLDSWORTH: op. cit., Volume 1, p. 531.

530 HOLDSWORTH: op. cit., Volume 1, pp. 546-547; POTTER: op. cit., pp. 181-182.

531 MARTIN: op. cit., p. 34; also HOLDSWORTH: op. cit., Volume 5, p. 150; PARDESSUS: ***Collection de Lois Maritimes*** Vol. 4, p. 212; PLUCKNETT: op. cit., p. 226; PARK: op. cit., p. xxxvii of the Introduction.

532 PARDESSUS: op. cit. Vol. 4, p. 212; POTTER: op. cit., p. 182.

533 POTTER: op. cit., p. 182.

534 HOLDSWORTH: op. cit., Volume 1, p. 571; PARDESSUS: op. cit., Vol. 4, p. 212.

535 MARTIN: op. cit., p. 34.

536 PARK: op. cit., p. xxxvii of the Introduction.

537 MARTIN: op. cit., pp. 34-35.

538 HOLDSWORTH: op. cit., Volume 1, p. 571; PARK: op. cit., p. xxxviii of the Introduction, both authors citing *Came v Moye* 2 Sid. 121.

539 MARTIN: op. cit., p. 34; PARK, J.A.: op. cit., p. xxxviii of the Introduction.

It was subsequently the Court of Admiralty which dealt with law and procedure and exercised jurisdiction in insurance matters, as well as matters relating to negotiable instruments, charterparties, bills of lading and other commercial business.[540] It administered the civil law.[541] In fact, only scholars of the civil law wrote about these topics during the sixteenth and seventeenth centuries and for years to come. Therefore, the lawyers that practised in the Court of Admiralty were taught in the civilian tradition and were familiar with the books of the civilians on the continent.[542] This led to a "...general Reception of the Romanized Italian mercantile law in England."[543]

The common law judges, however, wished to acquire this jurisdiction for themselves.[544] The reason appears to be the fact that merchants generally preferred to take their disputes to the Court of Admiralty, whereas the Common Law Courts rather wished to secure the profits arising therefrom.[545] This should, of course, be seen against the background of the blooming commercial relations between England and the Italian city-states in the sixteenth century.[546] The days of the Court of Admiralty were numbered when Coke came to the bench at the beginning of the seventeenth century.[547] Of Coke's antagonism towards the jurisdiction exercised by that court, it is said that he seemed "to have entertained not only a jealousy of, but an enmity against, that jurisdiction."[548] During his term in office, prohibitions were constantly issued to the admiralty courts.[549] He denied the Court of Admiralty its status as court of record and denied that it had any jurisdiction

[540] HOLDSWORTH: op. cit., Volume 5, p. 139; PLUCKNETT: op. cit., p. 227.
[541] HOLDSWORTH: op. cit., Volume 5, p. 138.
[542] Ibid., p. 140; PLUCKNETT: op. cit., p. 227.
[543] PLUCKNETT: op. cit., p. 227.
[544] Ibid.
[545] POTTER: op. cit., p. 183, where the author quotes from a pamphlet titled "*Reasons why the merchants both English and Foreign desire liberty to try cases by the Civil Law*" and then summarises the reasons as follows: "(i) foreigners only understood the civil law; (ii) if contracts were drawn abroad there were only civilians available for the purpose; (iii) civil law was the *Jus Gentium*; (iv) civil law was closer to the Law Merchant than was the Common Law; (v) process of the civil law was more effective where a party was absent and especially in the matter of reception of evidence; and (vi) the Common Law Judges forming a part of the High Court of Delegates could prevent injustice." The pamphlet alleged five reasons against the Common Law, summarised by the author as follows: "(i) it was purely English law; (ii) it had no terms of art suitable for a foreign language in which a commercial document might have to be framed; (iii) witnesses could not always be at hand to give oral evidence; (iv) the unsuitability of the Common Law was the cause of the merchant's importunate outcry for a Court Merchant; (v) the civil and not the Common Law being the birthright of foreigners they simply fled to prohibitions for the purpose of defrauding their creditors."
[546] PARK, Semin: op. cit., p. 21.
[547] HOLDSWORTH: op. cit., Volume 1, p. 553; PLUCKNETT: op. cit., p. 227; POTTER: op. cit., p. 184.
[548] HOLDSWORTH: op. cit., Volume 1, p. 553, quoting Buller, J. in *Smart v Wolff* (1789) 3 T.R. 348.
[549] PLUCKNETT: op. cit., p. 227.

over contracts made on land, in England, or abroad, whether or not they were to be performed upon the sea.[550] Although, toward the end of the eighteenth century, fewer prohibitions were issued against the Court of Admiralty, that institution never really recovered from the blow dealt to it by the Common Law Courts, particularly during the time that Lord Coke had been on the bench.[551] These courts recognised the customs of merchants, including the practise of insurance, as part of common law.[552] In order to obtain the jurisdiction in maritime cases over acts which took place in foreign countries, over which only the Court of Admiralty had jurisdiction, the common law courts introduced a strange fiction by which such a place was described as being under the jurisdiction of the court.[553] Consequently, the common law courts extended their jurisdiction to include mercantile matters such as insurance, whilst the Court of Admiralty was left with a jurisdiction limited to matters relating to a contract that was made *super altum mare*, i.e. on the high seas, and actually was to be performed there.[554] The law merchant was initially administered in the common law courts as a sort of foreign law, and these courts only administered mercantile custom once such a custom had been proved.[555] The common law judges, being dependent on the customs of the law merchant to decide commercial cases, attached great importance to these customs.[556] Rules of the civil law, however, were not afforded much respect by the common law judges, and the chances of such a rule finding favour with a common law judge were much better if the rule had been presented as a commercial custom.[557]

It was not until Lord Mansfield came to the bench that it became general practice for the courts to take notice of general mercantile custom without requiring proof thereof.[558] He introduced the rule that, once a custom had been given, the custom was judicially noticed and no proof of it was required.[559] Through the efforts of Lord Mansfield, the Law Merchant, and with it the civilian understanding of good faith, became a part of the common law[560] – though it turned out that the latter only found a foothold in marine insurance law and that at best in a mutated form. The Law Merchant, therefore, ceased to be a separate body of law administered by separate courts and became "...neither more nor less than the usages of merchants

[550] HOLDSWORTH: op. cit., Volume 1, p. 553.
[551] POTTER: op. cit., p. 185.
[552] PARK, Semin: op. cit., p. 21.
[553] Thus, the plaintiff "...alleged an act taking place outside the realm, and then asserted that that foreign place was situate at a place in England – 'to wit in the parish of St. Mary le Bow in the Ward of Cheap.' " HOLDSWORTH: op. cit., Volume 5, p. 140; also Volume 1, p. 554; PLUCKNETT: op. cit., p. 228.
[554] HOLDSWORTH: op. cit., Volume 5, p. 140; POTTER: op. cit., p. 185.
[555] PLUCKNETT: op. cit., p. 228.
[556] HOLDSWORTH: op. cit., Volume 5, p. 147.
[557] Ibid.
[558] PLUCKNETT: op. cit., p. 228.
[559] POTTER: op. cit., p. 191.
[560] Ibid., p. 192.

and traders ... ratified by the decisions of courts of law, which, upon such usages being proved before them, have adopted them as settled law."[561] Accordingly, the notion of good faith can indeed be said to have its origin in the common law, by virtue of the Law Merchant.[562]

4.3.3 Lord Mansfield and the remains of *Carter v Boehm*

Whether or not one accepts that the civilian notion of good faith became part of the English common law, the acknowledged origin of the concept of "utmost" good faith in common law is generally considered by both the courts and legal writers to be found in the speech of Lord Mansfield in the case of *Carter v Boehm.*[563] Not only is Lord Mansfield said to have had a profound influence on the development of the English case law relating to marine insurance,[564] or even to have created that branch of the law as such,[565] but he is also credited with incorporating "...the Law Merchant into the Common Law of England, while maintaining it as a special branch of that system with rules of its own."[566] "With consummate skill he introduced into the Common Law a scientific body of commercial law, modelled especially along the lines of the then new Roman-French maritime and commercial ordinances of Louis XIV and Louis XV."[567] Lord Mansfield was called to the King's Bench as Chief Justice in 1756.[568] Whereas most of his predecessors had been happy to learn about the legal principles through the customs of the law merchant presented as evidence in court, Lord Mansfield was a scholar of the civilian law and learned its principles from the writings of the foreign civilians.[569] He is also said to have made a study of all the continental codes of marine insurance which were in existence in his time.[570] In order for him to settle the law in a satisfactory manner, he had a practice of appointing special juries of city merchants to assist him in cases concerning the law merchant.[571]

It so happened that Lord Mansfield had to decide upon the validity of the marine insurance policy of a certain assured, called George Carter, who was the governor of Fort Marlborough. Governor Carter concluded a marine insurance policy in 1759 against the loss of Fort Marlborough, situated as it was in the island of

---

[561] *Per* Cockburn, C.J., in *Goodwin v Robarts* (1876) L.R. 10 Ex. 337 at p. 346, quoted with approval by HOLDSWORTH: op. cit., Volume 1, p. 573; POTTER: op. cit., p. 192.
[562] EGGERS et al.: **Good Faith and Insurance Contracts** par. 4.30; *contra*: RHIDIAN THOMAS, D. (editor): op. cit., p. 32, stating that the duty, particularly that of disclosure, in marine insurance derives from the historical equitable tradition in English law.
[563] (1766) 3 Burr. 1905.
[564] RöPLING: op. cit., p. 62.
[565] LAY: op. cit., p. 100.
[566] POTTER: op. cit., p. 191.
[567] SHERMAN: **Roman Law in the Modern World** § 397.
[568] LAY: op. cit., p. 99.
[569] HOLDSWORTH: op. cit., Volume 5, p. 147; MARTIN: op. cit., p. 121.
[570] LAY: op. cit., p. 100.
[571] POTTER: op. cit., p. 191.

Sumatra, from being destroyed by, taken by, or surrendered unto, any European enemy. The policy was underwritten by Charles Boehm. Fort Marlborough was subsequently lost to the French and the assured submitted a claim on the policy. Lord Mansfield stated the relevant legal principles in the following terms:

> "First. Insurance is a contract upon speculation. The special facts, upon which the contingent chance is to be computed, lie most commonly in the knowledge of the insured only: the underwriter trusts to his representation, and proceeds upon confidence that he does not keep back any circumstance in his knowledge, to mislead the underwriter into a belief that the circumstance does not exist, and to induce him to estimate the risque (*sic*), as if it did not exist.
>
> The keeping back such circumstance is a fraud, and therefore the policy is void. Although the suppression should happen through mistake, without any fraudulent intention; yet still the underwriter is deceived, and the policy is void; because the risque run is really different from the risque understood and intended to be run, at the time of the agreement.
>
> The policy would equally be void, against the underwriter, if he concealed; as, if he insured a ship on her voyage, which he privately knew to be arrived: and an action would lie to recover the premium.
>
> The governing principle is applicable to all contracts and dealings.
>
> Good faith forbids either party by concealing what he privately knows, to draw the other into a bargain, from his ignorance of that fact, and his believing the contrary.
>
> But either party may be innocently silent, as to grounds open to both, to exercise their judgement upon. *Aliud est celare; aliud, tacere; neque enim id est celare quicquid reticeas; sed cum quod tu scias, id ignorare emolumenti tui causa velis eos, quorum intersit id scire.* [572]
>
> This definition of concealment, restrained to the efficient motives and precise subject of any contract, will generally hold to make it void, in favour of the party misled by his ignorance of the thing concealed.
>
> There are many matters, as to which the insured may be innocently silent – he need not mention what the underwriter knows – *Scientia utrinque par pares contrahentes facit.*
>
> An underwriter can not insist that the policy is void, because the insured did not tell him what he actually knew; what way soever he came to the knowledge.
>
> The insured need not mention what the underwriter ought to know; what the takes upon himself the knowledge of; or what the waves being informed of.
>
> The underwriter needs not be told what lessens the risque (*sic*) agreed and understood to be run by the express terms of the policy. He needs not to be told general topics of speculation: as for instance – The underwriter is bound to know every cause which may occasion natural perils; as, the difficulty of the voyage – the kind of seasons – the probability of lightning, hurricanes, earthquakes, etc. He is bound to know every cause which may occasion political perils; from the ruptures of States from war, and the various operations of it. He is bound to know the probability of safety, from the continuance or return of peace; from the imbecility of the enemy, through the weakness of their counsels, or their want of strength, etc…
>
> Men argue differently, from natural phenomena, and political appearances: they have different capacities, different degrees of knowledge, and different intelligence. But the means of information and judging are open to both: each professes to act from his own

[572] Lord Mansfield was citing *Cicero, de Off.* 3, XII – 52 and XIII – 57 (Concealment is one thing, keeping silent, another. It is not necessarily concealment when you keep silent of something, but indeed so when, for your own advantage, you purposely keep another in a state of ignorance as to facts of which you know and which is in the interest of another to know.)

> skill and sagacity; and therefore neither needs to communicate to the other.
> The reason of the rule which obliges parties to disclose, is to prevent fraud, and to encourage good faith. It is adapted to such facts as vary the nature of the contract; which one privately knows, and the other is ignorant of, and has no reason to suspect.
> The question therefore must always be whether there was, under all the circumstances at the time the policy was under-written, a fair representation; or a concealment; fraudulent, if designed; or, though not designed, varying materially the object of the policy, and changing the risque (*sic*) understood to be run."[573]

Lord Mansfield was, as has been explained above, well versed in civil law[574] and in fact frequently referred in his judgements to works on marine insurance by European authors.[575] Apart from the quotation from the third book of *Cicero*'s *De Officiis*, no direct reference is made to any European authors or marine insurance legislation in this particular judgement. Nevertheless, the principles expounded in it were clearly in conformity with the civilian position. First, Lord Mansfield called the marine insurance contract a contract "upon speculation", which is perfectly in accordance with the writings of i.a. *Pothier*,[576] and later, *Emérigon*,[577] referred to above. Second, Lord Mansfield's explanation of the rules regarding concealment also corresponds with the principles laid down by the civilians.[578] Particularly the reference to *Cicero* is instructive thereof. The Latin quotation is an amalgamation of two sentences[579] from that part of *De Officiis*, referred to above, in which *Cicero* asked whether the grain merchant who arrived at the famine-stricken Rhodes, knowing that relief was on its way, could take advantage of the Rhodians' ignorance to obtain a higher price for his goods.[580] This *Ciceronian* case study was also pertinently referred to in the context of the principle of good faith in marine insurance in the works of civilian authors, such as *Emérigon*.[581] Thirdly, as we have seen above, all the important European legal commentators, writing before and during the time of Lord Mansfield, e.g. *Grotius*[582] and *Pothier*[583] stated that the principle of good faith applied in all contracts, and that it was also applicable to the marine insurance contract.[584]

But, this *dictum* or parts of it have been repeatedly cited by English judges and commentators alike as authority for what is known today as the principle of "utmost good faith". It is questionable whether this case does provide support for

---

573 (1766) 3 Burr. 1905, at pp. 1909-1911.
574 Cf. p. 96 *supra*.
575 Joubert, JA in *Mutual and Federal Ins v Oudtshoorn Municipality* 1985 (1) SA 419, at p. 431.
576 Cf. text to fn. 244, *supra*.
577 Cf. text to fn. 245, *supra*.
578 Cf. *Pothier*, fn. 277 and fn. 295; also *Emérigon*, fn. 293 and fn. 298.
579 *Cicero*, *de Off.* 3, XII – 52 and XIII – 57; cf. fn. 572, *supra*.
580 Cf. pp. 19 and 20 *supra*.
581 Cf. fn. 293, *supra*.
582 Cf. text to fn. 279, *supra*.
583 Cf. text to fn. 277, *supra*.
584 Cf. generally sub-chap. 2.3.1 *Stricti iuris* or *bonae fidei*, *supra*.

this principle as it stands today at all.[585] If one looks at this judgement with greater scrutiny, it appears that Lord Mansfield had a different principle in mind. Both Lord Mustill in *Pan Atlantic Insurance Co. Ltd. and Another v. Pine Top Insurance Co. Ltd*[586] (the *Pine Top* case) and Lord Hobhouse of Woodborough in *Manifest Shipping Co. Ltd. v. Uni-Polaris Insurance Co. Ltd. and la Réunion Européene (The Star Sea)*,[587] in discussing the origins of the duty of the utmost good faith, stated that Lord Mansfield at the time attempted to introduce into English commercial law a general principle of good faith.[588] In *Carter v Boehm* – so much is clear – he applied the civilian general principle of good faith to an insurance contract. Accordingly, neither the word "utmost" in describing good faith, nor the Latin equivalent "*uberrima fides*" is to be found in Lord Mansfield's speech.[589] That Lord Mansfield intended to apply good faith as a general legal principle to all contracts, was also recognised by Lord Pitmilly in *Smith v Bank of Scotland*[590] half a century after *Carter v Boehm*. Lord Pitmilly said, referring to the latter case:

> "I found on a statement of Lord Mansfield as laying down the regulatory principle of all contracts, in the following words: 'The governing principle is applicable to all contracts and dealings...' This opinion was given in an insurance case; but it was given as a doctrine applicable to all dealings."[591]

Also Park seemed to appreciate the general applicability of good faith to all contracts as envisaged by Lord Mansfield:

> "In every contract between man and man, openness and sincerity are indispensably necessary to give its due operation; because, fraud and cunning once introduced, suspicion soon follows, and all confidence and good faith are at an end."[592]

However, as we shall soon see, this attempt to introduce the principle of good faith into English contract law did not succeed[593] and the high standards of good faith prescribed by Lord Mansfield to be observed by parties to a contract in the particular circumstances of *Carter v Boehm* only survived in certain contracts e.g. insurance and partnership, whilst in general contract law the "...benefits of

[585] See in general HASSON: op. cit.
[586] [1994] 2 Lloyd's Rep. 427, at p. 444.
[587] [2001] 1 Lloyd's Rep. 389, at p. 398.
[588] This opinion is shared by commentators: see e.g. RHIDIAN THOMAS, D. (editor): op. cit., p. 29; SOYER: *Continuing duty of utmost good faith in insurance contracts: still alive?* [2003] LMCLQ 39, at pp. 39-40.
[589] Lord Hobhouse in *The Star Sea* [2001] 1 Lloyd's Rep. 389, at p. 398.
[590] (1829) 7 S 244.
[591] Ibid., at p. 253.
[592] See footnote 480 *supra*.
[593] RHIDIAN THOMAS, D. (editor): op. cit., p. 29.

simplicity and certainty which flow from requiring those engaging in commerce to look after their own interests"[594] were preferred.[595]

Since Lord Mansfield intended the principle of good faith to be generally applicable to all contracts and dealings, he favoured a narrow interpretation of the duty of disclosure, which flowed from that principle under certain circumstances, where one party privately knows of facts related to the risk of which the other is ignorant.[596] Accordingly, good faith required the duty of disclosure from the parties to a contract in so far as one party had exclusive knowledge of material facts, of which the other was ignorant.[597] In *Carter v Boehm*, it was the case of the insurer that the policy should be declared void, because the state and condition of the fort, i.e. it being badly supplied with stores, arms and ammunition and the impracticability of maintaining it against an European enemy, mentioned in a letter by the governor to the East India Company, as well as the likelihood that the French might attack Fort Marlborough, had not been disclosed.[598] Lord Mansfield set out by making the following general remark relating to these facts:

> "The underwriter at London, in May 1760, could judge much better of the probability of the contingency, than Governor Carter could at Fort Marlborough, in September 1759. He knew the success of the operations of the war in Europe. He knew what naval force the English and French had sent to the East Indies. He knew, from a comparison of that force, whether the sea was open to any such attempt by the French. He knew, or might know every thing which was known at Fort Marlborough in September 1759, of the general state of affairs in the East Indies, or the particular condition of Fort Marlborough, by the ship which brought the orders for the insurance."[599]

Lord Mansfield, therefore, placed the responsibility for obtaining the relevant material information squarely on the insurer.[600] This is supported by Lord Mansfield's treatment of the insurer's allegation that the vulnerability of the fort had not been disclosed:

---

[594] Lord Hobhouse of Woodborough in *The Star Sea* [2001] 1 Lloyd's Rep. 389, at p. 399; also see Lord Mustill in the Pine Top case [1994] 2 Lloyd's Rep. 427, at p. 444.

[595] SOYER: *Continuing duty of utmost good faith in insurance contracts: still alive?* [2003] LMCLQ 39, at p. 40. Also c.f. LOWRY and RAWLINGS: *Insurers, Claims and the Boundaries of Good Faith* (2005) 68(1) M.L.R. 82, at pp. 83-84.

[596] HASSON: op. cit., at p. 617, footnote 9 remarks in this regard: "It is submitted that the fact that Lord Mansfield regarded the principle of disclosure he was stating in the present case as 'applicable to all contracts and dealings,' ... tends to support the argument that he thought of the duty of disclosure in narrow terms. Certainly one would not expect so practical a judge to decree something as obviously impractical as a broad duty of disclosure applicable throughout the whole range of contractual dealings."

[597] PARK, Semin: op. cit., p. 25.

[598] (1766) 3 Burr. 1905, at p. 1914.

[599] Ibid., at pp. 1914-1915.

[600] HASSON: op. cit., at p. 616.

> "The underwriter knew the insurance was for the governor. He knew the governor must be acquainted with the state of the place. He knew the governor could not disclose it, consistently with his duty. He knew the governor, by insuring, apprehended, at least, the possibility of an attack. With this knowledge, without asking a question, he underwrote. By so doing, he took the knowledge of the state of the place upon himself. It was a matter, as to which he might be informed in various ways: it was not a matter, within the private knowledge of the governor only."[601]

The Lord Justice finally found for the assured and concluded his judgement in the following terms:

> "There is no imputation upon the governor, as to any intention of fraud. By the same conveyance, which brought his orders to insure, he wrote to the company every thing which he knew or suspected: he desired nothing to be kept a secret, which he wrote either to them or his brother. His subsequent conduct, down to the 8th of February 1760, shewed that he thought the danger very improbable.
> The reason of the rule against concealment is, to prevent fraud and encourage good faith. If the defendant's objections were to prevail, in the present case, the rule would be turned into an instrument of fraud.
> The underwriter, here, knowing the governor to be acquainted with the state of the place; knowing that he apprehended danger, and must have some ground for his apprehension; being told nothing of either; signed this policy, without asking a question.
> If the objection 'that he was not told' is sufficient to vacate it, he took the premium, knowing the policy to be void; in order to gain, if the alternative turned out one way; and to make no satisfaction if it turned out the other: he drew the governor into a false confidence, 'that, if the worst should happen, he had provided against total ruin;' knowing, at that same time, 'that the indemnity to which governor trusted was void.' ...
> What has often been said of the Statute of Frauds may, with more propriety, be applied to every rule of law, drawn from principles of natural equity, to prevent fraud – 'That it should never be so turned, construed, or used, as to protect, or be a means of fraud.' "[602]

It would therefore appear that Lord Mansfield intended that in so far as an insurer might have informed himself of matters material to his decision to underwrite, good faith did not require the assured to disclose such facts. Indeed, the assured's duty to disclose was a very narrow one.[603] Although one might conceive of the difficulty it afforded an insurer in London in the eighteenth century to obtain information on the security of Fort Marlborough and its vulnerability in case of an attack by European forces, this was, in fact, what Lord Mansfield required of the insurer.[604] It has even been suggested that this passage supports the view that "...the insurer has a positive responsibility to obtain access to the relevant material information in relation to the insured's duty of disclosure".[605] However, as far as

[601] (1766) 3 Burr. 1905, at p. 1915.
[602] Ibid., at pp. 1918-1919.
[603] HASSON: op. cit., at p. 617.
[604] Ibid.
[605] PARK, Semin: op. cit., p. 26; Sections 18(3)(b) and (c) of the Marine Insurance Act 1906 are said to be consistent with this view. It is questionable, however, if the wording of these two sections can be interpreted as establishing a positive responsibility on the part of the insurer.

the insurer relied on facts in the exclusive knowledge of the assured, i.e. facts that the insured "privately knows, and the [insurer] is ignorant of, and has not reason to suspect",[606] to make an informed decision, good faith dictated that the assured had a duty to disclose such facts.[607]

That this was in fact Lord Mansfield's intention is supported by other cases[608] over which he presided as judge, e.g. *Mayne v Walter* (1787).[609] The assured, in this case, lost his vessel after she had been captured by a French privateer. The French Admiralty condemned her on the ground that she carried an English supercargo. The insurer refused to settle the claim on the basis that this fact, i.e. that she had an English supercargo on board, should have been disclosed to him. The insurer argued that it was all the more material in this case, since at the time, a French ordinance was in force that allowed the seizure of any *Dutch* vessel as prize if such vessel carried the supercargo of a country at war with France. The insurer defended the insurance claim by averring that the assured should have disclosed that the ordinance was in force. Lord Mansfield found for the assured, holding:

> "If both parties were ignorant of it [the ordinance], the underwriter must run all risks: and if the defendant knew of such an edict it was his duty to enquire, if such a supercargo were on board. It must be a *fraudulent* concealment of circumstances, that will vitiate a policy."[610]
>
> (Emphasis added)

Once again, the Lord Justice's application of the legal principles relating to good faith and concealment corresponded with the civilian position, as it was expounded by, for instance, *Pothier* and *Emérigon*. The former, it will be remembered, stated that nothing but what was plainly injurious to good faith ought to be considered as a fraud sufficient to impeach a contract.[611] The latter stated that if the policy was not tainted by fraud, and if neither of the parties had been better informed than the other, the policy would be valid, as long as the event against which the insurance had been taken out was uncertain.[612]

In *Planché and Another v Fletcher*[613], two merchants in London, Messrs Planché and Jacquery, insured a cargo on board the "*Maria Magdalena*", due from London to Nantes, with liberty to call at Ostend. Although the goods were to be shipped directly from London to Nantes, the custom, which had also been practised in this

---

606 (1766) 3 Burr. 1905, at p. 1911.
607 HASSON: op. cit., at p. 617.
608 *Mayne v Walter, Noble and Another v Kennoway* (1780) 2 Doug. 510; *Court v Martineau* (1782) 2 Doug. 161.
609 PARK: op. cit., pp. 220-221; cf. also HASSON: op. cit., at p. 617.
610 PARK: op. cit., p. 221.
611 Cf. fn. 146 *supra.*
612 Cf. fn. 350, *supra.*
613 1 Dougl. 251; PARK: op. cit., pp. 217-220.

case, was to make out all the papers including bills of lading and customs clearances for Ostend, i.e. to create the impression that the cargo would have been shipped at Ostend. After the policy had been signed by the defendant underwriter on the 7th of July 1778 and before the vessel set sail on the 24th of August, hostilities broke out between England and France. On her way to Nantes, the vessel was taken by a King's cutter, but subsequently released. Her cargo, however, was condemned. Some of the underwriters defended the claim, arguing, firstly, that the fact that the vessel had been cleared out for Ostend and yet was heading for Nantes, constituted a fraud on them, and secondly, that since hostilities had been declared after the policy was signed, but before the vessel sailed, they ought to have had notice to give them an opportunity to reconsider the premium.

Lord Mansfield found for the assured, his reasons being twofold. First, the fact that the vessel cleared out for Ostend, although she was heading directly for Nantes, was not considered to be a fraud: "What had been practised in this case was proved to be the constant course of the trade; and notoriously so to every body."[614] As far as the second ground was concerned, Lord Mansfield found that every man in England and France at the time when the underwriters signed the policy expected immediate commencement of war. Since two underwriters, in fact, signed the policy after hostilities had been declared, it appeared to him that the risk of war had been present in the minds of the defendants when they underwrote: "Shall he avail himself of an event, which encreases (*sic*) the risk, but which he had in contemplation when he underwrote the policy?", the Lord Justice asked, before finding for the assured.[615]

Lord Mansfield also presided over *Noble and Another v Kennoway*[616], where the assured took out a policy upon two vessels, the "Hope" and the "Anne" for their journey at sea until they be arrived at their port of discharge and moored at anchor for twenty-four hours, as well as upon any kind of goods and merchandizes on these ships until it should be discharged, and safely landed. Both vessels arrived safely on the coast of Labrador, after which the various crews were employed in fishing and, therefore, in accordance with the trade and general usage in that region, did not discharge the cargoes but kept the goods on board. About one month after their arrival, an American privateer entered the harbour and took both vessels, which had been unattended at the time. The assured claimed on the policy for the loss of the goods. The insurer defended the claim, asserting that there was no general usage as contended by the assured, and for lack of an express stipulation to this effect, i.e. that the cargo need not be discharged within 24 hours after safe arrival and, therefore should be protected for such an extended period, they were not liable. Lord Mansfield, finding that there did exist such a usage in that region, held as follows:

[614] 1 Dougl. 251, at p. 253; PARK: op. cit., p. 219.
[615] 1 Dougl. 251, at pp. 253-254; PARK: op. cit., p. 219-220.
[616] (1780) 2 Doug. 510.

> "Every underwriter is presumed to be acquainted with the practice of the trade he insures, and that whether it is established or not. If he does not know it, he ought to inform himself."[617]

In *Court v Martineau*[618] a Liverpudlian shipowner wished to effect a marine policy on two vessels, captured off the Irish coast. On the Sunday night, the shipowner sent an express message to his broker in London, confirming the arrival of one of the vessels, but expressing great fears about the second and requested further insurance on her, adding that if she arrived the next morning, he would send a further express message. The broker received the message on the Tuesday and since he did not receive a second express message by the Wednesday, proceeded to insure the vessel. Amongst the underwriters was the plaintiff in this matter, who underwrote at a premium of fifty guineas per cent. On the Tuesday, one day before letters dispatched by normal post on the Sunday would have arrived in London, an entry was made in Lloyd's books, on account of the broker, that the first vessel was arrived, but that the second vessel was still awaited. No mention was made of the express message.

Lord Mansfield, found that the policy could only have been underwritten at such a high premium under circumstances where the insurer was informed that the ship had not arrived, and that the assured did not believe that she had arrived at that moment. In no uncertain terms, he found that the holding back of the express message did not constitute a ground to vitiate the policy:

> "Now it must have been known, that a merchant at Liverpool so circumstanced would send an express upon the ship's arrival, since the whole of the premium paid after that event would be thrown away. If the underwriter had wished to know by what means the broker acquired his information that the ship had not arrived, he should have made inquiry; but he waived the inquiry by putting no questions to him, though they naturally arose from the subject. By the course of the post from Liverpool, the underwriter must have known that the entry of Tuesday at Lloyd's did not arrive by post. The broker said nothing to mislead. We are all of opinion that there was no concealment, and that it was owing to himself that the underwriter did not receive the information which he now complains was withheld from him."[619]

This very narrow duty of disclosure envisaged by Lord Mansfield was initially subscribed to by other judges in subsequent decisions around the turn of the eighteenth century. One such a case was *Friere v Woodhouse*.[620] It concerned a policy of insurance against all common risks on the "Louisitania". According to a letter from her owners addressed to their broker, requesting the latter to effect an

---

617 Ibid., at p. 513.
618 (1782) 2 Doug. 161.
619 Ibid., at p. 163.
620 (1817) 1 Holt. 572.

insurance, she sailed from Maranham to Lisbon on the 1st of September, 1815. They stated, however, that they were not alarmed by the fact that she has been at sea for fifty-seven days, since there had been many contrary winds. It was subsequently established that the assureds, before writing this letter, received a letter from their agents in Maranham, which was brought by another vessel, the "Victorioso", that set sail together with the assureds' vessel, and which arrived 10 days before the assureds wrote their letter to the underwriters.

Burrow, J. found that the material facts were honestly disclosed in the letter. The fact that the assureds had not informed the underwriters of the arrival of the "Victorioso" did not vitiate the policy, since the arrival of vessels must be presumed to be known by the underwriters. This was a circumstance that they could easily verify by referring to Lloyd's printed Lists. He stated the legal principle on which he based his judgement as follows:

> "What is exclusively known to the assured ought to be communicated; but what the underwriter, by fair inquiry and due diligence, may learn from the ordinary sources of information need not be disclosed."[621]

The two latter matters appear to have been dictated by the same civilian rules as the French cases of the eighteenth century mentioned above.[622] In the civilian tradition, good faith dictated that the parties to the marine insurance contract should be on an equal footing as far as information regarding the risk was concerned. Both parties were presumed to have acted in good faith. In the same vein, ignorance of facts was presumed, unless proof to the contrary suggested otherwise. However, this position was balanced by the Roman rule that nobody was presumed ignorant of facts known to all the inhabitants of the town where he dwelled, or of what had been manifested in public advertisements.[623] In the light of these early cases, it seems clear that the assured's duty of disclosure was a limited and narrow duty that did not arise in respect of facts which the insurer could have discovered by a fair inquiry conducted with due diligence.[624] However, this clear and rational statement of principle, by which these cases were marked, did not survive the nineteenth century. The "good faith" ship that Lord Mansfield put to sea was subsequently run aground by his successors.

Probably the first case signalling a departure from civilian principles was *Lindenau v Desborough*.[625] The importance of this case has been questioned as a result of its "peculiar" facts.[626] Bayley, J. and Littledale, J., who delivered judgement in this case

[621] Ibid., at p. 573.
[622] Cf. pp. 60 and 62 *supra*.
[623] Cf. p. 62 *supra*.
[624] HASSON: op. cit., at p. 618.
[625] (1828) 8 B. & C. 586.
[626] HASSON: op. cit., at p. 618.

with Lord Tenterden, C.J., however, made statements of principle that unfortunately acquired undue importance. The case dealt with an insurance policy on the life of the Duke of Saxe Gotha. The Duke, it was said, lived a dissolute life in Germany and had lost the use of his speech and apparently that of his mental faculties. The Duke's doctors, in answering the questions on the proposal for the insurance, mentioned that the Duke had been hindered in his speech, but made no mention as to the state of his mental faculties. The insurers in London duly underwrote the policy. Upon the Duke's subsequent death, it was discovered that he had a large tumour pressing on his brain, which might have been the cause of his losing his speech and mental faculties. The insurer refused to pay on the policy, submitting that the physicians' failure to disclose the state of the Duke's mental faculties vitiated the policy. All medical evidence established, however, that the symptoms during the Duke's life were neither so as to draw attention to any particular illness, nor to suggest that his life was in danger. Still, an English surgeon said in cross-examination that he thought it right to mention the state of the Duke's mental faculties.

Lord Tenterden, C.J. found that the general question put to the medical practitioners, required information of every fact which any reasonable man would think material. The state of the Duke's mental faculties was such a fact. The Lord Justice made mention of the fact that the insurance had been "on the life of a foreigner"[627] which would suggest that, since the insurers, having their offices in London, could not examine the Duke themselves, they had to rely on the information provided by his medical practitioners, who in turn had exclusive knowledge of the state of his mental faculties. Put in this way, the judgement of Lord Tenterden, C.J. appears not to provide any broader principle of law.

The same cannot, unfortunately, be said of the judgements of his brethren. Bayley, J. stated the law in exceedingly broad terms:

> "I think that in all cases of insurance, whether on ships, houses, or lives, the underwriter should be informed of every material circumstance within the knowledge of the assured; and that the proper question is whether any particular circumstance was in fact material, and not whether the party believed it to be so. The contrary doctrine would lead to frequent suppression of information, and it would often be extremely difficult to show that the party neglecting to give the information thought it material."[628]

Littledale, J. was of the same opinion and held that it was the duty of the assured in all cases to disclose all material facts within its knowledge.[629] He thought that despite the fact that in the case of life insurance, certain specific questions were posed, the general question in this proposal was proposed to meet "...

[627] (1828) 8 B. & C. 586, at p. 591.
[628] Ibid, at p. 592.
[629] Ibid.

circumstances affecting particular individuals which are not likely to be known to the assurers and which had they been known would no doubt have been made the subject of specific enquiries."[630] The Judge also thought that the question was not whether a certain individual thought a particular fact material, but whether it was "in truth" material, thereby introducing an objective test of materiality.[631]

Probably one of the most important cases, signifying a departure from Lord Mansfield's application of the principle of good faith in English contract law requiring a narrow duty of disclosure in marine insurance, was *Bates v Hewitt*.[632] The "Georgia" had been a notorious Confederate cruiser during the American civil war,[633] before she was dismantled in Liverpool in May 1864. Her putting into Liverpool had also been a subject of public notoriety and was well documented in the London Press and in the House of Commons. Hewitt, the defendant and underwriter at Lloyd's, was familiar with these facts at that stage too. Bates bought the "Georgia" in Liverpool at a public auction, and converted her into a merchant vessel. In August of that year, Hewitt underwrote a policy for six months on the vessel. When Bates presented the risk, Hewitt was not mindful of her notorious past anymore, and Bates did not inform him thereof either. The vessel subsequently sailed from Liverpool and was shortly afterwards captured by a frigate from the United States. Bates instituted action to recover the loss. Hewitt defended the action, averring that the fact that the "Georgia" had formerly been a Confederate cruiser and therefore liable to capture, was concealed.

The court found in favour of the insurer. All three judges supported a broad view of the assured's duty of disclosure. The jury acknowledged that the insurer had abundant means to establish that the vessel had been a Confederate cruiser from viewing the particulars of the slip and the memorandum, from consulting Lloyd's Register and in view of his previous knowledge. If the insurer gave sufficient consideration to the matter, he could have identified the vessel.[634] Nevertheless, the court found that even when an assured failed to disclose a material fact of which the insurer had known at an earlier point in time, but which he did not recall when the policy was concluded, the insurer could avoid the contract. Lord Cockburn, L.J. considered the verdict of the jury, and then asked whether their finding entitled the assured to succeed on his claim on the policy. The Lord Justice came to the astonishing answer that it did not:

> "No proposition of insurance law can be better established than this, viz. that the party proposing the insurance is bound to communicate to the insurer all matters which will

[630] Ibid, at p. 593.
[631] Ibid.
[632] (1867) L.R. 2 Q.B. 595.
[633] 1861-1865.
[634] (1867) L.R. 2 Q.B. 595 at p. 604.

> enable him to determine the extent of the risk against which he undertakes to guarantee the assured."[635]

Without reference to any authority for his statements, Lord Cockburn, C.J. tried to establish, in even more glowing terms, the superiority of the English legal tradition in general, and the antiquity of his newly-found rule in particular:

> "I think that we should be sanctioning an encroachment on a most important principle, and one that is vital in keeping up the full and perfect faith which there ought to be in contacts of marine insurance, if we were to hold that a party, - who is under an obligation to communicate the material conditions and facts which constitute the basis of the contract into which he invites another to enter, - may speculate as to what may or may not be in the mind of the underwriter, or as to what may or may not be brought to his mind by the particulars disclosed to him by the assured, if those particulars fall short of the fact which the assured is bound to communicate. If we were to sanction such a course, especially in these days, when parties frequently forget the old rules of mercantile faith and honour which used to distinguish this country from any other, we should be lending ourselves to innovations of a dangerous and monstrous character, which I think we ought not to do."[636]

Mellor, J., in turn, came so far as to cite and quote from Lord Mansfield's judgement in *Carter v Boehm*.[637] This still did not preclude him from agreeing with the opinion of Lord Cockburn, C.J. Although he acknowledged that Lord Mansfield's judgement rested on "sound principle" and stated the "true rules" of marine insurance, which had "never been qualified"[638], he proceeded to disturb the principle and qualify the rule in his own terms:

> "I cannot help thinking that to enable a person proposing an insurance to speculate upon the maximum or minimum of information he is bound to communicate, would be introducing a most dangerous principle into the law of insurance."[639]

Shee, J. carried on in similar terms, stating the principle to be that the person proposing the insurance should take care that the underwriter was as well informed of the material facts as he himself was. He found that although the underwriter in this case might have discovered the material facts if he had instituted inquiries, he was "not obliged to do" so.[640] Shee, J. also did not make reference to any authority for his finding of law.

---

[635] Ibid., at pp. 604-605.
[636] Ibid., at pp. 606-607.
[637] Ibid., at p. 609.
[638] Ibid., at p. 610.
[639] Ibid, at p. 608.
[640] (1867) L.R. 2 Q.B. 595, at p. 611.

In Scotland, reference to *uberrima fides* was made in 1873 for the first time in *Life Association of Scotland v Foster*.[641] In his judgement, Lord President Inglis said:

> "Contracts of insurance are in this, among other particulars, exceptional, that they require on both sides *uberrima fides*. Hence without any fraudulent intent, and even in bona fide, the insured may fail in the duty of disclosure."[642]

This rather astonishing distinction prevailed in this case, although the Lord President did not refer to any authority, and, perhaps even more interesting, found no support for his point of view from his brethren, Lord Ardmillan and Lord Deas. The former stated that insurance contracts were subject to *bona fides*, whilst the latter considered insurance to be "a contract of good faith on both sides".[643] However, it has been argued that Lord President Inglis did not intend to attach any other meaning to *uberrima fides* than that which the other judges meant by their requirement of good faith.[644] By his use of the expression *uberrima fides*, the Lord President intended to convey the distinction that is to be drawn between contracts of insurance and other commercial obligations. This distinction was not the result of the fact that the contract was one of insurance and therefore of the utmost good faith; it was rather the case that the insurance contract generated distinct duties, e.g. the duty of disclosure as a result of the exceptional nature of the contract.[645]

The Court of Appeal put their seal of approval on the new doctrine of utmost good faith in the case of *Joel v Law Union and Crown Insurance*.[646] Fletcher Moulton, L.J. held that the insurer was entitled to be put in possession of all material information possessed by the insured.[647] The Lord Justice stated that "*uberrima fides*" was "more than an obligation to treat the insurer honestly and frankly, and freely to tell him what the applicant thinks it is material he should know".[648] It did not suffice that the assured should have performed these duties in good faith and to the best of his understanding.[649] Fletcher Moulton considered that in addition the assured had to stand up to the objective measure of the reasonable man.[650] Accordingly, the disclosure must have been of all the assured "ought to have realized to be material", not of that only which he "did in fact realise to be so."[651] It has been

---

641 (1873) 11 M 351.
642 Ibid., at p. 360.
643 Ibid., at p. 364.
644 FORTE: *Good Faith and Utmost Good Faith* **Good Faith in Contract and Property** p. 82.
645 Ibid.
646 [1908] 2 K.B. 863 (C.A.).
647 Ibid., at p. 883.
648 Ibid., at pp. 883-884.
649 Ibid., at p. 884.
650 Ibid.
651 Ibid.

convincingly argued that this duty to disclose facts in the knowledge of the assured, irrespective of whether he appreciated their materiality, is excessively high.[652]

These decisions marked a departure from the civilian principle of good faith and rules relating to disclosure laid down in *Carter v Boehm*.[653] In the former cases the rules relating to disclosure were severed from their civilian origins in the principle of good faith, in the sense that disclosure became a goal in itself. In the civilian tradition and in the *dicta* of particularly Lord Mansfield, the rules of disclosure were imperative to promote equality in accordance with good faith in all contracts. Accordingly, good faith enabled judges, in the context of marine insurance, to take into consideration the various degrees of knowledge regarding the risk of both the assured and insurer in which they were helped by certain rules and presumptions,[654] in order to decide whether the duty to disclose had been breached or not. In decisions like *Bates v Hewitt*[655] and *Lindenau v Desborough*[656], and later on *Joel*[657], no attempt was made to promote good faith and equity in the contract. The judges in these cases appear to have assumed from the start that there existed an imbalance in favour of the assured. The duty of disclosure was, therefore, necessary to correct this "assumed imbalance", instead of promoting equity in real terms in accordance with good faith.

4.3.4 Misrepresentation

As far as the subject of misrepresentation is concerned, the principles as laid down by Lord Mansfield were largely carried through into the nineteenth and twentieth centuries. On the basis of Lord Mansfield's judgements in this regards, Park stated the general rule regarding misrepresentations in marine insurance policies to be the following:

> "If a representation be made to the underwriter of any circumstance, which was false, this, if it be in a material point, shall vacate the policy, and annul the contract, although it happen by mistake, and without any fraudulent intention, or improper motive on the part of the insured..."[658]

This rule, according to Park, was based on the principle that the insurer could not be expected to run a risk that he had not intended to run: because the insurer had been led into erroneous belief, as a consequence of which he based his calculation of the risk on facts not really in existence, i.e. "that the underwriter has computed

---

[652] HASSON: op. cit., at p. 622.

[653] Cf. pp. 96 - 102 *supra*.

[654] E.g. the presumption of ignorance, and the rule against that presumption where certain facts were publicly known; cf. p. 105 *supra*.

[655] Cf. p. 107 *supra*.

[656] Cf. p. 105 *supra*.

[657] Cf. p. 109 *supra*.

[658] PARK: op. cit., p. 231.

the risk upon circumstances, which were false, or which did not exist."[659], the real risk would be different from the risk upon which the insurer intended to contract.[660]

The classic case in point of misrepresentation is *Pawson v Watson.*[661] The "Julius Caesar" was insured in the summer of 1776 for her journey to America. The instructions for the insurance stated that the ship mounted 12 guns and 20 men. After she set sail on the 23rd of July 1776, an American privateer took her. It was established that at that time she had on board 6 "four pounders", 4 "three pounders", 3 "one pounders", 6 "half pounders" – also known as "swivels" – and a crew of 27 of whom 16 were men and the rest were boys. Three underwriters defended the claim on the policy, averring, first, that the written instruction should be considered as a warranty inserted in the policy, and secondly, that the written instruction constituted a representation, which would avoid the policy, if fraudulent.

Lord Mansfield set out to distinguish warranties from representations. A warranty was part of the written policy and must be strictly performed as part of the written agreement. In this context, Lord Mansfield made the well-known statement of law with respect to representations:

> "But as, by the law of merchants, all dealings must be fair and honest, fraud infects and vitiates every mercantile contract. Therefore, if there is fraud in a representation, it will avoid the policy, as a fraud, but not as a part of the agreement."[662]

In *Macdowall v Fraser* [663], a broker caused insurance to be effected in London on the ship the "Mary and Hannah" from New York to Philadelphia on the 30th of January. The broker made the following representation to the underwriters: "The Mary and Hannah", a tight vessel, sailed with several armed ships, and was seen safe in the *Delaware on the 11th of December*, by a ship which arrived at *New York*." In reality, the ship was already lost on the 9th of December, after it ran against a *chevaux de frise* placed across the river. The underwriters defended the claim on the basis of the false representation as to the time when the ship was seen. Lord Mansfield explained the law with regard to misrepresentations:

> "A representation must be fair and true. It should be true as to all that the insured knows; and, if he represents facts to the underwriter, without knowing the truth, he takes the risk upon himself. But the difference between the fact as it turns out, and as represented, must be material."[664]

---

[659] Ibid., p. 222.
[660] Ibid., p. 231.
[661] 2 Cowp. 786; also reported in PARK: op. cit., pp. 222-228.
[662] 2 Cowp. 786, at p. 788
[663] 1 Doug. 247; PARK: op. cit., p. 231.
[664] 1 Doug. 247, at p. 261.

The Lord Justice distinguished *Pawson v Watson* on the basis that the insured in that case only said what was meant to be done, and that what had in fact been done, though different, proved to be as advantageous or more so than what had been represented. Accordingly, the difference between the fact as it turned out, and as represented, was not material. He then continued:

> "There was no evidence of *actual fraud* in the present case, and no question of that sort seemed to be made. But there was a positive averment, that the ship was seen in the *Delaware* on the 11th of *December*. The underwriter was deceived as to that fact, and entered into the contract under that deception."[665]

Much was made of the requirement of materiality in this case. According to Lord Mansfield, since the safety of the ship up to a certain day was always considered as a very important circumstance in insurances on ships over great distance, the representation in the current matter concerning the day was undoubtedly material. Indeed, Park stated in this regard that, in order to vitiate the contract, the thing concealed must be material. He did not elucidate Lord Mansfield's further requirement, that the difference between the representation and the real state of affairs must have been material in order to establish liability of misrepresentation. It must be some fact; a mere supposition or speculation of the insured would, accordingly, not suffice.[666] In what reminds one of the requirement of inducement, Park furthermore required that the underwriter "...must take advantage of any misrepresentation the first opportunity, otherwise he will not be allowed to claim any benefit from it at a future period."[667] Accordingly, if the insured merely represented that he expected a thing to be done, the contract would not be void, even though the event should turn out very different from his expectation."[668]

In *Barber v Fletcher* [669], a broker insured a vessel and stated to the underwriter that the vessel was expected "to leave the coast of Africa in November or December 1777". It turned out the vessel had sailed already in May 1777. In an action on the policy, the underwriter defended the assured's claim on the basis of misrepresentation. Lord Mansfield stated that the representation was not material: "It was only an expectation, and the underwriters did not inquire into the ground of the expectation."[670]

4.3.5 Remedies

Park concluded his chapter on fraud in marine insurance policies with a discussion on whether or not the premium should be returned to the assured in cases of

---

665 Ibid.
666 PARK: op. cit., p. 234.
667 Ibid.
668 Ibid.
669 (1779) 1 Dougl. 305.
670 Ibid., at p. 306.

fraud.[671] As far as fraud on the part of the underwriter was concerned, the author found the law to be clear, on authority of Lord Mansfield:

> "The policy would be void against the underwriter, if he concealed any thing; as, if he insured a ship on her voyage, which he privately knew to be arrived; and *an action would lie to recover the premium.*"[672]
> (Emphasis in Park)

This is also in accordance with the civilian position as set out by *Emérigon* in the case mentioned above of the policy underwritten on cargo that had already been in port for six days. *Emérigon* found that the assured was entitled to a return of the premium.[673]

As far as the position of the fraudulent assured was concerned, however, *Park* was careful not to lay down any hard and fast rules. The author referred to a number of cases.[674] In *Da Costa v Scandret*[675], a shipowner, having heard a doubtful account of a ship that had been taken, her description likening that of his own ship that was at sea at the time, proceeded to insure her. He did not give any notice to the insurers of what he heard, nor did he mention the circumstances which might induce him to believe she was in danger or to fear for her loss. When he finally claimed on the policy, the insurers defended the claim. Lord Macclesfield held that the assured had not acted fairly with the insurers.[676] He should have disclosed to them what intelligence he had of the ship, causing him to fear that she was lost, though the account had been uncertain. If this had been the case, the insurers would certainly not have insured against such a small premium, or might not have insured at all.[677] Accordingly, Lord Macclesfield found for the insurers that the concealment was a fraud. The policy was void and, importantly, the insurers ordered to pay back the premium.[678]

Another important case in respect of the correct remedy was that of *Wilson v Duckett*.[679] In this case, the question that came up for decision was whether, upon a policy of insurance being found fraudulent, the premium should be returned to the assured or retained by the insurer.[680] Lord Mansfield decided that although the common law did not lay down any general rule and although in all the cases that

---

671 PARK: op. cit., pp. 244-249.
672 Ibid., pp. 247-248.
673 Cf. p. 62 *supra*.
674 *Wittingham v Thornborough* 2 Vern. 206; *Da Coasta v Scandret* 2 P. Wil. 170; *Wilson v Duckett* 3 Burr. 1361; *Tyler v Horne* Hil. T. 1785.
675 2 P. Wil. 170.
676 Ibid, at p. 170.
677 Ibid.
678 Ibid.; PARK: op. cit., pp. 200 and 245.
679 3. Burr. 1361.
680 Ibid., at p. 361; PARK: op. cit., at p. 246.

had been stated the premium was restored, if the fraud was "notorious, palpable, and gross in its nature", the court could order, as it did in this case, the underwriters to retain the premium.[681] This was the case in *Tyler v Horne*[682], where it was proved that the assured caused his vessel to be insured, knowing that it had perished. Lord Mansfield held that the "fraud was so gross, that the premium should not be recovered from the underwriter."[683]

4.3.6. Toward codification

The common law principle of utmost good faith in marine insurance was first endorsed and regulated in sections 17-20 of the Marine Insurance Act 1906. The Act was drafted by Sir Mackenzie Chalmers, and intended to be a codification of the existing law.[684] Section 17 of this Act provides expressly that a contract of marine insurance is a contract based on the utmost good faith. It lays down the general obligation, whereas the following sections codify particular facets of the general obligation.

Section 17 does not include a definition of the duty of utmost good faith. This is understandable since in its nature, the concept of good faith is "flexible, imprecise and evolving".[685] In contradiction with the traditional common law position where "no contractor is his brother's keeper", the duty of utmost good faith requires i.a. honesty, candour, openness, equal bargaining, fair dealing, assistance, co-operation, protection and disclosure of material facts.[686]

Sections 18, 19 and 20, in turn, provide for certain pre-contractual duties flowing from the general principle of utmost good faith resting on the assured: section 18 and 19 require the assured and his agent to disclose all material facts before the contract is concluded, while section 20 requires the assured and his agent to refrain

---

[681] 3. Burr.1361, at p. 1362; PARK: op. cit., at p. 247.
[682] PARK: op. cit., at p. 247.
[683] Ibid.
[684] HANSELL, D.S.: op. cit., p. 175; SOYER: *The Star Sea – a lode star?* [2001] LMCLQ 428 at p. 429 and *Continuing duty of utmost good faith in insurance contractgs: still alive?* [2003] LMCLQ 39 at p. 40; MERKIN, Robert (editor): **Colinvaux's Law of Insurance** p. 115.
[685] RHIDIAN THOMAS, D. (editor): op. cit., p. 29.
[686] Ibid.

from making material misrepresentations during negotiations leading to formation of the policy.[687] The dominance of these sections, together with the doubtful suggestion that the application of the duty of utmost good faith is limited by these sections, resulted in there not being much use made of the general obligation established in section 17 of the M.I.A 1906.[688] Furthermore, the harsh remedy of section 17 does not allow a flexible application of the duty of utmost good faith.

687 Marine Insurance Act 1906; SOYER: *The Star Sea – a lode star?* [2001] LMCLQ 428 at p. 429.
688 RHIDIAN THOMAS, D. (editor): op. cit., p. 27.

5. THE MODERN PRINCIPLE OF "UTMOST GOOD FAITH"

5.1 THE PRINCIPLE OF "UTMOST GOOD FAITH"

Section 17 of the M.I.A. 1906 requires parties to a marine insurance contract to observe the utmost good faith:

> "A contract of marine insurance is a contract based upon the utmost good faith, and, if the utmost good faith be not observed by either party, the contract may be avoided by the other party."

It was already mentioned above that section 17 does not define "utmost good faith". Good faith, as the contractual principle from which "utmost" good faith mutated is known in the civilian legal tradition, is a principle that does not allow of a definition, it being by its very nature a flexible, imprecise and evolving concept.[689] This would, arguably, also hold good for the Common Law principle of "utmost good faith", which, as one commentator ironically remarks, "both legislature and judiciary ought not even attempt to define with precision."[690]

The principle of utmost good faith requires the assured to respond truthfully to questions put to him by the insurer. Written and oral questions alike are to be answered truthfully.[691] Since sections 18-20 of the M.I.A. 1906 is furthermore limited by the requirement of materiality, the duty of the assured to respond truthfully and accurately to questions of the insurer relating to non-material circumstances will be based upon the requirement of utmost good faith.[692] Furthermore, the assured is also under the duty to disclose spontaneously to the insurer those facts which are material for the insurer to know and which the assured exclusively knows.[693] Therefore, the assured cannot rely on the failure of the insurer to ask specific questions to argue in favour of an implied waiver of disclosure.[694] Such failure may nevertheless lead to a finding that the relevant facts were immaterial.[695] Utmost good faith also requires the assured to correct mistakes in the mind of the insurer, e.g. where the insurer is proceeding on the basis of a serious mathematical error, or a mistaken apprehension of fact.[696]

---

689 RHIDIAN THOMAS, D. (editor): **The Modern Law of Marine Insurance** p. 29.
690 Ibid.
691 MERKIN, Robert (editor): op. cit., p. 124.
692 BENNET: *Mapping the Doctrine of Utmost Good Faith in Insurance Contract Law* [1999] LMCLQ 165 at at p. 177.
693 MERKIN, Robert (editor): op. cit., p. 124.
694 Cf. *Arterial Caravans v Yorkshire Insurance* [1973] 1 Lloyd's Rep. 169.
695 Cf. *Newsholme Bros. v Road Transport & General* [1929] 2 K.B. 356, at pp. 362, 363.
696 BENNET: *Mapping the Doctrine of Utmost Good Faith in Insurance Contract Law* [1999] LMCLQ 165 at at p. 177.

It is clear from the wording of section 17 that the principle is to be observed by both parties to a marine insurance contract.[697] This is in accordance with Lord Mansfield's *dictum* in *Carter v Boehm*[698] regarding the mutuality of the civilian concept of good faith.[699] Although it was already recognised by Lord Mansfield as a mutual obligation operating in both ways, the principle of utmost good faith has until recently almost exclusively been explained in the context of the duties resting on the assured to disclose and to refrain from the misrepresentation of facts material to the risk.[700] This reducing of the principle to duties applicable only to the assured has been exemplified by statements to the effect that it is the assured who is the "natural and sole depositary"[701] of the information; or that he has the "advantage of information"[702] relating to the subject-matter of the risk, such as the time and place at which the goods are to be loaded, or the ship is to sail, the force and equipment of the vessel, etc.;[703] or that there exists an "inequality of ...knowledge"[704] between the assured and the insurer; and that the underwriter must rely solely on the good faith of the assured for the information that will enable him to calculate the nature of the risk and the rate of the premium.[705] These passages appear to be based on the well-known *dictum* of Lord Justice Scrutton:

> "As the underwriter knows nothing and the man who comes to him to ask him to insure knows everything, it is the duty of the assured... to make a full disclosure to the underwriters without being asked of all the material circumstances, because the underwriters know nothing and the assured knows everything. This is expressed by saying that it is a contract of the utmost good faith – *uberrima fides.*"[706]

---

[697] BAATZ: *Utmost Good Faith in Marine Insurance Contracts* **Marine Insurance at the Turn of the Millennium** Vol 1 p. 15; COLINVAUX, R.: **The Law of Insurance** at p. 92; RHIDIAN THOMAS, D. (editor): op. cit., p. 28.

[698] Cf. p. 96 *supra*; also cf. *Re Bradley and Essex Accident* [1912] 1 K. B. 415, at p. 430 *per* Farwell, L.J.

[699] GILMAN: **Arnould's Law of Marine Insurance and Average** Vol. III, par. 579B.

[700] EGGERS et al.: **Good Faith and Insurance Contracts** at par. 1.05.; RHIDIAN THOMAS, D. (editor): op. cit., pp. 28 and 32; also see the remarks of GILMAN: op. cit., Vol. III, at paras. 579A and B.

[701] CHORLEY and BAILHACHE: **Arnould on Marine Insurance** at par. 550.

[702] CLARKE: **The Law of Insurance Contracts** par. 23-1A.

[703] CHORLEY and BAILHACHE: op. cit., par. 550.

[704] EGGERS et al.: op. cit., par. 2.06.

[705] CHORLEY and BAILHACHE: op. cit., par. 550; also see COLINVAUX, R.: op. cit., p. 92.

[706] *Rozanes v Bowen* (1928) 32 Ll.L.R. 98, at p. 102; also cf. *Greenhill v Federal Insurance Co.*[1927] 1 K.B. 65, where Scrutton, L.J. held that the "underwriter knows nothing of the particular circumstances of the voyage to be insured. The assured knows a great deal, and it is the duty of the assured to inform the underwriter of everything that he is not taken as knowing, so that the contract may be entered into on an equal footing."

Only two recent cases in England, namely *Banque Keyser Ullmann S.A. v Skandia (U.K.) Insurance Co. Ltd.*[707] (*Banque Financière*), and *The Good Luck*[708] dealt with breach of the duty of utmost good faith by the insurer.[709] Since sections 18-20 of the M.I.A. 1906 are merely concerned with the duties of the assured, any duties of the insurer flowing from the principle of utmost good faith will have to be based on section 17.[710] In *Banque Financière* the assured was a bank which entered into a credit transaction. The bank secured its position in the event of default by the borrower by means of credit insurance. In fact, payment under the credit facility was conditional on the credit insurance being obtained. However, the broker who had been assigned by the bank to obtain the cover, issued cover notes without full cover being obtained. The insurer subsequently came to know of this state of affairs. As it turned out, the borrower defaulted and the whole transaction turned out to be fraudulent. The assured claimed on the policy, but the insurer refused to pay as a result of a fraud exception in all the policies. The assured resorted to claiming damages from the insurer for breach of the duty of utmost good faith. No case had been served previously before the English Courts where an *assured*, relying on the mutuality of the principle, sought relief for breach of the utmost good faith.[711]

At first instance, Steyn, J., as he then was, had no doubt that reciprocal duties rested on both assured and insurer to observe the utmost good faith by disclosing all material circumstances.[712] In describing the ambit of the duty resting on the insurer, he found that it covered matters peculiarly within the knowledge of the insurers, of which they knew the assured was ignorant, but which were material "in the sense of being calculated to influence the decision of the insured to conclude the contract of insurance."[713] The question that a court had to consider was: "Did

---

[707] [1987] 1 Lloyd's Rep. 69 (Queen's Bench Division); *Banque Financière de la Cité SA v Westgate insurance Co. Ltd.*. [1990] 2 Lloyd's Rep. 377 (Court of Appeal); [1990] 2 Lloyd's Rep. 377 (House of Lords).

[708] *Bank of Nova Scotia v Hellenic Mutual War Risks Association (Bermuda) Ltd. (The Good Luck)* [1988] 1 Lloyd's Rep. 514 (Queen's Bench Division); [1989] 2 Lloyd's Rep. 238 (Court of Appeal); [1991] 2 Lloyd's Rep. 191 (House of Lords); the House of Lords allowed the appeal, but on grounds not concerned with the principle of utmost good faith.

[709] GRIGGS, J.S.: *Is the Doctrine of Utmost Good Faith out of Date?* A Presentation at the Marine Insurance Seminar p. 9; see the remark of May, L.J. in *The Good Luck* 1989] 2 Lloyd's Rep. 238, at p. 263.

[710] BENNET: *Mapping the Doctrine of Utmost Good Faith in Insurance Contract Law* [1999] LMCLQ 165 at at p. 165 and also at p. 177, referring to i.a. *Gordon v Street* [1899] 2 Q.B. 641 and *The Bedouin* [1894] 1 P.I. 12; 69 LT 782 (CA).

[711] GILMAN: op. cit., Vol. III, par. 579G.

[712] [1987] 1 Lloyd's Rep. 69, at p. 93: "Indeed, it is difficult to imagine a more retrograde step, subversive of the standing of our insurance law and our insurance markets, than a ruling today that the great Judge erred in *Carter v Boehm* in stating that the principle of good faith rests on both parties. I unhesitatingly reject this contention."

[713] Ibid., at p. 94.

good faith and fair dealing require a disclosure?"[714] On the facts of the case, Steyn, J. found that it did and that the insurer, accordingly, had a clear duty to disclose the relevant facts to the banks.

In the Court of Appeal[715] Slade, L.J. considered "broad concepts of honesty and fair dealing" as too uncertain to serve as a basis for a duty of disclosure in commercial contracts.[716] He rejected Steyn, J's test for materiality as being too broad and formulated the duty of disclosure owed by insurers in the following terms:

> "In adapting the well established principles relating to the duty of disclosure falling upon the insured to the obverse case of the insurer himself, due account must be taken of the rather different reasons for which the insured and the insurer require the production of full disclosure. In our judgement, the duty falling upon the insurer must at least extend to disclosing all facts known to him which are material either to the nature of the risk sought to be covered or the recoverability of a claim under the policy which a prudent insured would take into account in deciding whether or not to place the risk for which he seeks cover with that insurer."[717]

Slade, L.J. found that the facts pointing to the dishonesty of the broker, of which the insurer knew, were material to the recoverability of a claim under the policy and added that "a prudent insured" would have taken these facts into account in deciding whether or not to make arrangements for the insurance.[718]

In the House of Lords, the majority concurred with Slade L.J. in this fairly broad view of the insurer's obligation to disclose.[719] However, the House of Lords found on the facts that the insurer did not shoulder a duty to disclose the fraud of which the assured bank's broker had been guilty.[720] Lord Bridge found that, since the fact of the broker's fraud would not have entitled the insurer to repudiate liability, it was not material to the recoverability of a claim under the policy.[721] Lord Templeman, whilst going to great lengths to point out that the assured's damages were caused by the fraud of the borrower and not by the failure of the insurer to disclose the fraud of the broker, did not expressly state any reasons why the insured did not have to disclose that fact.[722] Lord Ackner agreed with Lord Bridge that, since the insurers could not rely on the fraud exclusion clause in the policy to repudiate liability by reason of the broker's fraud, the principle of utmost good faith did not require the

---

[714] Ibid.
[715] [1988] 2 Lloyd's Rep 513.
[716] Ibid., at pp. 544-545.
[717] Ibid., at p. 545; also see GILMAN: op. cit., Vol. III, par. 579G.
[718] [1988] 2 Lloyd's Rep 513, at p. 545.
[719] [1990] 2 Lloyd's Rep. 377, at p. 380 (*per* Lord Bridge).
[720] Ibid.; p. 387 (*per* Lord Templeman); at p. 388 (*per* Lord Ackner); at p. 389 (*per* Lord Jauncey).
[721] Ibid., at p. 380.
[722] Ibid., at p. 387.

insurers to disclose the fraud.[723] Lord Jauncey favoured an extremely narrow duty of disclosure that he deduced from an almost literal interpretation of Lord Mansfield's example of the insurer knowing of the arrived ship in *Carter v Boehm*:[724] according to this view, the insurer's obligation to disclose was confined to facts which would reduce the risk.[725] Accordingly, Lord Jauncey was of the opinion that the insurer's duty should only entail matters which related directly to the insured's decision to contract, and at what premium. On the facts of the case, he found that the fraud of the broker was not relevant to the risk.[726] This was so since the risk, being the inability of the borrower to repay the loan except by reason of fraud, had not been affected by the fraud of the broker.[727] In short, therefore, the House of Lords recognised that at the heart of the bank's problems was the fraud of the borrower and not the agent's fraud.[728]

The second case dealing with the duties of an insurer as a result of the application of the principle of utmost good faith concerned the vessel, "The Good Luck". Upon entering a zone prohibited by the terms of the war risk cover granted by the defendant club of mutual war risk insurers, she was duly destroyed by a missile. The claimant bank, which had entered into refinancing agreements with her owners before the loss and to which the benefit of the insurance had been assigned, was under the impression that there was a valid claim on the war risks cover. In fact, there was a valid defence of breach of warranty to such a claim. Since the bank had not been duly informed in accordance with an undertaking by the club to notify the bank once the insurance ceased, it claimed damages from the insurers, i.a. for breach of utmost good faith which the bank asserted had been owed to it as assignees of the policy. Both Hobhouse, J. (as he then was) at first instance[729] and May, L.J. in the Court of Appeal[730] appear not to have had the slightest doubt that the insurer, too, may owe certain duties of disclosure under the principle of utmost good faith.[731]

[723] Ibid., at p. 388; also cf. GILMAN: op. cit., Vol. III, par. 579G.
[724] Cf. p. 96 *supra*.
[725] [1990] 2 Lloyd's Rep. 377, at p. 389: "Thus any facts which would increase the risk should be disclosed by the insured and any facts known to the insurer but not to the insured, which would reduce the risk, should be disclosed by the insurer." RHIDIAN THOMAS, D. (editor): op. cit., p. 30.
[726] [1990] 2 Lloyd's Rep. 377, at p. 389; also cf. GILMAN: op. cit., Vol. III, par. 579G; MERKIN, Robert (editor): op. cit., p. 126.
[727] [1990] 2 Lloyd's Rep. 377, at p. 389.
[728] RHIDIAN THOMAS, D. (editor): op. cit., p. 31.
[729] [1988] 1 Lloyd's Rep. 514, at pp. 545-547.
[730] [1989] 2 Lloyd's Rep. 238, at p. 262.
[731] Neither the insurer, nor the bank disputed the mutuality of the principle and the point was, therefore, not argued before the court.

Although the mutuality of the principle now seems to be settled, in practice the scales are still tipped in favour of the insurer.[732] This becomes apparent in, for instance, the context of the duty of disclosure. The insurer would normally not have much to disclose. In the rare occasion where the duty is activated and the insurer is under the obligation to disclose material information, and breaches the duty in failing to disclose, he will merely risk losing the premium. In turn, as will be seen below, the assured who is in breach of the duty to disclose stands to lose the whole amount which would have been due in the event of a loss.[733] The doctrine of the utmost good faith can, therefore, hardly be said to burden the insurer at all. Insurers, as a consequence, generally enjoy the full privilege of the doctrine of freedom of contract. Insurers can draft their policies as they please, and have, furthermore, what can be called an unfair advantage in applying the rules on warranties. These rules, which were developed by Lord Mansfield in the field of marine insurance, allow the insured to turn any term or condition in the policy into a warranty. Once it is proved that the assured did not comply with a term or condition which is stated to be a warranty, the insurer can rescind and the assured stand to lose all his rights under the policy.[734]

The general duty of utmost good faith transcends the requirements and peculiar application of sections 18-20 of the M.I.A. 1906,[735] demanding from the insurer and assured "honesty, candour, openness, equal bargaining, fair dealing, assistance, co-operation, protection and disclosure of material facts",[736] and furthermore, "is cast in terms sufficiently general to support some continuation of the duty beyond formation of the contract".[737] In fact, Sir Mackenzie Chalmers, the drafter of M.I.A. 1906, wrote that section 17 contained the "general principle" and that the

[732] For a critique of the practical effects of the mutuality of this principle, cf. FRIEDMANN, Daniel: *The Transformation of "Good Faith" in Insurance Law* **Good Faith in Contract, Concept and Context**.

[733] FRIEDMANN, Daniel: op. cit., p. 314; in case of fraud, the assured will also not be allowed to recover the premium already paid.

[734] FRIEDMANN, Daniel: op. cit., p. 315.

[735] E.g. the right of an underwriter, who is sued on a policy, to obtain an affidavit of ship's papers was before Ordinance 72 rule 10 of the Rules of the Supreme Court customarily associated with the duty of utmost good faith. However, Lord Hobhouse, referring to the legal basis for the disclosure of ship's papers, stated that –

"...it must also be recognized that, whatever the continuing duty was, it was of a different character to that which exists pre-contract. Its extent was different. Its enforcement was in the discretion of the Court and required an order from the Court. Its breach did not give rise to the right to avoid the contract: so, whatever it was, it was not the obligation referred to in s. 17 nor was it the subject matter of Lord Mansfield's judgement in Carter v. Boehm. Similarly, it can be taken to support the argument of the owners in the present case that the s. 17 obligation does not extend into litigation." Also in this regard, cf. BENNET: *Mapping the Doctrine of Utmost Good Faith in Insurance Contract Law* [1999] LMCLQ 165, at p. 199-201.

[736] RHIDIAN THOMAS, D. (editor): op. cit., p. 28-29.

[737] BENNET: **The Law of Marine Insurance** p. 46.

sections following were "not exhaustive".[738] It has been suggested that section 17 cannot be used to circumvent the limitations on the particular duties of the assured and his agent to disclose, contained in sections 18 and 19 of the M.I.A. 1906 (and arguably the duty not to misrepresent in section 20 of the Act).[739] Since these particular duties are pre-contractual in character, section 17 cannot, once they have been properly discharged, be used to revive the obligation to disclose after the contract of insurance is concluded.[740]

Accordingly, in so far as section 17 might find application in circumstances where the assured is found to be in breach of utmost good faith involving a question of pre-contractual non-disclosure or misrepresentation, the requirements of materiality and inducement as well as the other requirements in sections 18 and 20 will have to be met.[741] Similarly, it has been suggested that even in circumstances concerning the post-contractual application of utmost good faith, the governing principle remains materiality to a future decision or evaluation of risk, and the "scope of the doctrine or the level at which the obligation is owed", should be the same as during the formation of the contract of insurance.[742] "There is nothing in the wording of section 17 to suggest that there are any differences."[743]

However, Lord Clyde, in *The Star Sea*[744], had the following to say about the principle of utmost good faith:

> "Since even after the contract is entered into the relationship between the parties should in any event be coloured by considerations of good faith, the point is in some respects academic. But once it is recognized that in a contract of insurance, and indeed in certain other contracts, an element of good faith is to be observed, and that that element may impose certain duties particularly of disclosure between one party and the other, duties which may vary in their content and substance according to the circumstances, then a question may arise as to the utility of the concept of an utmost good faith or an uberrima fides. In my view the idea of good faith in the context of insurance contracts reflects the degrees of openness required of the parties in the various stages of their relationship. It is not an absolute. The substance of the obligation which is entailed can vary according to the context in which the matter comes to be judged. It is reasonable to expect a very high degree of openness at the stage of the formation of the contract, but there is no justification for requiring that degree necessarily to continue once the contract has been made."[745]

---

[738] CHALMERS & OWEN: *The Marine Insurance Act 1906* (London, 1907); GILMAN: op. cit., Vol. III, par. 579F; *Container Transport International Inc. v Oceanus Mutual Indemnity Association (Bermuda) Limited* [1984] 1 Lloyd's Rep. 476, at p. 525.
[739] RHIDIAN THOMAS, D. (editor): op. cit., p. 31.
[740] Ibid; however, cf. 5.7 Time of the Duty of "Utmost Good Faith" *infra* for instances where the post-contractual application of the principle has been established.
[741] GILMAN: op. cit., Vol. III, par. 579F.
[742] Ibid., par. 579K.
[743] Ibid.
[744] [2001] 1 Lloyd's Rep. 389.
[745] Ibid., at p. 392.

Although Lord Clyde said this in relation to the question whether the principle of utmost good faith applies after the inception of the policy it, would appear from this *dictum* that the utmost good faith is a general principle, which entails more than merely the duties of sections 18-20 M.I.A 1906 relating to disclosure and misrepresentation[746] and that it may change its colour according to the specific circumstances of a particular case. In contrast with sections 18-20, section 17 refers to mutual duties, it makes no mention of the concept of materiality and it is not expressly confined to the period leading up to the conclusion of the contract.[747] Moreover, the theory that the principle of utmost good faith continues at a level appropriate to each moment or stage in the contractual relationship is gaining acceptance among legal commentators.[748]

[746] GILMAN: op. cit., Vol. III, par. 579AA; earlier editions of *Arnould* – as is the case in most other works on marine insurance – whereas they dealt in great detail with non-disclosure, i.e. sections 18 and 19 of the M.I.A. 1906, and misrepresentation, i.e. section 20, did not give much attention to the general duty of "utmost" good faith. In the third volume of the latest and sixteenth edition of *Arnould*, this has been corrected: "It is now clear that there are important questions with regard to the general doctrine and as to the nature and scope of any duty of good faith continuing after the contract of insurance is made which require separate and fuller discussion." (par. 579A).
[747] Ibid.
[748] Ibid., Vol. III, par. 579K.

5.2 IMPLIED TERM OR A DUTY ARISING EX LEGE

The basis of the duty to comply with the standard of utmost good faith in marine insurance contracts is an important consideration in the context of remedies for the breach of the duty, particularly regarding the question whether damages should be allowed in an action based on non-disclosure. In English law the basis of the duty of utmost good faith, and disclosure particularly, has been a subject of controversy.[749]

There are two main theories to be discerned since the nineteenth century. The first can conveniently be called the "*ex contractu*-theory". Proponents of this theory argue that the duty of the utmost good faith is based on an implied term of the insurance contract.[750] According to this analysis, that seems to have "impressive support in precedent"[751] as well as elsewhere,[752] utmost good faith constitutes a contractual liability. Similarly it has been called "an incident of the contract of insurance".[753]

---

[749] EGGERS et al.: op. cit., par. 4.14; GILMAN: op. cit., Vol. III, par. 579H; Lord Mustill in *Pan Atlantic Insurance Co. Ltd. v Pine Top Insurance Ltd* [1994] 2 Lloyd's Rep 427 at pp. 448-449.

[750] EGGERS et al.: op. cit., par. 4.13.

[751] CLARKE: op. cit., par. 23-1A; cf. PARK, Semin: **The Duty of Disclosure in Insurance Contract Law** p. 48, citing *Moens v Heyworth* (1842) 10 M. & W. 147 at p. 157; *Proudfoot v Motefiore* (1867) L.R. 2 Q.B. 511, at pp. 521-522; *Blackburn Low Co. Vigors* (1886) 17 Q.B.D. 553, at pp. 578 and 583; (1887) 12 App. Cas. 531, at p. 539; *William Pickesgill & Sons Ltd. V London and Provincial Marine and General Insurance Co. Ltd.*. [1912] 3 K.B. 614, at p. 621; *Jester-Barnes v Licenses & General Ins. Co. Ltd.* (1934) 49 Ll.L.R. 231 at pp. 234-235; *Zurich General Accident and Liability Insurance Co. Ltd. v Morrison* [1942] 1 All E.R. 529, at p. 533; *Black King Shipping Corp. v Massie (The Litsion Pride)* [1985] 1 Lloyd's Rep. 437, at pp. 518-519; *The Bank of Nova Scotia v Hellenic Mutual War Risks Association (Bermuda) Ltd. (The Good Luck)* [1988] 1 Lloyd's Rep. 514, at p. 547.

[752] CLARKE: op. cit.,, seems to support the contractual analysis at par. 23-1A. The sixteenth edition (1981) of *Arnould* (MUSTILL & GILMAN: **Arnould's Law of Marine Insurance and Average** Vol.II, par. 595) still favours the analysis in *Blackburn v Vigors* according to which the rules of non-disclosure and misrepresentation are based on an implied condition of the contract, that there is not misrepresentation or concealment. However, the author of the third volume of this work (GILMAN: op. cit., Vol. III, par. 579H), published in 1997 and serving as a noting-up to the sixteenth edition, appears to break the tradition in following *dicta* of Steyn, J. (as he then was) and Slade, L.J in the *Banque Financière* case (see at p. 131 *infra*). *MacGillivray*, in the second edition (1937) at p. 465, states that the duty to disclose arises "out of an implied condition contained in the contract of insurance and is precedent to the liability of the insurers". As far as the correct basis for misrepresentation is concerned, the second edition offers the contractual theory as well – see at p. 404. The editors of the tenth edition (2003), appear to favour – at least regarding the post-formation duty – a contractual analysis at par. 17-2, whilst noting that House of Lords decided otherwise in *The Star Sea*. The explanation of the basis of the duty in the context of misrepresentation did not change in the tenth edition: see par. 16-8.

[753] CLARKE: op. cit., par. 23-1A, referring particularly to the assured's duty of disclosure, "the most important part ... of the general duty of good faith", and citing *The Good Luck* (see previous footnote); also see RHIDIAN THOMAS, D. (editor): op. cit., p. 32, who maintain that the duty

The second school of thought maintains that the duty of utmost good faith is a legal duty. In this scheme, it is "a general obligation recognised by the common law which exists outside of the terms of the contract".[754] Accordingly, the duty arises from a rule of law, or *ex lege*, and not from the contract, i.e. not as a result of an implied term.[755]

5.2.1 Fraud

It has recently been argued that as a result of the fact that the duty of utmost good faith is a common law duty, as distinct from a duty at equity, the type of fraud that would breach that duty is the common law variety.[756] This analysis rests on the premises that Lord Mansfield's attempts to fuse the common law, the law merchant and equitable principles into one coherent body of rules governed by the principle of good faith, failed and that accordingly the principle of utmost good faith came to belong to the common law via the law merchant.[757] Therefore, insofar as a party to the insurance contract fraudulently makes a representation or fraudulently fails to disclose a material circumstance, where fraud is defined as in *Derry v Peek*[758], i.e. the "common law variety"[759], the consent of the parties is disturbed.[760] The fraud, therefore, strikes at the root of the contract, upsetting it irrespective of the terms of the contract.[761] At first glance, this would appear to accord with the statement of Lord Mansfield in *Pawson v Watson*[762] to the effect that a fraudulent misrepresentation avoids the policy on account of the fraud and not as a result of non-compliance with the policy. It may be debatable whether Lord Mansfield's "fraud" in that case corresponds with fraud as defined in *Derry v Peek*.

---

is not contractual, but that it "arises as an incident of the contract of insurance, deriving from the historical equitable tradition in English law and now clothed in statutory form."

[754] EGGERS et al.: op. cit., par. 4.13; cf. GILMAN: op. cit., Vol. III, par. 579I for a position somewhere in the middle: "To the extent that there is still room for controversy on these points, the solution may... be that the *duty* at all stages (except arguably in particular contexts such as held-covered clauses) arises outside the contract, but there is *also* an implied condition precedent, which is not of a promissory nature and cannot give rise to claims for damages..." (Emphasis in the original text).

[755] PARK, Semin: op. cit. p. 48, citing *Joel v Union and Crown Insurance Co. Ltd.* [1908] 2 K.B. 863, at p. 886; *Taylor v Eagle Star Ins. Co.* (1940) 67 Ll.L.R. 136, at p. 140; *Merchants & Manufactures Ins. Co. v Charles & John Hunt* [1941] 1 K.B. 295, at p. 313; *Schoolman v Hall* [1951] 1 Lloyd's Rep. 139, at p. 142; *March Cabaret Club & Casino Ltd v London Assurance* [1975] 1 Lloyd's Rep. 169, at p. 175; *Banque Keyser Ullmann S.A. v Skandia (UK) Ins. Co. Ltd.* [1987] 1 Lloyd's Rep. 69, at p. 94; *The Bank of Nova Scotia v Hellenic Mutual War Risks Association (Bermuda) Ltd. (The Good Luck)* [1989] 2 Lloyd's Rep. 238, at p. 264; *Pryke v Gibbs Hartley Cooper Ltd.* [1991] 1 Lloyd's Rep. 602, at pp. 615-616.

[756] EGGERS et al.: op. cit., par. 4.21.

[757] Ibid., par. 4.15, also par. 4.30.

[758] (1889) 14 App Cas 337.

[759] EGGERS et al.: op. cit., par. 4.21.

[760] Ibid., par. 4.22.

[761] Ibid.

[762] (1778) 2 Cowp. 786

Nevertheless, the important point is that the policy will be avoided for fraud, irrespective of its terms, leading to the conclusion that good faith, at least in the context of fraud, operates *ex lege*.

As far as fraud in the performance of the contract is concerned, conceivably both parties to the contract agreed that they shall perform the contract in good faith and abstain from fraud. Accordingly, it has been suggested that the duty not to make a fraudulent claim is based on an implied term prohibiting fraud.[763] The better view, however, appears to be that that fraud at any stage of the contract would violate the *ex lege* duty to act in good faith and to abstain from fraud.[764]

5.2.2 Misrepresentation

In England, since 1963, an action is also available for a negligent misrepresentation in respect of any contract at common law.[765] Since the common law remedies for fraudulent or negligent misrepresentations turn on the moment of "placing in tort", the duty to abstain from fraudulent or negligent misrepresentations is a non-contractual duty.[766] In turn, it will be a fraud in equity "if a person permitted another to rely on a falsehood which arose because of the action or inaction of that person, no matter how innocent."[767] In these circumstances, equity provides the remedy of rescission to the "innocent" party to a contract to whom an innocent, non-negligent or non-fraudulent misrepresentation was made.[768] This is the position in general contract law. In marine insurance law, any material misrepresentation, "although it happen by mistake, and without fraudulent intention"[769], is against the utmost good faith.[770] That duty being a duty at common law, its breach constitutes a breach of duty at law.[771]

Lord Mansfield in *Pawson v. Watson*[772] stated that the remedy of avoidance of the policy as a result of a false representation, did not derive from the contract, but from a rule of law, holding that –

> " ...by the law of merchants, all dealings must be fair and honest, fraud infects and vitiates every mercantile contract. Therefore, if there is fraud in a representation, it will avoid the policy, on account of the fraud, but not on account of the non-compliance with any part of the agreement."[773]

---

[763] EGGERS et al.: op. cit., par. 4.23.
[764] Ibid.
[765] Ibid., par. 4.24.
[766] Ibid., par. 4.27.
[767] Ibid., par. 4.26.
[768] Ibid., par. 4.25 and 4.26.
[769] PARK: op. cit., p. 231.
[770] EGGERS et al.: op. cit., par. 4.28.
[771] Ibid.
[772] (1778) 2 Cowp. 786.
[773] Ibid., at p. 788; PARK: op. cit., p. 224.

Similarly, in *Merchants and Manufacturers Ins. Co. v John Hunt*[774], Lord Justice Luxmoore was satisfied that in a case of positive misrepresentation the right to avoid a contract, whether of insurance or otherwise, depended "not on any implied term of the contract but arises by reason of the jurisdiction originally exercised by the Courts of Equity to prevent imposition."[775]

5.2.3 Non-Disclosure

The earliest cases dealing with non-disclosure in the context of marine insurance and the principle of good faith, as it then was, do not appear to deal expressly with the question as to its basis, although it was recognised in the Common Law Courts that concealment of material facts rendered the policy void as a matter of law.[776] In the course of the nineteenth century the duty of disclosure provided fertile soil for the development of the *ex contractu*-theory of the utmost good faith. The tone was set in *Moens v Heyworth*[777] where it was stated – although *obiter* by all accounts – that policies of insurance "...are made upon an implied contract between the parties that everything material to the insurer should be disclosed. That is the basis on which the contract proceeds..."[778]

Cockburn, C.J., in *Proudfoot v Montefiore*[779], had to decide whether an agent's concealment of the fact that the vessel upon which his principal's cargo was carried had been lost, for the fraudulent purpose of allowing his principal to obtain insurance cover on that cargo, vitiated the policy. In stating the law with respect to concealment and misrepresentation, Cockburn, C.J. stated that the insurer was entitled to assume that the assured would communicate to him every material fact of which he, i.e. the assured, had, or, in the ordinary course of business, ought to have had knowledge.[780] This was a "condition"[781] which the Judge considered to form the "basis of the contract".[782]

In *Blackburn Low Co. v Vigors*[783], the Court was confronted by a similar set of facts to that in *Proudfoot*. The plaintiff instructed a broker to effect on his behalf a re-insurance upon an overdue ship. In the course of his mandate, the broker obtained intelligence of a material fact pointing at the loss of the ship. The broker did not communicate this fact to the assured, and failed to obtain the cover. The assured

---

774 [1941] 1 K.B. 295.
775 Ibid, at p. 312.
776 GILMAN: op. cit., Vol. III, par. 579H, referring to *Seaman v Fonerau* (1743) 2 St. 1183 and *Hodgson v Richardson* (1764) 1 Wm. B1. 463.
777 (1842) 10 M. & W. 147.
778 Ibid., at pp. 157-158.
779 (1867) L.R. 2 Q.B. 511.
780 Ibid., at pp. 521-522.
781 Ibid., at p. 522.
782 Ibid., at p. 521.
783 (1886) 17 Q.B.D. 553.

subsequently, through another broker, and acting entirely in good faith, reinsured the ship with the defendant underwriters. It was established that she was lost some time before the assured set out to reinsure her. Both Lords Lindley[784] and Lopes[785], finding that the assured could not recover upon the policy and relying heavily on *Proudfoot*, were of the opinion that it was a condition of the contract that there should be no misrepresentation or concealment by the assured (and his agent). Lord Esher, dissenting, held that the absence of misrepresentation or concealment was "a condition precedent to the right of the assured to insist on the performance of the contract, so that on a failure of the performance of the condition the assured cannot enforce the contract."[786] In the Court of Appeal[787], Lord Watson was of the opinion that the duty of disclosure was a condition precedent of the contract[788], whereas Lord Chancellor Halsbury pointed out that any discussion as to the character of the duty of utmost good faith in that case was *obiter*.[789] Lord Fitzgerald concurred in the judgement of Lord Esher, i.e. that the duty of disclosure was a condition precedent of the contract.[790]

This analysis of the duty to disclose – finding the favour of the editors of *Arnould* up to the sixteenth edition[791] of this work – has been criticised on the basis that if the duty were indeed a condition on which the *performance* of the contract depended, the result of a breach of the duty would have been that the insurer did not have to pay on the policy and retained the premium.[792] This is, of course, not in accordance with the law as it was stated by Lord Mansfield in *Carter v Boehm* to the effect that the premium was to be returned, accept in the case of fraud.[793] On the other hand, if it were, as was suggested by Lord Watson, a condition precedent to the contract, there would have been no contract to avoid once a court found that the duty was breached.[794]

Since the enactment of the duty of disclosure in the Marine Insurance Act in 1906, it is the law that the assured "…must disclose to the insurer, before the contract is concluded."[795] Subsequently a different view started to emerge early in the

---

784 Ibid., at p. 578.

785 Ibid., at p. 583, speaking of "the implied contract between the parties".

786 Ibid., at p. 562.

787 (1887) 12 App. Cas. 531.

788 Ibid., at p. 539: "It is, in my opinion, a condition precedent of every contract of marine insurance that the insured shall make a full disclosure of all facts materially affecting the risk which are within his personal knowledge at the time when the contract is made."

789 Ibid, at pp. 536-537.

790 Ibid., at p. 542.

791 MUSTILL & GILMAN: op. cit., Vol. II, par. 595; also see DE HART & SIMEY: **Arnould on the Law of Marine Insurance and Average** Vol. I, par. 535.

792 EGGERS et al.: op. cit., par. 4.33.

793 Ibid.

794 Ibid.

795 Section 18(1).

twentieth century.[796] The duty, in accordance with section 18 of the M.I.A. 1906, now had a pre-contractual nature. If the duty was based on an implied term, it could arguably not arise until the contract was made. One of the earliest cases dealing with this issue after the enactment of M.I.A. in 1906 was *Joel v Law Union & Crown Ins. Co.*,[797] where Fletcher Moulton L.J. stated that "[t]he applicant can be and is called on to answer all questions relevant to the matter in hand. But this is merely the fulfilment of a duty – it is not contractual."[798]

Four years later, in *William Pickersgill v London & Provincial Marine and General Ins. Co. Ltd.*, Hamilton J again favoured the view that the duty is based on an implied condition.[799] He was of the opinion that –

> "...the rule imposing an obligation to disclose upon the intending assured does not rest upon a general principle of common law, but arises out of an implied condition contained in the contract itself, precedent to the liability of the underwriter to pay."[800]

In *Bell v Lever Bros Ltd*[801] Lord Atkin said that "the duty does not arise out of contract; the duty of a person proposing in insurance arises before a contract is made." [802]

Scott L.J. attempted to untangle the judgements of his predecessors to this point, and came to the conclusion in the matter of *Merchants and Manufacturers Ins. Co. v John Hunt* that the duty is a legal one.[803] He disposed of the issue as follows:

> "I realized there were several reported cases in which learned judges have, in the course of their judgements, expressed an opinion that the duty of disclosure might be regarded as resting on an implied term, but I do not know of any case where the point had come up for actual decision. On principle it seems plain that the equitable jurisdiction to avoid a contract for misrepresentation could not rest on such a foundation... Even the common law duty of disclosure I find difficult to explain fully on the theory of its resting only on an implied term of the contract. If it did, it would not arise until the contract had been made; and then its sole operation would be to unmake the contract. Although the question has not been decided judicially, it is worthy of note that ss. 17 and 18 of the Marine Insurance Act 1906 seem to treat the twin duties of disclosing all the material facts and of misrepresenting none, as existing outside the contract and not as mere implications inside the contract; for that Act was intended to be declaratory of the Common Law."[804]

---

[796] PARK, Semin: op. cit., p. 50.
[797] [1908] 2 K.B. 863.
[798] Ibid., at p. 886.
[799] [1912] 3 K.B. 614.
[800] Ibid., at p. 621.
[801] [1932] A.C. 161.
[802] Ibid., at p. 227.
[803] [1941] 1 K.B. 295.
[804] Ibid., at pp. 312-313; also see p. 128 *supra*.

May J., in *March Cabaret Club & Casino Ltd. v The London Assurance*[805], after reviewing the authorities said the following about the basis of the duty to disclose:

> "Bearing in mind the basis of the rule, however, which is as Lord Justice Scrutton pointed out [in *Rozanes v Bowen* (1928) 32 Ll.L.Rep. 98, at p. 102] the fact that there is a disparity in negotiating position between the intending assured and insurers, in my judgement the duty to disclose is not based upon an implied term of the contract at all; it arises outside the contract; it applies to all contracts *uberrimae fidei* and is not limited to insurance contracts..."[806]

In his brilliant apology in favour of the Roman-Dutch Law in South Africa, Joubert JA in *Mutual and Federal Insurance Co. Ltd.v Oudtshoorn Municipality*[807] rejected the idea that the duty of disclosure was based on an implied term and favoured an *ex lege* analysis of the duty.

The basis of the duty of disclosure, although in the context of bringing a claim under a marine insurance policy, was one of various issues that came up for decision in *The Litsion Pride.*[808] Hirst, J., delivering the judgement, considered i.a. *Merchants and Manufacturers Insurance v Hunt*[809] as well as *Blackburn Low & Co. v Vigors*[810] and preferred the authority of the latter, holding that "the duty... not to make fraudulent claims and not to make claims in breach of the duty of utmost good faith is an implied term of the policy."[811]

In the judgement of Lord Steyn, in *Banque Keyser Ullmann S.A. v Skandia (U.K.) Ins. Ltd.*[812], it was incorrect to categorise the duties arising out of the body of rules known as the *uberrima fides* principle as implied terms. According to Lord Steyn, these rules were rules of law developed by judges, applicable to every contract of insurance and, indeed, before the contract come into existence.[813] The *ex lege* explanation for the duty of disclosure seemed to have found the support of the Court of Appeal too.[814] Slade, L.J. found that the weight of authority and of principle was against the conclusion that the duty of disclosure was founded upon an implied term of the contract.[815]

In the same year that the Court of Appeal made this judgement, Hobhouse, J., as

---

805 [1975] 1 Lloyd's Rep. 169.
806 Ibid., at p. 175.
807 1985 (1) SA 419.
808 [1985] 1 Lloyd's Rep. 437.
809 [1941] 1 K.B. 295; see p. 130 *supra*.
810 (1886) 17 Q.B.D. 553.; see p. 128 *supra*.
811 Ibid., at pp. 518-519.
812 [1987] 1 Lloyd's Rep. 69.
813 Ibid., at p. 94.
814 *La Banque Financière de la Cité S.A. v Westgate Insurance Co. Ltd.* [1988] 2 Lloyd's Rep. 513, at pp. 548-550.
815 Ibid., at p. 548.

he then was, delivered his judgement from the Queen's Bench in *The Good Luck*.[816] He preferred the view that the obligation of the utmost good faith at the time of the performance of the contract arose from an implied term of the contract.[817] The judge considered that the pre-contractual duty not to misrepresent any material facts arose as a matter of general law. As far as the duty to disclose material facts was concerned, he merely said that it had a different character from the post-contractual duty, which he thought to be contractual.[818] The Court of Appeal rejected this interpretation, holding in the words of May, L.J. that the "...mutual obligation of utmost good faith arose by operation of law as an incident of the contract of insurance."[819] The Court saw no reason why the source of the duty, or the remedy for its breach, should be different after the contract was made, from what it was at the pre-contractual stage.[820] The different duties were all part of the same principle of "utmost" good faith, taking shape only to meet the circumstances in which the parties found themselves.[821]

Over a decade later the House of Lords was confronted with, amongst other issues, the question of the basis of the duty of disclosure in *The Star Sea*.[822] Hobhouse, J. in the meanwhile became Lord Hobhouse of Woodborough and now held the view that the duty arose *ex lege*:

> "There are certain contracts expressed by the law to be contracts of the utmost good faith, where material facts must be disclosed; if not, the contract is voidable. Apart from special fiduciary relationships, contracts for partnership and contracts of insurance are the leading instances. In such cases the duty does not arise out of contract; the duty of a person proposing an insurance arises before a contract is made, so of an intending partner."[823]

It would appear in the light of these *dicta* that the weight of judicial authority is in favour of describing the duty of utmost good faith as deriving *ex lege*, and not as an implied term of the contract, at least with regard to the pre-contractual duty of utmost good faith.[824]

Some of the leading authorities in favour of an *ex contractu*-basis have been criticised in the past. The *Pickersgill* case is one such an authority which has found its way as support for an *ex contractu*-analysis into *The Litsion Pride* judgement. The reason why

[816] Cf. pp. 119 and 121 *supra*; [1988] 1 Lloyd's Rep. 514.
[817] [1988] 1 Lloyd's Rep. 514, at p. 547.
[818] Ibid.
[819] [1989] 2 Lloyd's Rep. 238, at p. 264.
[820] [1989] 2 Lloyd's Rep. 238 at p. 263.
[821] EGGERS et al.: op. cit., par. 4.46 and 4.48
[822] [2001] 1 Lloyd's Rep. 389; also see Lord Atkin in *Bell v Lever Brothers* [1932] A.C. 161 at p. 227.
[823] [2001] 1 Lloyd's Rep. 389 at p. 399.
[824] Cf. COLINVAUX, R.: op. cit., par. 5-02; FORTE: op. cit., p. 83; PARK, Semin: op. cit. p. 50; Other authority for the proposition that the duty of the utmost good faith arises from an implied term is *Orakpo v Barclays Bank* [1995] 1 LRLR 443.

Hamilton, J. in *Pickersgill* based the duty of disclosure on an implied term of the contract was to vitiate the argument of the assignee of the policy that he was not responsible for a breach by the assignor of his duty to disclose. It has subsequently been pointed out that this argument could be resolved by reference to section 50(2) of the Marine Insurance Act 1906, which provides in the following terms:

> "Where a marine policy has been assigned so as to pass the beneficial interest in such policy, the assignee of the policy is entitled to sue thereon in his own name; and the defendant is entitled to make any defence arising out of the contract which he would have been entitled to make if the action has been brought in the name of the person by or on behalf whom the policy was effected."

The foundation for the *ex contractu*-analysis in this case, therefore, seems to be weak.[825]

As for the judgement of Hirst, J. in *The Litsion Pride*, his analysis has been said to be concerned with the scope of the duty of the utmost good faith and not with its basis.[826] Since the case dealt with a failure to observe the duty of disclosure after conclusion of the policy, it has furthermore been argued that his judgement cannot be relevant in deciding the basis of the duty of disclosure in section 18 of the Marine Insurance Act 1906, which is essentially a pre-contractual duty.[827]

It has been suggested, however, that there is no reason why an implied term providing for a right of avoidance where the duty has been breached, could not be generated by the law.[828] *Arnould* too appears to favour a position somewhere between the contractual and *ex lege* analysis, stating that the "the *duty* at all stages (except arguably in particular contexts such as held-covered clauses) arises outside the contract, but there is *also* an implied condition precedent, which is not of a promissory nature and cannot give rise to claims for damages..."[829]

---

[825] PARK, Semin: op. cit., p. 55.
[826] Cf. the judgement of Steyn, L.J. in *Banque Keyser Ullmann S.A. v Skandia (U.K.) Ins. Ltd.* [1987] 1 Lloyd's Rep. 69, at p. 94.
[827] PARK, Semin: op. cit., p. 55.
[828] BAATZ: *Utmost Good Faith in Marine Insurance Contracts* **Marine Insurance at the Turn of the Millennium** Vol. 1 p. 23.
[829] GILMAN: op. cit., Vol. III, par. 579I.

5.3 NON-DISCLOSURE

The common law principle in contract law applicable to all parties – not only to buyers – to commercial contracts, is *caveat emptor*, i.e. let the buyer be aware.[830] The common law does not prescribe a general duty to provide information; in fact, it puts the responsibility on the parties to obtain the information material to their undertakings before concluding the contract by themselves.[831] Accordingly, even if *Hansell* were to be correct that all contracts are subject to good faith,[832] in common law there exists no duty upon the contracting parties to disclose their peculiar knowledge regarding the subject-matter of their contract to one another. The general common law rule in contract law is that mere non-disclosure by a party to a contract does not entitle the other party to rescind the contract. The latter party will be able to rescind where he had been induced by a misstatement to enter into the contract.[833]

In certain contracts however, where a party to a contract concealed something he knew to be material, the contract will be *voidable* at the instance of the aggrieved party. These contracts are known as contracts of *the utmost good faith*, or *uberrima fides*, the prime example of which is of course contracts of insurance.[834] There have been different explanations for the basis of the duty of disclosure in English marine insurance law. Some commentators suggest that insurance contracts are of a fiduciary nature, i.e. they are based upon mutual trust and confidence between the insurer and the assured.[835] It would therefore be inequitable to apply the *caveat emptor* rule, as the information needed by the parties in order to contract is not as apparent as with e.g. a contract of sale, where the buyer can inspect the subject-matter of the sale. Therefore the common law duty that applies to insurance contracts is the "...much more stringent one of *uberrima fides* (utmost good faith)".[836]

Lord Hobhouse in *The Star Sea* arguably offered the most acceptable explanation for the duty of disclosure with reference to Lord Mansfield's judgement in *Carter v Boehm*:

> "It was based upon the inequality of information as between the proposer and the underwriter and the character of insurance as a contract upon a 'speculation'. He (Lord Mansfield) equated non-disclosure to fraud. He said at p1909: 'The keeping back [in] such circumstances is a fraud, and therefore the policy is void. Although the suppression

[830] EGGERS et al.: op. cit., par. 1.08, also see par. 1.15 and par. 2.04.
[831] Ibid., par. 1.07.
[832] Cf. p. 13 *supra*.
[833] BAATZ: *Utmost Good Faith in Marine Insurance Contracts* **Marine Insurance at the Turn of the Millennium** Vol. 1, p. 15; BENNET: **The Law of Marine Insurance** pp. 44-45.
[834] MERKIN, Robert (editor): op. cit., p. 115.
[835] HANSELL, D.S.: **Introduction to Insurance** p. 175; SCHNEIDER: op. cit., p. 109.
[836] Ibid.

> should happen through mistake, without any fraudulent intention; yet still the underwriter is deceived, and the policy is void.'
> It thus was not actual fraud as known to the common law but a form of mistake of which the other party was not allowed to take advantage. "[837]

Lord Hobhouse made this remark in his discussion of the origin of section 17 of the M.I.A 1906 and the principle of "utmost good faith". He agreed with Lord Mustill in the *Pine Top* case that Lord Mansfield attempted at the time to introduce a general principle of good faith into English commercial law.[838] Accordingly, when Hobhouse, L.J. spoke of an inequality of information as the basis of the duty, he appreciated at the same time the real intention of Lord Mansfield, namely that the general principle of good faith dictated in the particular circumstances of contracts upon "speculation", or *contrats aléatoires* as Pothier referred to them,[839] that neither the assured nor the insurer should hide from the other what is privately known in order to obtain the advantage of cover or premium. Some authors maintain that the duty of disclosure in sections 18 and 19 of the M.I.A. 1906 is essential to the marine insurance contract, because the "material information is peculiar to the assured and his broker".[840] Such a basis would not accord with Lord Mansfield's intention as expressed in *Carter v Boehm*, and which has now – more than two centuries later – also been appreciated by the House of Lords. By placing "material information" *per se* and from the outset in the private or exclusive sphere of knowledge of the assured, there is no room left for the equitable operation of the principle of good faith. Disclosure was never intended to be a rule upon itself, i.e. a rule for the sake of disclosing material information. It was also not intended to be only applicable to a limited class of contracts. It was intended, in the first place, to serve good faith and to prevent a party to any contract from taking unfair advantage of an inequality of information during the formation of the contract. It was *good faith* that directed a contractual party not to draw his counterpart into a bargain by concealing material information of which he privately knew.

In 1906, the duty of utmost good faith was entrenched in section 17 of the Marine Insurance Act. The duties of non-disclosure, and not to misrepresent, were codified in sections 18-20 as particular facets of the duty of utmost good faith.[841] Section 18 of M.I.A. 1906 enacts the duty of disclosure as follows:

> "**Disclosure by assured**
> (1) Subject to the provisions of this section, the assured must disclose to the insurer, before the contract is concluded, every material circumstance which is known to

[837] *The Star Sea* [2001] 1 Lloyd's Rep. 389 at p. 398.
[838] Cf. the discussion at p. 99 *supra*.
[839] Cf. the text to footnote 244 *supra*.
[840] RHIDIAN THOMAS, D. (editor): op. cit., p. 33; cf. other examples of similar statements at fns. 701, 702, 703, 704, and 705 *supra*.
[841] Ibid: op. cit., p. 27.

the assured, and the assured is deemed to know every circumstance which, in the ordinary course of business, ought to be known by him. If the assured fails to make such disclosure, the insurer may avoid the contract.

(2) Every circumstance is material which would influence the judgement of a prudent insurer in fixing the premium, or determining whether he will take the risk.

(3) In the absence of inquiry the following circumstances need not be disclosed, namely:-
(a) Any circumstance which diminishes the risk;
(b) Any circumstance which is known or presumed to be known to the insurer. The insurer is presumed to know matters of common notoriety or knowledge, and matters which an insurer in the ordinary course of his business, as such, ought to know;
(c) Any circumstance as to which information is waived by the insurer;
(d) Any circumstance which it is superfluous to disclose by reason of any express or implied warranty.

(4) Whether any particular circumstance, which is not disclosed, be material or not is, in each case, a question of fact.

(5) The term 'circumstance' includes any communication made to, or information received by, the assured."

Section 19 deals with the situation where an agent effects the insurance on behalf or the assured:

"**Disclosure by agent effecting insurance**
Subject to the provisions of the preceding section as to circumstances which need not be disclosed, where an insurance is effected for the assured by an agent, the agent must disclose to the insurer –

(a) every material circumstance which is known to himself, and an agent to insure is deemed to know every circumstance which in the ordinary course of business ought to be known by, or to have been communicated to, him;
(b) and every material circumstance which the assured is bound to disclose, unless it
(c) come to his knowledge too late to communicate it to the agent."

The duty of disclosure as described in these sections is but an aspect of the overriding principle of the utmost good faith.[842] Since the duty to disclose, in the context of the principle of utmost good faith in marine as well as non-marine insurance, has been the point of much litigation and academic discussion, it has led to the misconception that utmost good faith is to be equated with the duty of disclosure.[843] The duty of disclosure contained in section 18, however, is only a pre-contractual duty resting on the assured:[844] section 18 is quite clear in requiring

---

[842] Cf. p.136 *supra*; also, *Container Transport International Inc. v Oceanus Murual Indemnity Association (Bermuda) Limited* [1984] 1 Lloyd's Rep. 476, at p. 492; GILMAN: op. cit., Vol. III, par. 579F; RHIDIAN THOMAS, D. (editor): op. cit., p. 32.

[843] RHIDIAN THOMAS, D. (editor): op. cit., p. 32; see also p.118 *supra*.

[844] COLINVAUX, R.: op. cit., par. 5-06, citing *British Equitable v G.W.R.* (1869) 20 L.T. 422 and *Canning v Farquhar* (1886) 16 Q.B.D. 727 as authority for this proposition; see however footnote 1202 *supra*.

the assured to disclose "*before the contract is concluded*", and similarly section 19 in requiring disclosure from the agent who "*effects*" the policy. Accordingly the duty of disclosure and the section 17 principle of "utmost" good faith cannot be equated: section 17 is not and should not be limited to the period before the contract is concluded, whereas the wording of sections 18 and 19 is clear in limiting the duty to disclose to the pre-contractual period. On the other hand, Hoffmann, L.J. in *Societe Anonyme d'Intermediaries Luxembourgeois v Farex Gie*[845] remarked that "the obligations in sections 18 and 19, although derived from the basic principle in section 17, go a good deal further".[846] The Lord Justice said this in the light of those parts of sections 18 and 19 allowing an insurer to repudiate for non-disclosure of imputed knowledge, which he considered to be "far from any ordinary understanding of lack of good faith".[847]

Primarily the duty to make full disclosure applies to negotiations preceding the formation of the policy. Where the policy consists of a Lloyd's slip, the assured owes a duty to disclose to each individual underwriter. The reason for this is that every initialling constitutes a separate contract.[848] This was confirmed in *General Reinsurance Corporation v Forsakringsaktiebolaget Fenna Patria*[849], where the Court of Appeal stated that it was a well-established principle that a binding contract was created by the initialling of the slip, whether it was an original initialling or in order to amend the slip.[850]

In accordance with sections 18 and 19 of the M.I.A. 1906, both the assured and his broker must make a fair representation of the risk in order for the underwriter to assess the risk on the correct basis.[851] They should do so by disclosing "every material circumstance" of which they have knowledge.[852] They are therefore under no obligation to disclose information of which they do not have knowledge.[853] A "man can only disclose what he knows".[854] The duty is dependant on the knowledge of the assured and his broker,[855] but knowledge is not confined to actual knowledge: both assured and broker are deemed to know every circumstance which, in the ordinary course of business, ought to be known by them.[856]

---

845 [1995] L.R.L.R. 116.
846 Ibid., at p. 149; GILMAN: op. cit., Vol. III, par. 579F.
847 [1995] L.R.L.R. 116, at p. 149; GILMAN: op. cit., Vol. III, par. 579F.
848 MERKIN, Robert (editor): op. cit. p. 118.
849 [1982] Q.B. 1022.
850 MERKIN, Robert (editor): op. cit., p. 25.
851 *Container Transport International Inc. v Oceanus Mutual Underwriting Association (Bermuda) Ltd.* [1984] 1 Lloyd's Rep. 476 at pp. 496-497; RHIDIAN THOMAS, D. (editor): op. cit., p. 33.
852 Sections 18 (1) and 19 (a) of the M.I.A. 1906.
853 COLINVAUX, R.: op. cit., par. 5-06; RHIDIAN THOMAS, D. (editor): op. cit., p. 33.
854 COLINVAUX, R.: op. cit., par. 5-06; *Wheelton v Hardisty* (1857) 8 E. & B. 232, at p. 269; also cf. *Joel v Law Union and Crown Insurance Company* (1908) 2 K.B. 899, at p. 884.
855 RHIDIAN THOMAS, D. (editor): op. cit., p. 33.
856 Sections 18 (1) and 19 (a) of the M.I.A. 1906.

Certain facts need not be disclosed by the assured and his broker. These circumstances are listed in section 18 (3) of the M.I.A. 1906. The list of circumstances should, however, be read together with the discussion of Lord Mansfield in *Carter v Boehm* regarding facts as to which either party "may be innocently silent"[857], in order to put it into the correct perspective. Lord Mansfield managed to balance the duty to disclose perfectly against the ignorance of a contractual party of those facts of which his counterpart privately knew.[858] It is clear from the judgement that although the Lord Justice acknowledged that the "special facts, upon which the contingent chance is to be computed, lie most commonly in the knowledge of the insured only"[859], he did not accept as a starting point that the assured knows everything and the insurer nothing, as Scrutton, L.J. observed[860] almost two centuries later. Lord Mansfield's observation that the "special facts" upon which the risk turned were commonly in the assured's knowledge, served to explain why the insurer "trust[ed] to his representation"[861], i.e. that it (the representation) was true, and that nothing had been concealed to induce a false estimation of the risk. In short, Lord Mansfield intended the duty to disclose to operate in those circumstances where in fact there existed an inequality between the parties with regard to the degree of knowledge of facts relating to the risk, i.e. where one party privately knows of a fact or facts of which the other is ignorant. Nowhere does he lay down as a rule that that should *per se* be the case in the contractual relationship between assured and insurer. In this context, the exceptions listed by Lord Mansfield denote subjective considerations relating to the position of the actual insurer.[862] They serve to promote the fairness in the policy, as good faith dictated, by holding the actual insurer to the contract notwithstanding a non-disclosure of a material fact.[863]

Accordingly, non-disclosure of facts within the knowledge of the insurer is excused; also circumstances which are presumed to be known by the insurer, need not be disclosed.[864] The insurer is presumed to know matters of common notoriety or knowledge, as well as matters which an insurer in the ordinary course of business ought to know.[865] Once the insured has the means of knowing the fact,[866] or if he ought to know it,[867] such a fact cannot be the subject of an action for non-disclosure. An example of how these rules find application in non-marine

[857] 3 Burr. 1909, at p. 1910.
[858] Ibid., at p. 1911.
[859] Ibid., at p. 1909.
[860] In *Rozanes v Bowen* (1928) 32 Ll.L.R. 98 at p. 102.
[861] 3 Burr. 1909, at p. 1909.
[862] RHIDIAN THOMAS, D. (editor): op. cit., p. 37.
[863] Ibid.
[864] COLINVAUX, R.: op. cit., par. 5-06; section 18 (3) (b) of the M.I.A. 1906.
[865] Section 18 (3) (b) of the M.I.A. 1906.
[866] COLINVAUX, R.: op. cit., par. 5-06; *Foley v Tabor* (1861) 2 F. & F. 663, at p. 672.
[867] *Carter v Boehm* 3 Burr. 1905, at p. 1911.

insurance is the case of *Woolcott v Excess Insurance* [868], where an assured claimed on a house insurance policy after the dwelling and its contents had been destroyed by fire. A peculiar fact about the assured was that he had lived a life of crime before he was convicted for armed robbery in 1960 and sentenced to 12 years imprisonment. The assured did not disclose his criminal record before signing the policy and the insurer refused to pay on that ground. It turned out that the brokers acting as agents for the insurers had knowledge of his criminal record before the fire broke out in 1974. Caulfield, J. found for the assured.[869] The Court of Appeal confirmed the judge's finding of law: if the insurers were deemed to have knowledge of the material facts, they could not rely upon the assured's non-disclosure.[870] It had reservations about his finding on the facts and accordingly ordered a new trial, where the judgement of Caulfield, J. was upheld.[871]

The M.I.A. 1906[872] follows a *dictum* of Lord Mansfield in *Carter v Boehm*[873] in stating that the assured need not disclose facts of which information is waived by the insurer.[874] Thus, if the insurer fails to ask further questions where he has been put on guard by the information provided by the assured, the insurer will not be heard to complain of non-disclosure.[875]

---

[868] [1978] 1 Lloyd's Rep. 633; [1979] 1 Lloyd's Rep. 231, Court of Appeal; [1979] 2 Lloyd's Rep. 210, Queen's Bench Division (retrial).
[869] [1978] 1 Lloyd's Rep. 633.
[870] [1979] 1 Lloyd's Rep. 231, cf. the findings of Megaw, L.J. at pp. 240-241.
[871] [1979] 2 Lloyd's Rep. 210.
[872] Section 18 (3) (c).
[873] 3 Burr. 1905, at p. 1910: "The insured need not mention what the underwriter ... waives being informed of."
[874] COLINVAUX, R.: op. cit., par. 5-08.
[875] *Becker v Marshall* (1922) Ll. L. R. 413, at p. 414; COLINVAUX, R.: op. cit., par. 5-08.

5.4 MISREPRESENTATION

Section 20 of the M.I.A 1906 provides that the contract of marine insurance will be voidable for misrepresentation. The fundamental considerations underlying the rules of misrepresentation in marine insurance are the same as those relating to the duty of disclosure, i.e. it derives from the general duty to observe the utmost good faith, and more particularly to provide the underwriter with all the material facts in order to assess the risk properly.[876] Section 20 of the M.I.A. 1906 reads:

> "**Representations pending negotiation of contract**
> (1) Every material representation made by the assured or his agent to the insurer during the negotiations for the contract, and before the contract is concluded must be true. If it be untrue the insurer may avoid the contract.
> (2) A representation is material which would influence the judgement of a prudent insure in fixing the premium, or determining whether he will take the risk.
> (3) A representation may be either a representation as to a matter of fact, or as to a matter of expectation or belief.
> (4) A representation as to matter of fact is true, if it be substantially correct, that is to say, if the difference between what is represented and what is actually correct would not be considered material by a prudent insurer.
> (5) A representation as to matter of expectation or belief is true if it be made in good faith.
> (6) A representation may be withdrawn or corrected before the contract is concluded.
> (7) Whether a particular representation be material or not is, in each case, a question of fact."

In the *Pan Atlantic* case, Lord Mustill said of sections 18-20 that "in practice the line between misrepresentation and non-disclosure is often imperceptible."[877] It would appear that the courts, as a result of insurers often pleading misrepresentation and non-disclosure together, failed always to distinguish clearly between these concepts, and expressly to base the remedy of avoidance of the policy on one or the other.[878] In fact, the line between the duty not to misrepresent and to disclose may be barely discernable,[879] for although the requirements that need to be fulfilled to establish misrepresentation or non-disclosure are conceptually different, there are some basic similarities.[880] The effect of misrepresentation and non-disclosure is the same, i.e. it affords the aggrieved party with the remedy of avoidance of the contract.[881] Section 20(2) effectively mirrors section 18(2). The question of materiality will therefore be approached in the same way as non-disclosure. In accordance with the interpretation of the House of Lords in the *Pine Top* case, the standard to be

876 RHIDIAN THOMAS, D. (editor): op. cit., p. 40.
877 [1994] 2 Lloyd's Rep. 427 at p. 452.
878 RHIDIAN THOMAS, D. (editor): op. cit., p. 42.
879 CLARKE: op. cit., par. 22-1, and par. 23-1.
880 RHIDIAN THOMAS, D. (editor): op. cit., p. 42.
881 COLINVAUX, R.: op. cit., par. 5-12 ; however, cf. 5.6.1 Remedy of the Insurer *infra*, where it is suggested that there might be circumstances where damages could be awarded for misrepresentation.

applied is that of the hypothetical prudent insurer.[882] Furthermore, the correct test for materiality of fact is the "right to know" test, and not the "decisive influence" test.[883]

According to *Arnould*, a representation, for the purposes of section 20 of the Act, is a –

> "... verbal or written statement made by the assured to the underwriter, at or before the time of the making of the contract, as to the existence of some fact or state of facts which is likely to induce an underwriter more readily to assume the risk, by diminishing the estimate he would otherwise have formed of it."[884]

The statement must be a positive affirmation of facts that do (or will) exist, or a declaration of belief or expectation that such facts do (or will) exist.[885] A representation may be oral, in writing or even based on conduct, as long as it is a positive statement; mere silence cannot amount to a representation.[886] In most instances the representation will be a written instruction or verbal communications by the broker to an underwriter.[887] Nevertheless, there is no rule that a representation must be inserted in the policy to be a valid representation. This constitutes the main and formal distinction between a representation and warranties, the latter having to be in writing and inserted in the policy[888], i.e. "part of the written policy".[889] In turn, this formal distinction gives rise to an important difference in effect: a warranty, being a part of the written contract, requires rigid and literal compliance, whereas in the case of a representation not carried on the face of the policy, a substantial compliance with the terms of the representation is the only requirement.[890]

---

[882] RHIDIAN THOMAS, D. (editor): op. cit., p. 33.

[883] Ibid., pp. 34-35; cf. the full discussion of this theme under 5.5.1 Materiality *infra*.

[884] MUSTILL & GILMAN: op. cit., Vol. II, par. 588; also see the previous (fifteenth) edition, CHORLEY and BAILHACHE: op. cit., at par. 554, where the words "calculated to induce" were still used. The editors of the sixteenth edition, at note 41 to par. 588, felt that "a definition in those terms is nowadays ambiguous, as possibly importing a requirement that the statement must be made with the intention of inducing the underwriter more readily to assume the risk." For a more concise definition, cf. CLARKE: op. cit., at par. 22-2.

[885] MUSTILL & GILMAN: op. cit., Vol. II, par. 588; the third volume of this work, GILMAN: op. cit., Vol. III, did not add anything to or qualify this paragraph. However the addition "*or will*" hints at promissory representations, of which in par. 603 of the latter volume the author says does not constitute a proper representation for purposes of section 20 of the M.I.A. 1906 (see p. 144 *infra*).

[886] CLARKE: op. cit., par. 22-2A.

[887] MUSTILL & GILMAN: op. cit., Vol. II, par. 589.

[888] Ibid.

[889] *Pawson v Watson* (1778) 2 Cowp. 785, *per* Lord Mansfield at p. 787.

[890] MUSTILL & GILMAN: op. cit., Vol. II, par. 591.

A representation must be a statement of fact and therefore neither a promise, nor a statement of opinion or law will suffice for that purpose.[891] An opinion is a statement which, as it appears or should appear to the person to whom the statement is made, the speaker does not have sufficient information to guarantee.[892] Since it would not be reasonable for a person to whom a statement of opinion is made to rely on such a statement, and since the person making the statement cannot be expected to take the same legal responsibility as would be the case when making a statement of fact, an opinion is usually not actionable.[893] The legal position maintained by Lord Mansfield in *Barber v Fletcher*[894] - where he stated that a broker's representation that a vessel departed at a certain date which proved to be false was not material, since it had only been "an expectation, and the underwriters did not inquire into the ground of the expectation"[895] – therefore, still holds good today. Accordingly, an opinion or expectation held by an assured that proved to be not in accordance with the actual facts will not constitute an actionable misrepresentation, except when it can be shown that the opinion was not honestly held, in which case it would amount to a fraudulent misstatement.[896] Another example of how these rules operate in practice is *Anderson v Pacific Fire and Marine Insurance Co.*[897] The policy in this case was for the cargo aboard the "Clarendon". It stated that she was to sail "from Belize to Rendezvous Point, thence back to Belize, and thence to London". Neither of the parties knew of a place called Rendezvous Point. A letter by the Master was shown to the underwriter, which stated i.a. that the local pilot considered it to be "a good and safe anchorage, and well sheltered." Said the master: "I have been out and seen the place, and consider it quite safe." During the subsequent trial, it was proved that Rendezvous Point was a dangerous place at which to anchor during the hurricane months. A jury found that the pilot and the master considered Rendezvous Point not to be dangerous and that the master honestly entertained that opinion. Willes, J. had to decide whether the statement by the master amounted to an absolute statement of fact, or only to a statement of opinion. He found that it was not an absolute statement of fact. The master merely stated, on strength of the consideration of and information received from the pilot, as well as on the basis of his own inspection, that he considered it safe. Fraud being out of the question, misrepresentation could not be established.[898]

---

[891] CLARKE: op. cit., par. 22-2B.

[892] Ibid., par. 22-2B2, citing i.a. *Hubbard v Glover* (1812) 3 Camp 313, at pp. 314-315 and *Brine v Featherstone* (1813) 4 Taunt 869, at p. 873.

[893] CLARKE: op. cit., par. 22-2B2.

[894] (1779) 1 Dougl. 305; cf. the text to footnote 669 *supra*.

[895] (1779) 1 Dougl. 305, at p. 306.

[896] COLINVAUX, R.: op. cit., par. 5-10; EGGERS et al.: op. cit., par. 7.49; also see CLARKE: op. cit., par. 22-2B2.

[897] (1872) L.R. 7 C.P. 65.

[898] For a summary of this case cf. MUSTILL & GILMAN: op. cit., Vol. II, par. 605.

For purposes of the M.I.A. 1906, a statement "as to a matter of expectation or belief"[899] will also constitute a representation, but such a representation will be considered as true for purposes of the Act "if it be made in good faith".[900] This distinction between statements of fact and opinion is considered to be "of secondary importance"[901] in the context of commercial insurance contracts: in this context, it is said, "the opinions of others do have influence, because an opinion may be valued as an opinion, and such reliance may be reasonable."[902] Thus, a man, who says that he expects or believes something to be the case, is making an affirmative representation as to the present condition of his mind.[903] Such a representation is, therefore, also one of fact, i.e. the fact of the condition of mind of the representor.[904] Accordingly, the statement that the element of fraud must be present in order to avoid the policy for misrepresentation of belief is superfluous, "for it is impossible to make a false representation as to one's own belief without at the same time being conscious that the representation is false."[905] Moreover, it has been suggested that a statement of opinion leads one to believe that such an opinion is justified by facts that are impliedly known to the person holding it.[906]

As mentioned above, a promise also cannot constitute a statement of fact, it being a statement of the future.[907] A promise can neither be true nor false at the time it is made.[908] Similar to the legal position as regards opinions, a promise, as far as it can be described as a statement of current intention, could be actionable as a misrepresentation if it turns out that the statement was not made in good faith, i.e. the intention was not honestly held.[909] It is much rather the true entertainment of intention that constitutes a representation as opposed to the resultant promise that a certain circumstance will be the case in the future.[910] The insurer may avoid the policy if the assured did not make a *bona fidei* representation of intention, i.e. that his intention was, in fact, different from that which he had represented, provided the difference in intention is material.[911] Moreover, it has been suggested that by making a promise, a person impliedly states that he has grounds for believing that

---

[899] Section 20(3).
[900] Section 20(5).
[901] CLARKE: op. cit., par. 22-2B2; MUSTILL & GILMAN: op. cit., Vol. II, go even further in par. 604, stating that the distinction, on their view, becomes unnecessary.
[902] CLARKE: op. cit., par. 22-2B2.
[903] MUSTILL & GILMAN: op. cit., Vol. II, par. 604.
[904] Ibid.
[905] Ibid.
[906] CLARKE: op. cit., par. 22-2B2, citing *i.a. Highlands Ins Co.v Continental Ins Co* [1987] 1 Lloyd's Rep. 109, at p. 112.
[907] CLARKE: op. cit., par. 22-2B1.
[908] Ibid.
[909] Ibid.
[910] EGGERS et al.: op. cit., par. 7.61; see also GILMAN: op. cit., Vol. III, par. 603.
[911] EGGERS et al.: op. cit., par. 7.61.

he will fulfil his promise.[912] It will, however, be close to impossible to prove it was the implied representation and not the promise which induced the contract,[913] as Staughton, J. suggested in *The Anemone*[914] by approving of the following paragraph in *Spencer Bower & Turner on Estoppel by Representation* (3rd ed.) p. 33:

> "An even more formidable difficulty, however, though this again does not negative the main proposition, generally stands in the way of one who seeks, whether for purposes of misrepresentation, or estoppel, to extract a representation from expressions of intention, the difficulty, that is, of proving that he regarded the supposed fact (that is, the existence of a then present intention on the part of the representor) as of the slightest importance. What the representee is generally found in the last resort to complain of, or to protest against, is that the representor is refusing to carry out his intention, not that he is setting up that he never had any such intention in the first instance – which is tantamount to an acknowledgment by the representee that he attached weight to the declared intention only in the belief that it would ripen into accomplishment, or, in other words, that he regarded the statement as a promise and not a representation."[915]

As a general rule, a representation of the legal position under English law will not be a representation of fact for the purposes of an action for misrepresentation.[916] In contrast, a representation of the position under foreign law will be treated as a statement of fact and as such will be actionable if untrue.[917] The general position is qualified in some instances, i.a. in that it will not hold good where a contractual party made a dishonest or fraudulent representation of the English legal position.[918]

[912] CLARKE: op. cit., par. 22-2B1; see the text to footnote 906 *supra*; also EGGERS et al.: op. cit., par. 7.61.
[913] GILMAN: op. cit., Vol. III, par. 603.
[914] *Clipper Maritime Ltd v Shirlstar Container Transport Ltd (The Anemone)* [1987] 1 Lloyd's Rep. 546.
[915] Ibid., at p. 558.
[916] CLARKE: op. cit., par. 22-2B3; EGGERS et al.: op. cit., par. 7.67.
[917] CLARKE: op. cit., par. 22-2B3; EGGERS et al.: op. cit., par. 7.69; GILMAN: op. cit., Vol. III, par. 609.
[918] CLARKE: op. cit., par. 22-2B3; EGGERS et al.: op. cit., par. 7.68; MUSTILL & GILMAN: op. cit., Vol. II, par. 609.

5.5 MATERIALITY OF FACT AND INDUCEMENT

The insurer needs to fulfil two requirements in order to succeed with a claim for non-disclosure (and misrepresentation): first, the fact which was not disclosed (or misrepresented) needs to have been material, and second, the insurer must have been induced by the non-disclosure to enter into the policy.[919]

5.5.1 Materiality

The concept of materiality in marine insurance law is necessary in order to delimit the obligation to disclose.[920] It has been suggested that such a limitation is not a "logically necessary requirement" to the duty to refrain from misrepresentation, a suggestion which holds true in the general English law of contract.[921] However, the concept of materiality is different under marine insurance law, where it has now developed an "overtly objective nature".[922] Materiality is required in the M.I.A 1906 both in the context of disclosure and misrepresentation.[923] The insurer will have no cause of action if the fact misrepresented or concealed by the assured is not material.[924]

Section 18(2) of the M.I.A. 1906 suggests that the test of materiality is objective.[925] Section 18(2) provides:

> "Every circumstance is material which would influence the judgement of a *prudent insurer* fixing the premium, or determining whether he will take the risk."
> (Emphasis added)

In similar terms, section 20(2) provides:

> "A representation is material which would influence the judgement of a *prudent insurer* in fixing the premium, or determining whether he will take the risk."
> (Emphasis added)

Materiality – the *prudent underwriter* and the *reasonable man*

It is now settled that it is on the mind of the *prudent underwriter*, as oppose to the mind of the *reasonable assured*, that the materiality of a circumstance depends.[926] The

[919] MERKIN, Robert (editor): op. cit., p. 130.
[920] *Container transport International Inc v Oceanus Mutual Underwriting Association (Bermuda) Ltd* [1984] 1 Lloyd's Rep. 476, at p. 496; EGGERS et al.: op. cit., par. 14.10.
[921] BENNET: op. cit., p. 46; cf. CHITTY: par. 6-036, where it is argued that objective materiality is not a *sine qua non* for obtaining relief for misrepresentation in the general English law of contract.
[922] EGGERS et al.: op. cit., par. 14.09; as will be seen below, the concept of materiality has developed into an objective test in the context of marine insurance, whereas the focus in general contract law is much rather on whether the *representee* – as opposed to the *reasonable man* – had been influenced by a representation; cf. CHITTY: par. 6-036.
[923] Ibid., p. 47.
[924] EGGERS et al.: op. cit., par. 14.10.
[925] RHIDIAN THOMAS, D. (editor): op. cit., p. 33.

test of the reasonable assured came aboard with the judgement of Fletcher Moulton, L.J. in *Joel v Law Union and Crown Insurance Company.*[927] The judge stressed the objectivity of the test, but related it to the reasonable man:

> "That duty [to disclose], no doubt, must be performed, but it does not suffice that the applicant should bona fide have performed it to the best of his understanding. There is the further duty that he should do it to the extent that a reasonable man would have done it; and, if he has fallen short of that by reason of his bona fide considering the matter not material, whereas the jury, as representing what a reasonable man would think, hold that it was material, he has failed in his duty, and the policy is avoided... If a reasonable man would have recognized that it was material to disclose the knowledge in question, it is no excuse that you did not recognize it to be so..."[928]

In the lower courts, the reasonable man had already done his rounds a few years earlier. In *Life Association of Scotland v Foster*[929], it was held by the Scottish Court of Session that it was the duty of the assured to –

> "...carefully and diligently... review all the facts known to himself bearing on the risk proposed to the insurers, and to state every circumstance which any reasonable man might suppose could in any way influence the insurers in considering and deciding whether they will enter into the contract."[930]

The propositions of Fletcher Moulton, L.J. in *Joel's* case subsequently found support in a string of judgements,[931] all of which were discussed and approved of by McNair, J in *Roselodge, Ltd. v Castle.*[932] The judge concluded with an appreciation of the merit of the reasonable man test. According to the judge, it emphasised the fact that materiality still had to be determined "as it was in Lord Mansfield's day by the view of the Jury of reasonable men."[933] It was MacKenna, J in *Lambert v Co-operative Insurance Society*[934] who gave the reasonable man test a fatal blow. The judge considered *Roselodge Ltd. v Castle* as well as the authorities cited there, but was content to take the law regarding the test for materiality as stated in the report of the Law Reform Committee in 1957.[935] Although the committee did not include

---

926 EGGERS et al.: op. cit., par. 14.17.
927 [1908] 2 K.B. 863.
928 Ibid., at p. 884.
929 (1873) 11 Macph. 351.
930 Ibid., at p. 359.
931 *Horne v Poland* (1922) 10 Ll.L.Rep. 275, *per* Lush, J; *Becker v Marshall* (1922) 11 Ll.L.Rep. 114, (1922) 12 Ll.L.Rep. (Court of Appeal, where Lord Sterndale, M.R. accepted the reasonable man test, but Scrutton, L.J. understood the test to be contained in sub-section 18(2) of the M.I.A. 1906; *Regina Fur Company, Ltd. v Bossom* [1957] 2 Lloyd's Rep. 466; *Godfrey v Britannic Assurance Company, Ltd.* [1963] 2 Lloyd's Rep. 515.
932 [1966] 2 Lloyd's Rep 113, at pp. 129-131.
933 Ibid., at p. 131.
934 [1975] 2 Lloyd's Rep 485.
935 Ibid., at p. 491.

marine insurance in the scope of its inquiries, it stated that there was no reason to doubt that –

> "...the definition of 'material'... namely that the fact, if disclosed, might have led a reasonable insurer to decline the risk or to stipulate for a higher premium... would be applied in all classes of insurance. This definition is substantially the same as that laid down in the Marine Insurance Act, 1906..."[936]

Earlier decisions which referred to the prudent assured as the measure were also rejected in *Pan Atlantic Insurance Co. Ltd. v Pine Top Insurance Co. Ltd.*[937] (the *Pine Top* case), which still is the leading case on this subject,[938] and cannot be supported by the wording of sections 18(2) and 20(2) of the Marine Insurance Act.[939] It is thus well established in recent authorities that the relevant question to ask in testing for materiality is whether the hypothetical prudent underwriter would have liked to consider a particular fact or circumstance in assessing the risk.[940]

Relevant to the test of materiality, is the judgement of the *hypothetical* prudent underwriter,[941] and not that of the *actual* underwriter.[942] The duty of the assured to disclose therefore does not only relate to facts which he thought would be material: the test to be applied in establishing materiality of fact is an *objective* test, namely that of the reasonable or prudent insurer.[943] One of the first cases in which the prudent underwriter test was applied, was *Ionides v Pender*[944], where Blackburn, J. relying on two other commentators, i.e. Duer[945] and Parsons[946], held that facts "which would affect the judgement of a rational underwriter governing himself by the principles and calculations on which underwriters do in practice act..."[947] would have to be disclosed. This position was confirmed in the *Pine Top* case too.[948] Lord Mustill could not state with certainty when the objective test of the prudent insurer entered into the equation, but thought it was at least as old as 1823 when it had been

---

936 Ibid., at p. 489.
937 [1994] 2 Lloyd's Rep. 427; [1994] 3 All E.R. 581.
938 GILMAN: op. cit., Vol. III, par. 610.
939 MERKIN, Robert (editor): op. cit., pp. 130-131.
940 EGGERS et al.: op. cit., par. 14.22; GILMAN: op. cit., Vol. III, par. 610; RHIDIAN THOMAS, D. (editor): op. cit., p. 33.
941 Cf. EGGERS et al.: op. cit., par. 14.26, where the authors offer together with the supporting authority various other descriptions of the hypothetical underwriter, i.e. "experienced", "rational", "ordinary", "prudent and intelligent", "reasonable" and "fair and reasonable".
942 RHIDIAN THOMAS, D. (editor): op. cit., p. 34.
943 FRIEDMANN, Daniel: *The Transformation of "Good Faith" in Insurance Law* **Good Faith in Contract, Concept and Context** pp. 314-315.
944 (1874) L.R. 9 Q.B. 531; also see EGGERS et al.: op. cit., par. 14.25.
945 Duer wrote the treatise, *The Law and Practice of Marine Insurance* in 1846.
946 Parsons was the author of *A treatise on the Law of Marine Insurance and General Average* (1868).
947 (1874) L.R. 9 Q.B. 531, at p. 539.
948 [1994] 2 Lloyd's Rep. 427, at p. 445.

described by the commentator, Marshall.[949] The principles stated by Lord Mansfield required fair dealing, and Mustill, L.J. thought "it would have been unfair to the assured to require disclosure of matters which a reasonable underwriter would not have taken into account."[950] Another ground for the objective test was that, until the Evidence Act of 1851, a party to a suit could not testify on his own behalf so that an underwriter would have been barred from providing evidence on the question of materiality. The question of materiality, therefore, would have to be approached on the assumption that the underwriter had been reasonable and "asking what effect the information would have had on a reasonable underwriter in his situation."[951]

Some commentators point out that the test for materiality, being objective, may lead a perfectly honest assured to lose his rights under a policy where he was unaware that a particular fact was relevant to a reasonable or prudent insurer and thus ought to have been disclosed, or where such a fact lay completely outside the assured's field of experience.[952] However, apart from the probability of such a situation occurring being very small,[953] the objective test of the hypothetical prudent underwriter may be justified in that the assured is protected from the "potential subjective capriciousness and idiosyncrasies of the actual underwriter", whose professional ways may be "uncertain, variable and impossible to predict".[954]

Lord Mustill in the course of his speech in the House of Lords in *Pine Top* described the hypothetical prudent underwriter as "those who know their job and perform it carefully, without exceptional timidity or boldness."[955] The hypothetical prudent underwriter is the manifestation of reasonable underwriting practice.[956] Evans, L.J. in *St. Paul Fire & Marine Insurance Co. (UK) Ltd. v McConnell Dowell Constructors Ltd.*[957] approved of a *dictum* of Lord Radcliffe in *Davis Contractors Ltd. v Fareham U.D.C.*[958] in which the prudent insurer was described as being "no more than the anthropomorphic conception of the standards of professional

---

949 Lord Mustill cited the second edition of Marshall's work, *A treatise on the Law of Insurance*, p. 465.
950 [1994] 2 Lloyd's Rep. 427, at p. 445.
951 Ibid.
952 Cf. the remarks of Hoffmann, L.J. in *Societe Anonyme d'Intermediaries Luxembourgeois v Farex Gie*, referred to in the text to fn. 847 *supra*; EGGERS et al.: op. cit., par. 14.22; FRIEDMANN, Daniel: *The Transformation of "Good Faith" in Insurance Law* **Good Faith in Contract, Concept and Context** p. 315; also see the comments of MacKenna, J. in *Lambert v Co-operative Insurance Society Ltd.* [1975] 2 Lloyd's Rep 485, at p. 491.
953 EGGERS et al.: op. cit., par. 14.22.
954 RHIDIAN THOMAS, D. (editor): op. cit., p. 34.
955 [1994] 2 Lloyd's Rep. 427, at p. 441; see also RHIDIAN THOMAS, D. (editor): op. cit., pp. 33-34.
956 BENNET: op. cit., p. 47.
957 [1995] 2 Lloyd's Rep. 116.
958 [1956] A.C. 696, at p. 728.

underwriting which the Court finds it appropriate to uphold."[959] However, the prudent underwriter will have to be examined in the light of the underwriting practice for the type of insurance concerned and in the market chosen by the assured.[960] The standard is ascertained by expert evidence.[961]

Materiality – the degree of knowledge

One of the more complex problems relating to the test of materiality is the extent or degree of the knowledge needed by the hypothetical prudent underwriter, which would constitute material facts. It has been suggested that a material circumstance could belong to one of four types of information by reference to the degree of influence that it may have on the prudent underwriter.[962] Firstly, there is information that is such that, if the insured had known about it, he would not have made the contract at all. Secondly, there are facts that are such that, if the prudent underwriter had known about them, he would have made the contract, but on different terms, e.g. on an increased premium. The third type includes information that would have affected the judgement of the prudent underwriter in any manner, be that by reinforcing his decision to contract, or be it that together with other information it might have led the prudent underwriter to contract on other terms. The point here is that the fact on its own need not make any difference to the contract or its terms. Finally, it has been suggested that there exists a category of information between the second and third types pointed out above.[963] It appears that this category has merely been created to provide for the situation where the evidence of the prudent underwriter does not provide a palpable answer, since some prudent insurers might have insisted on different terms and others not.[964]

The M.I.A. 1906 defined a "material circumstance" as one "which would influence the judgement of a prudent insurer in fixing the premium, or determining whether he will take the risk".[965] It is generally accepted that this Act was a statutory statement of the common law in respect of marine insurance.[966] However, the judicial *dicta* dealing with this aspect of materiality before, as well as after the Act, do not exhibit any uniformity.[967] On the one hand there are *dicta* supporting the so-called "contributing influence" test,[968] also known as the "right to know" test.[969]

---

[959] [1995] 2 Lloyd's Rep. 116, at p. 122.

[960] EGGERS et al.: op. cit., par. 14.27.

[961] BENNET: op. cit., p. 47; RHIDIAN THOMAS, D. (editor): op. cit., p. 34.

[962] CLARKE: op. cit., par. 23-7A.

[963] Ibid.

[964] Ibid.

[965] See sections 18(2) and 20(2).

[966] HANSELL, D.S.: op. cit., p. 175; SOYER: *The Star Sea – a lode star?* [2001] LMCLQ 428 at p. 429 and *Continuing duty of utmost good faith in insurance contracts: still alive?* [2003] LMCLQ 39 at p. 40; MERKIN, Robert (editor): op. cit., p. 115; also see EGGERS et al.: op. cit., par. 14.35, and the cases cited there.

[967] EGGERS et al.: op. cit., par. 14.35.

[968] Ibid., par. 14.39.

This test renders every fact material, which might play a role in the insurer's assessment of the risk, i.e. any fact that the insurer would have liked to take into consideration when deciding whether to accept the risk and at which rate, even if that fact on its own may not have influenced his decision to underwrite.[970] It would, therefore, encompass facts belonging to the third and fourth categories mentioned above, and has also been called the "awareness" test of materiality.[971] On the other hand, support can be found for the "decisive influence" test.[972] According to this test, a circumstance that would have influenced the decision of the prudent underwriter to take the risk and at a particular premium if it were not concealed or misrepresented would be considered material to the risk.[973] Accordingly, the "decisive influence" test would include facts belonging to the first two categories mentioned above.

One of the most important cases to deal with this issue after the M.I.A. 1906 came into effect[974] was *Mutual Life Insurance Company of New York v Ontario Metal Products Company Limited.*[975] The insurer in this case refused to pay on a life policy, submitting that the assured made certain misrepresentations in answering negatively to questions in the proposal form as to whether he suffered any illnesses, diseases etc., and whether he had consulted a doctor in the past five years. The insurer's medical agent considered the over-worked assured to appear "sallow complexioned" but otherwise "healthy". The doctor of the assured's wife subsequently prescribed a tonic to improve his condition. The Judicial Committee of the Privy Council had to decide whether this fact, in the light of the assured's negative answer to the above-mentioned questions, had been material. Lord Salvesen found that the test for materiality was concerned with whether the reasonable insurer "would have acted differently" if the fact concealed had been disclosed. In the view of their Lordships, it was a question of fact in each case whether, if the matters concealed or misrepresented had been truly disclosed, they would, on a fair consideration of the evidence, have influenced a reasonable insurer to decline the risk or to have stipulated for a higher premium.[976] On the facts of the case, Salvesen, L.J. found that "had the facts concealed been disclosed, they would not have influenced a reasonable insurer so as to induce him to refuse the risk or alter the premium",[977] and consequently came to the conclusion that "the non-disclosure or misstatement was not material to the contract".[978] Lord Mustill suggested in *The Pine Top case* that this decision, whilst establishing the general law

[969] RHIDIAN THOMAS, D. (editor): op. cit., p. 34.
[970] EGGERS et al.: op. cit., par. 14.39.
[971] CLARKE: op. cit., par. 23-7A.
[972] RHIDIAN THOMAS, D. (editor): op. cit., p. 34.
[973] EGGERS et al.: op. cit., par. 14.39.
[974] See *The Pine Top case* [1994] 2 Lloyd's Rep. 427, at p. 445 (*per* Lord Mustill).
[975] [1925] A.C. 344.
[976] Ibid., at p. 351.
[977] Ibid., at p. 352.
[978] Ibid.

as to materiality, could not be taken to establish any finer distinctions.[979] It has subsequently been argued that the Council's judgement does, in fact, support the "decisive influence" test.[980] Lord Salvesen, in his judgement, stressed the fact that materiality would not have been established if the effect of the undisclosed fact were merely to cause the insurer to delay his acceptance and if that delay were the only difference in action.[981] It was, therefore, necessary to establish the inducement of the reasonable insurer in order to satisfy the decisive influence test.[982]

The "decisive influence" test also found support in *Gallé Gowns Ltd. v Licenses & General Insurance Co. Ltd.* [983] and in *Zurich General Accident and Liability Insurance Company Ltd. v Morrison.*[984] The most recent and last analysis in favour of the "decisive influence test" was offered by Lloyd, J. (as he then was) at first instance in *Container Transport International Inc. v Oceanus Mutual Underwriting Association (Bermuda) Ltd.*[985] (the *C.T.I.* case), who held as follows:

> "In general I would say that underwriters ought only to succeed on a defence of non-disclosure if they can satisfy the Court by evidence or otherwise that a prudent insurer, if he had known the fact in question, would have declined the risk altogether or charged a higher premium. It seems to me that this should be the general rule, if only because the defence under s. 18 is capable of working such great hardship on the assured... The fairness of the English rule is not at once obvious and hardly seems to reflect the duty of utmost good faith under s. 17 which, be it noted, is owed both ways. Why, if the insurer would have accepted the risk in any event, albeit at an increased premium, should he be able to avoid the claim altogether? Since the English law is so favourable to the

[979] [1994] 2 Lloyd's Rep. 427, at p. 447; Lord Mustill thought that the Council stated four propositions, namely "(1). Materiality was not to be judged by reference to the opinion of a reasonable assured. This had been the common law for very many years. (2). The fact that the insurers had inserted a question in the proposal form was not ipso facto a demonstration of its materiality. (3). The fact that if the information had been correctly stated it would have caused the insurers to delay in reaching a decision was not in itself enough to make it material. (4). The test was whether the information would have influenced a reasonable insurer to decline the risk or to have stipulated for a higher premium." According to Mustill, L.J.'s interpretation, once the Council found on the first three propositions in favour of the assured, it was not necessary to make a decision as to the fourth.

[980] For a discussion of this case, cf. EGGERS et al.: op. cit., paras. 14.40-42.

[981] [1925] A.C. 344, at p. 351.

[982] Cf. text to fn. 977 *supra*; EGGERS et al.: op. cit., par. 14.42.

[983] (1933) 47 Ll.L.Rep. 186, where the members of the jury had to avail themselves of the question: " 'If I were a reasonable underwriter would I have considered it one of the things that I had to take into consideration in deciding whether I should accept the risk or refuse it?' and if the answer is 'Yes', then it is a material fact; if the answer is 'No', then it is immaterial..." (at p. 191).

[984] [1942] 2 K.B. 53, the Court of Appeal in this case, however, merely applied the test in *Mutual Life Insurance Company of New York v Ontario metal Products Company Limited* and was more concerned with the requirements of the Road Traffic Act 1934, particularly the requirement of inducement.

[985] [1982] 2 Lloyd's Rep. 178.

> underwriter in this respect, the least that should normally be expected of the underwriter is to show that a prudent insurer would have charged an increased rate."[986]

The judge pointed out that section 18 was cast in wide terms requiring the "judgement" of the prudent underwriter, and not the premium, to be influenced. He acknowledged that there might be cases in which the prudent underwriter could say that if a particular fact were disclosed, it would have affected his judgement, although he would nevertheless have charged the same rate. Still, he was of the opinion that in such a case the defendant must prove that the judgement of the prudent underwriter "would" have been affected and not that it "might" have been affected.[987]

The Court of Appeal[988] did not approve of this test, holding that materiality flowed from the relevance of the circumstance, and not from its weight. A circumstance, therefore, would be material if it would have an impact on the formation of the prudent underwriter's opinion of the risk, as Stephenson, L.J. concluded from the language of the M.I.A. 1906 and the authorities:

> "...everything is material to which a prudent insurer, if he were in the proposed insurer's place, would wish to direct his mind in the course of considering the proposed insurance with a view to deciding whether to take it up and on what terms, including premium."[989]

The leading judgement was delivered by Kerr, L.J., who concluded after an analysis of the wording of section 18(2) that in order to prove materiality, the insurer must satisfy the Court that the *judgement* – by which the Lord Justice meant to convey the dictionary meaning, i.e. "the formation of an opinion" – of a prudent insurer would have been influenced if the circumstance in question had been disclosed.[990] The word "influenced", said Kerr, L.J., meant that the disclosure was one which "would have had an impact on the formation of his opinion and on his decision-making process in relation to the matters covered by section 18(2)."[991] Accordingly, a fact would still be material even if it did not have a discernable effect on the final decision, as long as it was a fact that the prudent insurer wished to be aware of,[992] i.e. a fact of which the prudent insurer "should have been told... before being asked to make up [his] mind".[993] After this statement of the law, he pointed to a range of authorities[994] that had apparently not been cited at first instance and which

[986] Ibid., at pp. 188-189.
[987] Ibid., at p. 189.
[988] [1984] 1 Lloyd's Rep. 476.
[989] Ibid., at p. 529.
[990] Ibid., at p. 492.
[991] Ibid.
[992] EGGERS et al.: op. cit., par. 14.49.
[993] [1984] 1 Lloyd's Rep. 476, at p. 492.
[994] *Carter v Boehm* (1766) 3 Burr. 1905, at p. 1909; *Traill v Baring*, (1864) 4 De G. J. & S. 318; *Bates v Hewitt*, (1867) L.R. 2 Q.B. 595, at p. 604; *Ionides v Pender* (1874) L.R. 9 Q.B. 531, at pp. 537 and

he considered to have been concerned with "the issue whether undisclosed circumstances would have been regarded as material by reference to the 'judgement' of a prudent insurer".[995] The Lord Justice was careful to put aside statements that were not concerned with this question[996] – however, it is doubtful whether all of the authorities cited could be described as such.[997] Kerr, L.J. concluded the part of his judgement dealing with materiality with a reference to Lord Mansfield's judgement in *Carter v Boehm*[998], stating that the London market practice as well as the law were based on the test of "fair representation".[999] This test was concerned with the answer to the question whether a "fair and substantially accurate presentation of the risk" had been made so that "a prudent insurer could form a proper judgement" in deciding whether or not to accept the risk and on what terms.[1000]

The Court of Appeal considered the very question again in the *Pine Top* case.[1001] The court was bound by precedent to the decision in the *C.T.I.* case to reject the "decisive influence" test. However, Steyn, L.J. was of the opinion that the *C.T.I.* case was merely authority for the negative proposition that the "decisive influence" test was wrong, and that a positive statement of the correct test was still to be formulated.[1002] In the result, Steyn L.J. distinguished two alternatives to the "decisive influence" test: first, a fact will be considered material if a prudent

---

539; *Rivaz v Gerussi* (1880) 6 Q.B.D. 222, at pp. 227 and 229; *Tate v Hyslop* (1885) 15 Q.B.D. 368, at pp. 375 and 379; *Glicksman v Lancashire and General Assurance Co.* (1926) 26 Ll.L.Rep. 69, at p. 71; *Scottish Shire Line Ltd. v London and Provincial Marine and General Insurance Co. Ltd.*. [1912] 3 K.B. 51, at pp. 70-71.

[995] [1984] 1 Lloyd's Rep. 476, at p. 493.

[996] Ibid.

[997] See the comment of Lord Justice Mustill in the *Pine Top case*, [1994] 2 Lloyd's Rep. 427, at p. 443: "With one crucial exception, nothing would be gained by rehearsal of the score of authorities through which the House was taken with great care during argument, for although it is possible to find expressions in the various judgements which support one or another of the conflicting interpretations, examination shows that in none of them did it make any difference which formula was used. Either the case was not about the extent of the duty at all, or the outcome would have been the same however the test was described. Accordingly, without intending disrespect to the diligent arguments or to the judgements in the C.T.I. case, where importance was attached to a number of the older authorities, I shall not occupy space by analysing them."

[998] (1766) 3 Burr. 1905, at p. 1912.

[999] [1984] 1 Lloyd's Rep. 476, at p. 496.

[1000] Ibid., at pp. 496-497.

[1001] [1993] 1 Lloyd's Rep. 496; Lord Mustill said during his speech in the House of Lords in *Pine Top*: "In substance this is an appeal against the decision in the C.T.I. case. In his judgement (at p. 505) Lord Justice Steyn said quite bluntly that C.T.I. had proved to be a remarkably unpopular decision not only in the legal profession but also in the insurance markets. Whether this generalisation about the markets is correct I cannot judge, but the books and articles produced in argument all adopt a critical stance." Cf. the judgement in the House of Lords [1994] 2 Lloyd's Rep. 427, at p. 438.

[1002] [1993] 1 Lloyd's Rep. 496, at pp. 505-506.

insurer shall have wished to be aware of that fact in reaching a decision whether to underwrite or not and on what premium. The second alternative – which may conveniently be referred to as the "increased risk" test of materiality – is based on Lord Mansfield's *dictum* in *Carter v Boehm* that the keeping back of special facts, upon which the risk falls to be judged and which lie most commonly in the knowledge of the assured, has the effect that the actual risk is different from the risk which was intended to be run.[1003] Accordingly, Steyn, L.J. said that this test was concerned with "whether a prudent underwriter, if he had known of the undisclosed facts, would have regarded the risk as increased beyond what was disclosed on the actual presentation."[1004] The Lord Justice, although not doubting that there were passages in the *C.T.I. case* consistent with the first test, nevertheless, thought that there were also parts of that judgement in favour of the second alternative.[1005] The "increased risk" test was not only in line with Lord Mansfield's rationale of the doctrine of non-disclosure, set out in *Carter v Boehm*, but also provided a "fairer and more balanced solution" than the first alternative.[1006] Thus, Steyn L.J. concluded with a ruling that "as the law now stands, the question is whether the prudent insurer would view the undisclosed material as probably tending to increase the risk."[1007] This test, which was also accepted as the correct test by a minority[1008] in the House of Lords in *the Pine Top* case, would have improved the position of the assured whose duty to disclose would have been less burdensome, whilst limiting the possibilities of underwriters to escape liability under policies.[1009]

However, the test which found favour with the majority in the House of Lords in the *Pine Top* case – it is now settled[1010] – was the "contributing influence" test[1011], which has also been called the "right to know" or the "would be of interest" test.[1012] Lord Mustill in the leading speech also rejected the "decisive influence" test, holding that there was no statutory support for such a test, as the words "influence" and "judgement" in the M.I.A. 1906 referred to thought processes, and not the final decision of the insurer.[1013] The "influence" of the "judgement" of the

[1003] Ibid., at p. 505.
[1004] Ibid., at p. 505; RHIDIAN THOMAS, D. (editor): op. cit., p. 35.
[1005] [1993] 1 Lloyd's Rep. 496, at p. 505.
[1006] Ibid., at pp. 505-506.
[1007] Ibid., at p. 506.
[1008] See e.g. Lord Lloyd, with whom Lord Templeman agreed in the minority judgement of the *Pine Top case* (at p. 559), who was in favour of a test that the undisclosed fact needs to have a *decisive influence* on a prudent insurer. He thought that the ordinary meaning of influence was to "affect or alter" something, and that the primary dictionary meaning of "judgement" referred to the decision itself and not merely the process of decision-making – see also CLARKE: op. cit., par. 23-7A.
[1009] RHIDIAN THOMAS, D. (editor): op. cit., p. 35.
[1010] In *St. Paul Fire & Marine v McConnel* [1995] 2 Lloyd's Rep. 116, see p. 157 *infra*.
[1011] EGGERS et al.: op. cit., par. 14.54.
[1012] MERKIN, Robert (editor): op. cit., p. 130.
[1013] [1994] 2 Lloyd's Rep. 427, at pp. 440-441.

insurer, was to be contrasted with the final state of mind of the underwriter which materialised in his decision. Lord Mustill held that the "decisive influence" test would require second-guessing on the part of the assured.[1014] Furthermore, it would presuppose that insurers based their assessments of risk on single factors, rather than on a combination of factors.[1015] The Lord Justice then set out with a discussion of texts and judicial *dicta* of the nineteenth century and found nothing in them to suggest that materiality had been understood, before the M.I.A. came into operation in 1906, "as extending only to such circumstances as would definitely have changed the underwriter's mind".[1016] In fact, these texts provided support for the view that material facts included "all matters which would have been taken into account by the underwriter when assessing the risk".[1017] That, in the opinion of Mustill, L.J., was what the 1906 Act had been intended to convey, and what it was actually saying.[1018]

The "decisive influence" test was unnecessary as the assured was afforded protection in that the test for inducement was a subjective one, requiring the insurer himself to show that he would have been influenced by the facts.[1019] Thus, according to Lord Mustill, it was not necessary to show that the disclosure would have had a "decisive influence" on the prudent insurer, i.e. that he would not have taken on a particular risk or took it on at a higher premium, had the facts been disclosed. Section 18(2) required any circumstance that the insurer would have liked to consider in his assessment of the risk to be disclosed. In the words of Lord Mustill:

> "A circumstance may be material even though a full and accurate disclosure of it would not in itself have had a decisive effect on the prudent underwriter's decision whether to accept the risk and if so at what premium."[1020]

In *St. Paul Fire & Marine Insurance Co. (UK) Ltd. v McConnell Dowell Constructors Ltd.*[1021] the Court of Appeal was confronted with the *Pan Atlantic* decision and particularly with the two tests for materiality formulated by Steyn, L.J. in his judgement in that case in the Court of Appeal.[1022] The assureds were construction companies. They took out a Contractors All Risks policy with the insurers. The risk was represented to the insurers as one concerning the construction of a building on piled foundations. In fact, the building was constructed on shallow strip footing foundations. It also surfaced that the assureds did not disclose two

[1014] Ibid., at p. 441.
[1015] Ibid.
[1016] Ibid., at p. 445.
[1017] Ibid.
[1018] Ibid.
[1019] Cf. 5.5.2 Inducement *infra*.
[1020] [1994] 2 Lloyd's Rep. 427, at pp. 452-453.
[1021] [1995] 2 Lloyd's Rep. 116.
[1022] See p. 155 *supra*.

reports that were compiled by engineers and concerned the consistency of the soil and recorded certain suggestions regarding the type of foundation that should be used. The insurers, after learning of this state of affairs, claimed that they had validly avoided the policy on the basis of non-disclosure of the reports and misrepresentation. An issue was raised whether the House of Lords in *Pine Top* – apart from rejecting the "decisive influence" test – also formulated the lesser standard and what the terms of that standard were.[1023] It was argued by the assured that the House of Lords did not disapprove of the test favoured by Steyn, L.J.[1024] Evans, L.J. analysed the judgements of the Law Lords in *Pine Top* and came to the conclusion[1025] that the definition of materiality was to be found in a passage in the judgement of Lord Mustill, referred to above, where he stated that materiality extended to "all matters which would have been taken into account by the underwriters when assessing the risk",[1026] and that the object of the rules was "to enable the underwriters to judge accurately of the risk."[1027] Lord Mustill, in the judgement of Evans, L.J.[1028], therefore, approved of Steyn, L.J.'s formulation of the test for materiality to the extent that the underwriter "would have appreciated that it was a different ... risk".[1029] However, there was no support for the further requirement that a circumstance would only be material if it increased the risk as opposed merely to altering the risk.[1030] Lord Evans supported his conclusion on the ground that materiality stood rather in relation to the subject-matter than to a prediction of its effect.[1031]

Accordingly, it is now settled that it will be irrelevant whether the decision of the insurer in the end will have been different. What is relevant is only whether his thought processes will have been influenced by the non-disclosed facts, i.e. whether he will have liked to consider these facts in his assessment of the risk and the premium.[1032]

The relevant date at which the materiality of a fact should be tested, is the date on which the contract was made. When at this date a fact appears to be material, the assured is obliged to disclose such to the insurer;[1033] if not, the assured is under no obligation to disclose.[1034]

[1023] [1995] 2 Lloyd's Rep. 116, at p. 122.
[1024] Ibid., at p. 123.
[1025] Ibid., at p. 124.
[1026] [1994] 2 Lloyd's Rep. 427, at p. 445.
[1027] Ibid.
[1028] [1995] 2 Lloyd's Rep. 116, at p. 124.
[1029] [1993] 1 Lloyd's Rep. 496, at p. 505.
[1030] [1995] 2 Lloyd's Rep. 116, at p. 124.
[1031] Ibid.
[1032] EGGERS et al.: op. cit., par. 14.54; MERKIN, Robert (editor): op. cit., pp. 130-131; RHIDIAN THOMAS, D. (editor): op. cit., pp. 34-35.
[1033] See e.g. *Seaman v Fonnereau* (1734) 2 Str. 1183 and *Lynch v Hamilton* (1810) 3 Taunt. 37.
[1034] See e.g. *Seaton v Burnand* [1900] A.C. 135; MERKIN, Robert (editor): op. cit., pp. 130-131.

It has furthermore been established in the *Pine Top* case, that once an undisclosed fact is found to be material, it will be irrelevant whether there was a connection between the fact in question and the circumstances of the loss.[1035]

Types of material facts

Facts may be material for various reasons and in each case materiality is purely a question of fact. Facts may be material because they show that the subject-matter is very likely to be destructed by the risk insured against.[1036] These are called the physical hazards, and includes amongst other things the condition of the insured subject-matter and the uses to which it is to be put,[1037] the duration and geographical limits of the voyage,[1038] and any particular risks which operate in the port of loading or discharge.[1039] Previous refusals will not constitute material facts for the purpose of marine insurance.[1040] Generally, however, in non-marine insurance these have been held to constitute material facts, especially since insurers constantly include questions in this regard in their proposal forms.

Facts which influence the premium, but not the moral[1041] or physical hazard, have been held to be material as well. Thus, in *The Dora*, where the assured fixed a premium taking into consideration that the assured supposedly was of the intention to insure four yachts every year, the failure of the assured to do so was found to be a misrepresentation relating to a material fact.[1042]

1035 The inverse is of course true as well, following *dicta* in *Dawsons v Bonnin* [1922] 2 A.C. 413: simply because the non-disclosure of a fact resulted in a loss, it does not follow automatically that such a fact will be a material fact.
1036 MERKIN, Robert (editor): op. cit., p. 133.
1037 Cf. *Berger v Pollock* [1973] 2 Lloyd's Rep. 442 and *Inversiones Maria v Sphere Drake, The Dora* [1989] 1 Lloyd's Rep 65.
1038 *Scottish Shire v London and Provincial Marine* [1912] 3 K.B. 51.
1039 *Marc Rich v Portman* [1996] 1 Lloyd's Rep. 430; cf. generally MERKIN, Robert (editor): op. cit., p. 486.
1040 *Glasgow Assurance Corporation v William Symondson and Co* (1911) 104 L.T. 254.
1041 Facts which will be material because they tell something about the character of the insured indicating that his proposal should be carefully considered, are called the moral hazard. Facts which may affect the so-called moral hazard are facts which relate to previous claims under other policies (e.g. *Arterial Caravans v Yorkshire Insurance* [1973] 1 Lloyd's Rep. 169) especially where there is a connection between that loss and the policy under consideration (*Ewer v National Employees Mutual* [1937] 2 All E.R. 193). Convictions material to the risk insured against will also be a moral hazard (e.g. *Schoolman v Hall* [1951] Lloyd's Rep 139). Even where the insured has been charged with an offence, but intends to plead innocence, he will need to disclose the charge to the insurer before the policy is issued (e.g. *The Dora*). Another moral hazard is where the assured changes his name, or any other concealment of his identity (e.g. *The Moonacre* [1992] 2 Lloyd's Rep 501). MERKIN, Robert (editor): op. cit., p. 133.
1042 MERKIN, Robert (editor): op. cit., p. 133.

Fraud and Materiality

There exists authority at common law for the proposition that materiality need not be established where the assured in a marine insurance policy has been guilty of fraud.[1043] On the other hand, certain commentators are of the opinion that fraudulent misrepresentation or non-disclosure *per se* on the part of the assured will not be enough to avoid the contract and that the misleading representation will have to relate to a material fact.[1044] The lack of clarity in this context seems to be part of the bigger dispute in general English contract law about the role of materiality in misrepresentation and the discrepancy between the concepts of materiality in general contract and marine insurance law.[1045]

Chitty defines a "material" misrepresentation in general contract law as one that "was likely to induce the contract".[1046] Moreover, *Chitty* states that objective materiality "in the sense that a reasonable man would have been influenced by it [i.e. a misrepresentation] in deciding whether to enter into the contract" is not a requirement.[1047] As far as a misrepresentation was fraudulent, *Chitty* states that it would be no defence for the representor to show that the representee would still have made the contract if there had been no misrepresentation.[1048] According to the author this is a "special rule in fraud cases" intended to deter fraud.[1049] In turn, *Treitel* defines materiality in objective terms, stating that a material misrepresentation "must be one which would affect the judgement of a reasonable person in deciding whether, or on what terms, to enter into the contract", a statement which mirrors the definition of that concept in marine insurance law.[1050] The author does not consider materiality to be a requirement in cases of fraudulent misrepresentation.[1051]

[1043] *The Bedouin* [1894] 1 P. 1; 69 LT 782 (CA); BENNET: *Mapping the Doctrine of Utmost Good Faith in Insurance Contract Law* [1999] LMCLQ 165, at p. 177, who writes that "it is well established that a fraudulent misrepresentation will be actionable even if not material..."; EGGERS et al.: op. cit., par. 14.16; TREITEL: **The Law of Contract** p. 311; cf. CHITTY: op. cit., par. 6-034, where it is stated that the "but for" causation test is not required for rescission for fraud.

[1044] MERKIN, Robert (editor): op. cit., par. 5-29.

[1045] Cf. p. 147 *supra*.

[1046] CHITTY: op. cit., par. 6-035; Chitty qualifies this position in stating that this would only be the case in a claim for rescission, since damages can only be recovered where the fraud also caused the loss for which damages are claimed.

[1047] Cf. fn. 921 *supra*.

[1048] Ibid., par. 6-034, citing *Re Leeds Bank* (1887) 56 L.J. Ch. 321, and *Edgington v Fitzmaurice* (1885) 29 Ch. D. 459, at p. 483.

[1049] Ibid.

[1050] TREITEL: op. cit., p. 311, citing i.a. the *Pine Top* and *St. Paul Fire & Marine Insurance cases* as authority.

[1051] Ibid., citing as authority *Smith v Kay* (1859) 7 H.L.C. 750, *Gordon v Street* [1899] 2 Q.B. 531, and *Rafsanjan Pistachio Producers Co-operative v Bank Leumi (UK) plc* [1992] 1 Lloyd's Rep. 514, at p. 542.

As far as marine insurance law is concerned, the position is not unequivocal either. Older editions of *Arnould* state that a fraudulent misrepresentation will avoid the policy, whether the false statement is material to the risk or not.[1052] "Material representation" is defined as a statement of fact "calculated to induce an underwriter more readily to assume the risk by diminishing the estimate he would otherwise have formed of it" which may "reasonably be presumed likely to have such an influence on the judgement of a prudent underwriter.[1053] However, the statement is qualified by another, i.e. that the fraudulent statement must have influenced the underwriter when he concluded the policy.[1054] The most recent addition to *Arnould*, however, confirms the legal position regarding materiality and inducement laid down in the *Pine Top case* and confirmed in *St Paul*.[1055] As to fraudulent misrepresentations, it confirms the position in the earlier editions:

> "The principles ... are confirmed by the *Pan Atlantic* case, where Lord Mustill states that the texts and the relevant cases leave no room for doubt that if the representation inducing the contract was fraudulent its falsehood would invariably give a right to avoid."[1056]

Indeed, certain parts of the judgement of Lord Mustill in the *Pine Top case* do appear to support this proposition.[1057] On the other hand, the latest edition of *Colinvaux* entertains the opinion that fraud alone will not *per se* render the policy voidable unless the misstatement related to a material circumstance.[1058] These authors also purport to base their opinion upon the *Pine Top* decision. It is said that a general desire was stated in this decision to apply normal principles of contract law to insurance contracts and that in general law fraud woüld not be enough to render the contract voidable. Furthermore, so the argument goes, Lord Mustill made it clear that the purpose of the doctrine of the utmost good faith was to ensure a fair representation of the risk and did not include any punitive element.[1059] It is submitted that this judgement does not provide the support sought for *Colinvaux*'s take on materiality. First of all, Lord Mustill expressly stated that materiality is not a requirement in the event of fraud.[1060] Secondly, even though Lord Mustill did express the desire to apply normal principles of contract law, this does not bring

---

[1052] CHORLEY and BAILHACHE: **Arnould on Marine Insurance** (fifteenth edition) par. 562.
[1053] Ibid., par. 557.
[1054] Ibid., par. 562
[1055] GILMAN: op. cit., (sixteenth edition) Vol. III, par. 610; cf. 5.5.1 Materiality *supra* and 5.5.2 Inducement *infra*.
[1056] Ibid., par. 596.
[1057] [1994] 2 Lloyd's Rep. 427, at pp. 441-442, where Lord Mustill held that "the texts and the relevant cases leave no room for doubt that whereas if the representation inducing a contract was either fraudulent or a "warranty" of the contract its falsehood would invariably give a right to avoid an innocent misrepresentation inducing the contract would give the underwriter a right to avoid only if it was material. Proof of actual effect was not necessarily proof of materiality."
[1058] MERKIN, Robert (editor): op. cit., par. 5-29; also cf. EGGERS et al.: op. cit., par. 14.16.
[1059] MERKIN, Robert (editor): op. cit., par. 5-29.
[1060] Cf. fn. 1057 *supra*.

the argument anywhere, since in general contract law fraud will be enough to render the contract voidable.[1061]

The case usually cited as authority for the proposition that materiality is not required in case of fraud, is *The Bedouin*.[1062] In the Court of Appeal, Lord Esher, M.R., declared in what can at best be called *obiter*, that an assured was bound to tell the underwriter "not every fact, but the material facts."[1063] He then proceeded:

> "[H]is other obligation is this, that if he is asked a question – whether a material fact or not – by the underwriters, he must answer it truly. If he answers it falsely, with intent to deceive, though it may not be a material fact, it will vitiate the policy."[1064]

A case on which both *Treitel* and *Arnould* rely, as proponents of the position that materiality need not be proved in case of fraud, is *Gordon v Street*.[1065] The question that came up for decision was "whether a person, whose evil reputation in business is such that no man will deal with him, can, after fraudulently concealing this identity and thus inducing another to enter into a contract which he otherwise would not have done, prevent that other, when sued by the defrauding party upon the contract, from insisting upon the ordinary defence of the defrauded – namely, that he had been induced by the fraud of the plaintiff to enter into the contract sued on."[1066] The jury found that a fraud had been committed, whereupon the plaintiff argued that the finding was immaterial "because the fraud proved was not material to the contract sued on."[1067]

A.L. Smith, L.J. considered that the point was not "whether the fraud was material to the contract entered into, but whether the fraud was material to the inducement which brought about the contract."[1068] Upon the jury finding the fact of fraud, the Lord Justice found that he could not doubt that the fraud also induced the contract, and was therefore material to the contract.[1069] As to the question whether the fraud had been material to the contract, the Lord Justice approved of a passage in the judgement of the House of Lords in *Smith v Kay*, [1070] to the effect that "a party who has practised deception, with a view to a particular end, which has been attained by it", could not be permitted "to speculate upon what might have been the result if there had been a full communication of the truth." [1071]

[1061] Cf. the references to *Chitty* and *Treitel supra*.
[1062] Cf. fn. 1043 *supra*.
[1063] [1894] 1 P. 1, at p. 12.
[1064] Ibid.
[1065] [1899] 2 Q.B.D. 641.
[1066] Ibid., at p. 644.
[1067] Ibid., at p. 645.
[1068] Ibid.
[1069] Ibid.
[1070] (1859) 7 H.L.C. 750; cf. fn. 1051 *supra*.
[1071] Ibid., at p. 759.

In the light of these *dicta*, the problem seems to turn on the essence of the concept of "materiality" in the context of misrepresentation. The focus of materiality in this context is on the capacity of the representation to induce the representee to conclude the contract.[1072] The concept of materiality in marine insurance corresponds with the definition of materiality under general contract law because a misrepresentation induces the making of the contract and it will be inequitable to allow the insurer to be so deceived or misled without giving him the opportunity to rescind the contract, provided certain conditions are fulfilled.[1073] This explanation would account for the first *dictum* of A.L. Smith, L.J. quoted above[1074] (*albeit* made in the context of concealment) and for the respective positions taken in *Chitty* and *Treitel* referred to above.[1075] Since the aim of a fraudulent representor is to induce the representee to contract by making a misstatement, the courts and legal commentators state that in these circumstances it is not for the representor to argue that the misrepresentation has been immaterial, where materiality, indeed, is focused on the capacity of the representation to induce the representee to conclude the contract and this goal, in fact, has been achieved. However, to this general position, marine insurance law added an objective test, namely that of the prudent underwriter.[1076] Statements to the effect that materiality remains a requirement even in the case of fraudulent misrepresentation, should therefore, be read in the light of the additional requirement of marine insurance law of the prudent underwriter in the context of materiality. It has also been pointed out – and quite rightly so – that neither section 18, nor section 20 of the M.I.A. 1906 provide for this exception and that accordingly materiality will remain relevant in case of fraud.[1077]

5.5.2 Inducement

Neither section 18(2) nor section 20(2) of the M.I.A 1906 indicates expressly whether there should be a causal connection between the non-disclosure or misrepresentation and the conclusion of the policy of marine insurance.[1078] In general English contract law – i.e. in law and in equity – a party to a contract would have to prove inducement in order to get relief for even a fraudulent misrepresentation.[1079] Further to this, under ordinary law the materiality of the representation is intertwined with the requirement of inducement.[1080] In turn,

[1072] EGGERS et al.: op. cit., par. 14.85.

[1073] Ibid., citing i.a. *Iron Trades Mutual Insurance Co. Ltd. v Companhia de Seguros Imperio* [1991] 1 Re. L.R. 213 and the *CTI* case [1984] 1 Lloyd's Rep. 476, at p. 490.

[1074] Cf. text to fn. 1068 *supra*.

[1075] Cf. fns. 1046 and 1050 *supra*.

[1076] EGGERS et al.: op. cit., par. 14.85.

[1077] EGGERS et al.: op. cit., par. 14.16.

[1078] RHIDIAN THOMAS, D. (editor): op. cit., p. 35.

[1079] EGGERS et al.: op. cit., pars. 14.01 and 14.88; The *Pine Top case* [1994] 2 Lloyd's Rep. 427, at p. 447 (*per* Lord Mustill).

[1080] EGGERS et al.: op. cit., pars. 14.02 and 14.89.

under insurance law, as was described above, the requirement of materiality developed into a wholly objective requirement, mainly to protect the assured from any particular insurer burdening the assured with an unreasonable requirement of information to be disclosed.[1081] Before this development, however, the courts appeared to have been interested merely in the effect of a non-disclosure or misrepresentation on the actual insurer.[1082]

A case in point was *Harrower v Hutchinson*,[1083] in which the assured purposely failed to advise the underwriter that the insured vessel was to call at a port called Laguna de los Padres in the province of Buenos Aires. The assured also did not disclose that, as a result of the lack of development of the port, the vessel had to be loaded by lighters whilst at anchor a quarter mile offshore. It was established that the insurers would have increased the premium if they had known these facts. Chief Justice Baron Kelly did not make explicit reference to the requirement of inducement, but held that the "fact which was concealed... was a material fact, that is to say, one which if made known to the underwriter would have affected his estimate of the character and degree of the risk."[1084] It appears, therefore, that the requirement of inducement was indeed intertwined with that of materiality. In turn, Willes, J. stated that the "policy was ***obtained*** at a less premium than the underwriters would have stipulated for had they known the facts" (emphasis added) as a result of the concealment of the condition of the port, which was "material to the underwriters' estimate of the character and degree of the risk".[1085] Said the judge:

> "This is a case, not of mere concealment of the port from which the vessel was intended to sail, but of *procuring* a policy by this concealment of circumstances beyond and besides, though including, that fact, and which if disclosed would have enhanced the premium."[1086]
>
> (Emphasis added)

The use of phrases by Willes, J. such as "the policy was ***obtained***" and "***procuring*** a policy" seems to suggest that the judge considered it necessary to point out that the insurers were induced to underwrite the risk at a premium below what they would have charged if the material facts had been disclosed. Nevertheless, Willes, J. did not expressly state that inducement was a separate requirement in order to establish a case for concealment or non-disclosure.[1087] Similarly, Lord Halsbury, L.C. stated

---

[1081] *Ionides v Pender* (1874) L.R. 9 Q.B. 531; EGGERS et al.: op. cit., par. 14.89.
[1082] EGGERS et al.: op. cit., par. 14.89; The *Pine Top case* [1994] 2 Lloyd's Rep. 427, at p. 441 (*per* Lord Mustill).
[1083] (1870) L.R. 5 Q.B. 584.
[1084] Ibid., at p. 590.
[1085] Ibid., at p. 594.
[1086] Ibid.
[1087] For a discussion of this case, cf. EGGERS et al.: op. cit., pars. 14.89-14.91.

in *Blackburn Low & Co. v Vigors*[1088] that an action for non-disclosure was concerned with –

> "...a policy which the defendant was *induced* to subscribe by the wrongful concealment by the plaintiffs and their agents of certain facts then known to the plaintiffs or their agents, and unknown to the defendant, and which were material to the risk."[1089]
> (Emphasis added)

It is noteworthy that the courts referred to the "obtaining" or "inducement" of insurance policies in these cases towards the end of the nineteenth century.[1090] But, since materiality was tested for by reference to the effect of the non-disclosure on the actual underwriter, inducement was closely connected to the requirement of materiality. Accordingly, there was no need to state inducement as a separate requirement. These cases, therefore, cannot be relied on to establish a separate requirement of inducement.[1091] Similarly, it has been held that the twentieth century cases do not provide any clear answers regarding the issues surrounding inducement.[1092] The first case to deal explicitly with the issue of inducement in marine insurance was *Container Transport International Inc. v Oceanus Mutual Underwriting Association (Bermuda) Ltd.*[1093] (the *C.T.I. case*). In the Court of Appeal, Parker, L.J. looked at the language used in sections 18 and 20 of the M.I.A. 1906 and came to the conclusion that there was "no requirement that the particular insurer should have been induced to take the risk or charge a lower premium than he would otherwise have done as a result of the non-disclosure."[1094] He saw no justification for importing a requirement of inducement either in relation to non-disclosure or misrepresentation.[1095] Kerr, L.J, thought that his judgement in *Berger & Light Diffusers Pty Ltd. v Pollock*,[1096] where he expressed the opinion that the prudent underwriter merely provided a yardstick to test for materiality, and that it was still necessary to show that the judgement of the actual underwriter was "influenced", had been wrong.[1097] Both Parker, L.J.[1098] and Kerr, L.J.,[1099] as well as Stephenson, L.J.,[1100] distinguished earlier decisions in which inducement was held

---

[1088] (1887) 12 App. Cas. 531.
[1089] Ibid., at p. 536.
[1090] Also cf. *Brownlie v Campbell* (1880) 5 App. Cas. 925, at p. 950; EGGERS et al.: op. cit., par. 14.93.
[1091] *Berger & Light Diffusers Pty. Ltd. V Pollock* [1973] 2 Lloyd's rep. 442, at p. 463; also see EGGERS et al.: op. cit., par. 14.95.
[1092] *The Pine Top case* [1994] 2 Lloyd's Rep. 427, at pp. 451-452 (*per* Lord Mustill).
[1093] [1982] 2 Lloyd's Rep. 178; [1984] 1 Lloyd's Rep. 476 (Court of Appeal).
[1094] [1984] 1 Lloyd's Rep. 476, at p. 510.
[1095] Ibid., at p. 510.
[1096] [1973] 2 Lloyd's rep. 442.
[1097] Ibid., at pp. 463-464.
[1098] [1984] 1 Lloyd's Rep. 476, at pp. 508-509.
[1099] Ibid., at p. 495.
[1100] Ibid., at p. 528.

to be a requirement,[1101] on the basis of their being subject to legislation that required a subjective element in order to establish an action based on non-disclosure.[1102]

The House of Lords in the *Pine Top case*, however, unanimously held that in order to resort to the remedy of rescission, the underwriter needed to show that he had been induced to conclude the contract by reason of the failure of the assured to disclose material facts.[1103] The underwriter's remedy of avoidance of the contract, therefore, did not only depend on the objective test of materiality, but also on subjective considerations.[1104] Lord Mustill pointed out by reference to the conflicting views of nineteenth century scholars that the controversy surrounding the requirement of inducement was nothing new.[1105] The difference in opinion resulted from the uncertainty about the legal basis for the duties to disclose and torefrain from misrepresenting material circumstances.[1106] As was explained above, Lord Mansfield introduced the general principle of good faith into English law.[1107] In *Carter v Boehm*, he proceeded on the basis of good faith to pronounce the duty not to draw someone into a bargain by concealing or misrepresenting material circumstances.[1108] Whereas the principle of good faith did not become part of the general English commercial law, these two particular duties and the remedy of avoidance for their breach remained part of marine insurance law. Without the general principle of good faith providing the natural legal basis for these duties and the remedy of avoidance, various theories were offered in support thereof. Lord Mustill referred to some of these theories in the course of his judgement:

> "...that the policy failed for want of agreement on the subject- matter; that non-disclosure was constructive fraud; and that contracts of marine insurance were subject to an implied condition precedent that there had been full and accurate disclosure."[1109]

[1101] *Mutual Life and Insurance Co. of New York v Ontario Metal Products Ltd.* [1925] A.C. 344, and *Zurich General Accident and Liability Insurance Co. Ltd.. V Morrison* (1942) 72 Ll.L.Rep. 167.

[1102] In the *Mutual Life case*, the Ontario Insurance Act, 1914 required in section 156 (3) that "[t]he proposals or application of the assured shall not as against him be deemed part of or considered with the contract of insurance except in so far as the court may determine that it contains a material misrepresentation by which the insurer was induced to enter into the contract." In the *Zurich case*, the court was concerned with section 10(3) of the Road Traffic Act 1934, which provided that insurer could only avoid the policy if it was "obtained" by the non-disclosure or misrepresentation of a material fact.

[1103] [1994] 2 Lloyd's Rep. 427, at p. 431 (*per* Lord Goff); at pp. 447-453 (*per* Lord Mustill); at pp. 463-466 (*per* Lord Lloyd).

[1104] EGGERS et al.: op. cit., par. 14.99; RHIDIAN THOMAS, D. (editor): op. cit., p. 36.

[1105] [1994] 2 Lloyd's Rep. 427, at p. 448.

[1106] Ibid.

[1107] Cf. 4.3.3 Lord Mansfield and the remains of *Carter v Boehm supra*.

[1108] Cf. the discussion of this case at p. 96 ff. *supra*.

[1109] [1994] 2 Lloyd's Rep. 427, at p. 448, where Mustill, L.J. refers to some of the old scholars.

Lord Mustill thought that this uncertainty had "at least some bearing on the need for proof of inducement",[1110] but did not go into any detail. The point appears to be that the principle of good faith, as Lord Mansfield correctly conceived, forbade either party to all contracts and dealings "to draw the other into a bargain"[1111] by concealing what he privately knew and the other was ignorant of. This position fitted into the civilian scheme: civilian lawyers thought that one of the functions of the principle of good faith was that neither party should be allowed to obtain an unfair advantage over the other by misleading him.[1112] In the mind of *Pothier*, the great French civilian lawyer, good faith dictated that a contract would be "vicious" if a party to it had been *induced* to make such contract as a result of the fraud of another and, consequently, the party so induced could institute an action to rescind the contract.[1113] Indeed, Lord Mansfield stated that the crucial question was whether there had been a "fair representation"[1114] of the risk, i.e. a representation not intended to "mislead the underwriter into a belief that the [concealed] circumstance does not exist, and to induce him to estimate the risque, as if it did not exist."[1115] If the underwriter had been deceived in this manner, "the policy [was] void" against the assured.[1116] It is, therefore, clear from these *dicta* and the texts of the civilian lawyers that the principle of good faith was aimed at ensuring that one contractual party did not *take advantage* of the ignorance of the other. It did not merely suffice that there had been a discrepancy between the underwritten and actual risk:[1117] "Only if the actual risk is prejudicially different from the underwritten risk can it be said that the assured has failed to make adequate disclosure."[1118] Accordingly, inducement of the contract by fraud – in the broadest sense of that word – was a central issue in establishing whether the good faith that should reign in the contract had been disturbed and whether the contract should be avoided. However, since the principle of good faith was not received in English law, English lawyers did not appreciate the real civilian origins of the duties to disclose and not to misrepresent material information as Lord Mansfield did.

Lord Mustill scrutinised the development of the M.I.A. 1906 by referring to the Digest of Sir Mackenzie Chalmers that preceded the Act as well as Chalmers' subsequent commentary to the Act and stated that there was no room for doubt "that in the minds of those who prepared the statute the ordinary rules of law were to apply."[1119] By 1906, of course, the law had become a fusion of the common law

[1110] Ibid., at p. 449.
[1111] 3 Burr. 1905, at p. 1910
[1112] See p. 25 *supra*.
[1113] POTHIER: **Law of Obligations** 1.III.2.29; see footnote 145 at p. 29 *supra*.
[1114] 3 Burr. 1905, at p. 1911.
[1115] Ibid., at p. 1909.
[1116] Ibid, at p. 1909.
[1117] Cf. Lord Mansfield in *Carter v Boehm* 3 Burr. 1905, at p. 1910, where he held that the underwriter needed not be told what lessens the risk; also section 18(3)(a) of the M.I.A. 1906.
[1118] RHIDIAN THOMAS, D. (editor): op. cit., p. 39.
[1119] [1994] 2 Lloyd's Rep. 427, at p. 449.

and equity and the rules Lord Mustill referred to were those mentioned in Chalmer's Digest, i.e. "rules relating to the effect of fraud, illegality, misrepresentation, and mistake", which included the requirement of inducement or at least some element of causation in the requirement of materiality.[1120] As far as the case law of the twentieth century was concerned, he stated that nothing could be gathered from these judgements.[1121] The Lord Justice then concluded that there was to be implied in the 1906 Act "a qualification that a material misrepresentation will not entitle the underwriter to avoid the policy unless the misrepresentation induced the making of the contract, using 'induced' in the sense in which it is used in the general law of contract."[1122] This proposition was concerned only with *material* misrepresentations, and moreover, was to be transferred to the case of non-disclosure.[1123] Lord Mustill based the requirement of inducement on considerations of justice and the spirit of the duty of the utmost good faith required by section 17 of the M.I.A. 1906.[1124]

The decision of the House of Lords in the *Pine Top* case did not go free of criticism. It has been argued that the standard laid down in the "right to know" test, and the separation of the test of inducement from the question of materiality, only served to dilute the duty of disclosure.[1125] To start with, the separation between materiality and inducement does not appear on the face of the law.[1126] Further to this, as has been explained above, testing for inducement was a natural step in deciding whether a contract could be avoided for breach of the principle of good faith through non-disclosure or misrepresentation. This had been the position in the civilian tradition and was correctly perceived as such by Lord Mansfield in *Carter v*

[1120] Ibid.

[1121] Ibid., at pp. 451-452, referring to *Cantiere Meccanico Brindisino v Janson* [1912] 2 K.B. 112 (since the judge decided that no representation had been made, nothing turned on inducement), *Visscherij Maatschappij Nieuw Onderneming v Scottish Metropolitan Assurance Co. Ltd.*. (1922) 10 Ll.L.Rep. 579, (Lord Scrutton only vaguely touched on the issue of inducement by stating that the underwriters should have given evidence on how they were influenced by the alleged non-disclosure.), *Mutual Life and Insurance Co. of New York v Ontario Metal Products Ltd.* [1925] A.C. 344, and *Zurich General Accident and Liability Insurance Co. Ltd.. v Morrison* (1942) 72 Ll.L.Rep. 167 (both cases were concerned with legislation requiring inducement, cf. text to fn. 1102 *supra*) and *Marene Knitting Mills Pty. Ltd. v Greater Pacific General Insurance Ltd.* [1976] 2 Lloyd's Rep. 631 (nothing turned on causation). Lord Mustill did not discuss *Berger & Light Diffusers Pty Ltd v Pollock* (cf. fn. 1096), in which Kerr, J. (as he then was) favoured an approach in which the actual underwriter had to show that he would have been "influenced" by the non-disclosed circumstance in determining whether to take the risk and at what premium (cf. text to fn. 1097 *supra*). Although, admittedly, "the instinct of Mr. Justice Kerr... was right" (Lord Mustill in *Pine Top* (*supra*) at p. 452), he stopped short of holding that the underwriter had to be induced (EGGERS et al.: op. cit., par. 14.95).

[1122] [1994] 2 Lloyd's Rep. 427, at p. 452.

[1123] Ibid.

[1124] Ibid.

[1125] Cf. generally RHIDIAN THOMAS, D. (editor): op. cit., pp. 38-40.

[1126] Ibid., at p. 39.

Boehm. Taking cognisance of the role of inducement in the making of what he called a "*fair representation*" of the risk, the "decisive influence" test might indeed appear more cogent. This test would render the artificial division between "materiality" and "inducement" superfluous, bringing the law as it is interpreted in line with the written law, and moreover, bringing it in line with the true character of the principle of good faith. However, by bringing back subjective considerations and causation into the equation by means of the requirement of inducement, the House of Lords took a step in the right direction.

Furthermore, it does not appear from the *Pine Top* case whether there exists a presumption of inducement. It was presumed by the Court of Appeal that a presumption of inducement existed in favour of the insurer in *St Paul Fire & Marine Insurance Co. (UK) Ltd. v McConnell Dowell Constructors Ltd.*[1127] It has been suggested however, that the presumption only operates in limited circumstances, and that the exceptional facts[1128] of the particular case justified the operation of such a presumption.[1129]

[1127] [1995] 2 Lloyd's Rep. 116

[1128] Three of the four underwriters who took on a risk, gave evidence before the decision of the House of Lords in the *Pine Top* case as to why the policy should be avoided, the fourth being unwilling to testify. Judgement was given by the Court of Appeal after the House of Lords required inducement in the *Pine Top* case. In these circumstances, it was presumed that the fourth underwriter had been induced into writing the cover.

[1129] BAATZ: *Utmost Good Faith in Marine Insurance Contracts* **Marine Insurance at the Turn of the Millennium** Vol 1 pp. 117-8.

5.6 EFFECT OF BREACH OF THE DUTY OF UTMOST GOOD FAITH

The duty of good faith may be breached in four ways: namely by ***non-disclosure*** which is a failure to disclose a material fact by accident or because the fact was mistakenly thought not to be material; or the duty will be breached by ***concealment***, i.e. the wilful failure to disclose a material fact; or the disclosure of false or misleading information, ***i.e. misrepresentations***, whether ***fraudulent*** or ***innocent*** will constitute breaches of the duty of utmost good faith.[1130]

5.6.1 Remedy of the Insurer

Section 17 of the M.I.A. 1906 affords the "victim" of a breach of the duty of utmost good faith the opportunity to avoid the contract. A breach of the duty of utmost good faith, therefore, renders the marine insurance policy voidable ***ab initio***. Avoidance of the contract, or rescission as it is also called, is a retrospective remedy. The parties are to be returned to the position that they were in before conclusion of the contract: the insurer will be put in a position as if he never took on the risk at all, the implication being that he will not be liable for any future claims under the policy, any outstanding liabilities will be discharged, and any claims paid under the policy will be recoverable.[1131] This remedy is reinforced in sections 18(1) and 20(1) of the M.I.A. 1906 to the effect that the contract may be avoided at the instance of the insurer where the assured failed to disclose material facts, or misrepresented material facts.[1132]

The only remedy available for non-disclosure of a material fact, in accordance with section 18(1) of the M.I.A. 1906, is avoidance of the whole contract. The contract of insurance will not be automatically void once a breach of duty is established: the aggrieved party will have the right to avoid the contract.[1133] Lord Mansfield, it will be remembered, said that the keeping back of a circumstance of which the underwriter is ignorant, inducing him to estimate the risk as if that circumstance did not exist, "is a fraud and therefore the policy is void."[1134] This proposition was favoured by judges until the middle of the nineteenth century.[1135] However, since Lord Campbell, in *The Deposit and General Life Assurance Company v Ayscough*,[1136] held that fraud rendered a contract ***voidable*** and not ***void***, and the equitable remedy of rescission for non-fraudulent misrepresentation entered the scene during the latter

[1130] HANSELL, D.S.: op. cit., pp. 182-183.
[1131] BENNET: op. cit., p. 67; EGGERS et al.: op. cit., par. 16.14.
[1132] BAATZ: *Utmost Good Faith in Marine Insurance Contracts* **Marine Insurance at the Turn of the Millennium** Vol 1 p. 25.
[1133] EGGERS et al.: op. cit., pars. 16.18-22; HANSELL, D.S.: op. cit., p. 182.
[1134] *Carter v Boehm*, cf. p. 96 *supra*.
[1135] Cf. EGGERS et al.: op. cit., par. 16.18, fn. 43, who suggests that references by judges to a policy being *void* as opposed to *voidable* might be due to the terms of the policies that had been the subject of these cases, or as a result of a poor choice of words by those judges, or because the policy had already been avoided by the underwriter.
[1136] (1856) 6 Ell & Bl 761.

part of the nineteenth century, it came to be accepted that avoidance of the policy was the correct remedy for breach of the duty of disclosure.[1137] It is, therefore, imperative that the insurer elects whether to avoid or carry on with the policy. Until such election, the contract will remain valid.[1138] The policy will, of course, also remain valid and avoidance will not be available if the insurer has elected to affirm or created the impression through unequivocal conduct that he has elected to affirm the policy. In order for an affirmation to be valid, the insurer must have full knowledge of all the facts, including the breach of the duty to disclose and his right to avoid.[1139] There must have been an unequivocal act on the part of the insurer which can be reasonably taken to constitute an informed affirmation of the policy.[1140] The fact that an insurer accepted premiums under the policy, or paid a claim, or made a statement that a claim under the policy would be paid, would constitute such acts affirming the policy.[1141] Also, where the insurer's failure to make his election within a reasonable period was prejudicial or suggested that he was not of the intention to avoid, the courts may infer affirmation of the policy.[1142]

Avoidance is the *only* remedy provided for in section 18(1) for non-disclosure of a material fact before the policy has been concluded.[1143] Accordingly, it has been argued that once the insurer has elected not to avoid, but to affirm the policy, he shall not have a right to reject a claim based on the policy by reason of the assured's non-disclosure.[1144] This would be in accordance with the purpose of the remedy of avoidance expressed in section 18(1), i.e. offering the insurer the chance to elect whether the contract should be cancelled from its inception or whether it should remain valid. If the latter, both parties will remain bound to it and liable to fulfil their respective obligations. Also, where the assured notified the insurer of a material fact not disclosed or misrepresented and the insurer nevertheless pays the claim, the insurer cannot recover such payment.[1145] Indeed, section 18(1) provides

---

[1137] EGGERS et al.: op. cit., par. 16.20.
[1138] Ibid., par. 16.39.
[1139] Ibid.; MERKIN, Robert (editor): op. cit., par 5-03; In *Orakpo v Barclays Insurance Services* [1995] L.R.L.R. 443, Staughton L.J. suggested that an insurer may be estopped from electing to avoid the contract, even where the insurer had no actual knowledge of the relevant facts, but caused the assured to rely on his conduct in treating the policy as subsisting. This appears to be an extraordinary protection to the assured, as the insurer stands to lose its only remedy for want of knowledge of the fraudulent actions of the assured.
[1140] Ibid., par. 16.41; MERKIN, Robert (editor): op. cit., par. 5-03.
[1141] *Wing v Harvey* 5 DE G. M. & G. 265, at pp. 269-271; cf. also *The Litsion Pride* [1985] 437, at pp. 516-517; EGGERS et al.: op. cit., par. 16.41, listing more examples of instances constituting an affirmation; MERKIN, Robert (editor): op. cit., par. 5-03.
[1142] EGGERS et al.: op. cit., par. 16.40; MERKIN, Robert (editor): op. cit., par. 5-03.
[1143] *Glasgow Assurance v Symondson* (1911) 104 L.T. 254, at p. 258; *Le Banque Financière v Westgate* [1988] 2 Lloyd's Rep. 513, at p. 550; MERKIN, Robert (editor): op. cit., par. 5-03.
[1144] *West v National Motor and Accident* [1955] 1 All E.R. 800; cf. generally EGGERS et al.: op. cit., pars. 16.27-32.
[1145] *Bilbie v Lumley* (1802) 2 East 469; *Wing v Harvey* (1854) 5 De G.M. & G. 265.

the underwriter with "an all or nothing remedy".[1146] The English courts have not been prepared to allow a claim for damages in the event of non-disclosure.[1147] However, damages will be available if the duty of disclosure is included as an express term of the contract.[1148] It has also been proposed that where the duty is held to be included as an implied term of the contract,[1149] it will be in accordance with principle that a breach of the duty sound in damages.[1150]

Where the insurer sets out to avoid the contract but has not established a proper case of non-disclosure, he "would himself be guilty of want of utmost good faith"[1151] and such rescission will amount to a repudiatory breach of contract.[1152] The assured may then choose to treat it as such and institute proceedings, or reject the repudiation. In the latter instance the repudiation will have no legal consequence.[1153] In the former case, there is authority for the proposition that, apart from having a right to cancel the contract, the assured may claim damages for its breach.[1154]

The effect of misrepresentation on the insurance contract in terms of section 20 will be the same as that of a non-disclosure, i.e. the contract is voidable at the election of the aggrieved party.[1155] However, the rules of misrepresentation are not completely foreign to the general English contract law.[1156] Although at common law, an innocent, i.e. a non-negligent and non-fraudulent misrepresentation is not a ground for avoidance of the contract, equity was prepared to grant the remedy of rescission where a person had been induced to make a contract as a result of an

[1146] EGGERS et al.: op. cit., par. 16.29; *Pan Atlantic Insurance Co. Ltd.. v Pine Top Insurance Co. Ltd.* [1993] 1 Lloyd's Rep. 496, at p. 508 (*per* Sir Donald Nicholls, V-C); *The Star Sea* [1995] 1 Lloyd's Rep. 651, at p. 667 (*per* Tuckey, J.); [1997] 1 Lloyd's Rep. 360.
[1147] *Glasgow Assurance v Symondson* (1911) 104 L.T. 254, at p. 258; *Le Banque Financière v Westgate* [1988] 2 Lloyd's Rep. 513, at p. 550.
[1148] EGGERS et al.: op. cit., par. 16.112.
[1149] Some English judges favoured an implied term analysis particularly in relation to fraudulent claims, cf. Hoffmann, L.J. in *Orakpo vo Barclays Insurance Services* [1995] L.R.L.R. 443.
[1150] EGGERS et al.: op. cit., par. 16.113.
[1151] Lord Lloyd in *Pine Top* [1994] 2 Lloyd's Rep. 427, at p. 456; Lord Lloyd appears to base his proposition on the authority of Lord Mansfield in *Carter v Boehm* (cf. p. 101 *supra*). However, Lord Mansfield never employed the phrase "utmost good faith". He considered the duty not to conceal to be based on the principle of good faith, which main function was "to prevent fraud". In this context, he warned that the duty not to conceal should "never be so turned construed, or used, as to protect, or be a means of fraud."
[1152] EGGERS et al.: op. cit., par. 16.17.
[1153] MERKIN, Robert (editor): op. cit., par. 5-03.
[1154] Cf. *Sprung v Royal Insurance* [1999] Lloyd's Rep. IR 111; EGGERS et al.: op. cit., par. 16.114.
[1155] MERKIN, Robert (editor): op. cit., par. 5-14.
[1156] Cf. Lord Lloyd in *Pine Top* [1994] 2 Lloyd's Rep. 427, at p. 456: "...whereas the right to avoid for non-disclosure is peculiar to contracts of utmost good faith, the right to avoid for misrepresentation is part of the general law of contract."

innocent misrepresentation.[1157] At common law, the contract would remain valid, except in those cases where the representation amounted to a total failure of consideration.[1158] Apart from that, the common law would allow an action for misrepresentation in all contracts, where the misrepresentation had been negligent, i.e. where a contractual party had been obliged to exercise due care in making a representation and failed to do so.[1159] Since the Misrepresentation Act of 1967 came into operation, rescission of the contract is permitted for misrepresentation, even where the representation has been incorporated as a term of the contract.[1160] More importantly though, the Misrepresentation Act allows the courts to award damages for non-fraudulent misrepresentation, thereby going where the common law feared to tread: at common law, damages were only available for fraudulent misrepresentation and in some circumstances, for negligent misrepresentation.[1161] Section 2(1) of this Act provides:

> "Where a person has entered into a contract after a misrepresentation has been made to him by another party thereto and as a result thereof he has suffered loss, then, if the person making the misrepresentation would be liable to damages in respect thereof had the misrepresentation been made fraudulently, that person shall be so liable notwithstanding that the misrepresentation was not made fraudulently, unless he proves that he had reasonable ground to believe and did believe up to the time the contract was made that the facts represented were true."

Theoretically, a court may award damages for a negligent misrepresentation inducing a contract of insurance.[1162] The Act goes even further in affording the court the discretion to award damages for innocent misrepresentation instead of the equitable remedy of rescission, where rescission is sought.[1163] Where rescission is available and prayed for, it is within the discretion of the court to decline and award damages in order to prevent the annulment of the contract.[1164] Arguably, it would be in the power of the court to use its discretion under section 2 (2) of the Misrepresentation Act to award damages in the context of an insurance contract that was induced by misrepresentation.[1165] On the other hand, it has been said that that Act "is wholly irrelevant to insurance law".[1166] The courts would indeed

---

1157 COLINVAUX, R.: op. cit., par. 5-09; EGGERS et al.: op. cit., par. 4.25 ; cf. MERKIN, Robert (editor): op. cit., par. 5-14.

1158 EGGERS et al.: op. cit., par. 4.25.

1159 Ibid., par. 4.24.

1160 Ibid., par. 6.18.

1161 Ibid., par. 6.19.

1162 CLARKE: op. cit., par. 23-14 and par. 23-15B.

1163 Section 2(2) of the Misrepresentation Act 1967; EGGERS et al.: op. cit., par. 6.20.

1164 EGGERS et al.: op. cit., par. 6.20.

1165 Ibid., par. 6.21.

1166 COLINVAUX, R.: op. cit., par. 5-09; however, cf. the seventh edition of this work under the editorship of Mr. Robert Merkin at par. 5-15 where it is conceded that the 1967 Act could find application, although only "to relieve a consumer or private assured who has acted innocently in falsely stating a fact."

appear to be wary of applying section 2(2) of the Misrepresentation Act in the context of insurance.[1167] In fact, there has been no such case reported yet.[1168]

The remedy of rescission is particularly harsh on the assured. Not only is the assured deprived of cover, but is also obliged to return payments received for legitimate claims, regardless of whether the breach in fact relates to the loss and regardless of culpability. The consequences of a breach as a result of an innocent mistake will be the same as that of a calculated concealment.[1169]

5.6.2 Remedy of the Assured

The remedy to avoid the contract is particularly harsh on the assured, as he would hardly wish to rescind where a loss was already suffered upon discovery of a breach of the duty of utmost good faith by the insurer. In such circumstances the assured would wish to recover under the policy, leading to the question whether an action against the insurer can sound in damages.[1170] Generally, damages would be available where there has been a breach of an express or implied term of the contract. Further to this, damages may also be awarded for breach of a common law duty of care. In order to establish a duty of care at common law, three requirements will have to be satisfied: firstly, there has to be a sufficient relationship of proximity or neighbourhood between the alleged wrongdoer and the person who has suffered damage; secondly, it must have been in the reasonable contemplation of the former that it is likely that his carelessness may cause damages to the latter and; thirdly, it must be fair and reasonable that a duty of care should exist.[1171]

In *Banque Keyser v Skandia*,[1172] the courts had the opportunity to consider whether damages would be an appropriate remedy. The assured based its claim for damages i.a. on breach of utmost good faith, contending that "the utmost good faith principle was …an implied term of the contract."[1173] The assured also argued that an action in tort should be entertained against the insurer for a breach of its duty of care. It asserted that the fact that the insurance contract was a contract of the utmost good faith established a special relationship between the assured and the

---

[1167] EGGERS et al.: op. cit., par. 6.21; MERKIN, Robert (editor): op. cit., par. 5-15; *Highlands Insurance v Continental Insurance Co* [1987] 1 Lloyd's Rep. 109, at pp. 117-118.
[1168] CLARKE: op. cit., par. 23-15B.
[1169] BENNET: op. cit., p. 68
[1170] BAATZ: *Utmost Good Faith in Marine Insurance Contracts* **Marine Insurance at the Turn of the Millennium** Vol 1 p. 26.
[1171] Cf. Steyn, J. (as he then was) in *Banque Keyser v Skandia* [1987] 1 Lloyd's Rep. 69, at pp. 98-99, referring to *Anns v Merton London borough Council* [1978] A.C. 728, at pp. 751G-752C; *Donoghue v Stevenson* [1932] A.C. 562; *Hedley Byrne & Co. Ltd.. v Heller & Partners Ltd.* [1964] A.C. 465; *Dorset Yacht Co. Ltd.. v Home Office* [1970] A.C. 1004; *Governors of the Peabody Donation Fund v Sir Lindsay Parkinson* [1985] A.C. 210, at pp. 240F-241C; also cf. EGGERS et al.: op. cit., par. 16.119.
[1172] [1987] 1 Lloyd's Rep. 69.
[1173] Ibid., at p. 93.

insurer, which was of sufficient proximity to infer a duty of care in tort. This duty would include an obligation resting on the insured to disclose material facts. Failure to disclose would accordingly result in a breach of the duty of care, giving rise to damages in tort. In the Commercial Court, Steyn, J. (as he then was) considered that although it was incorrect to categorize the duties arising from the principle of utmost good faith as implied terms,[1174] from the point of view of legal principle and policy it would be "anomalous that there should be no claim for damages for breach of those duties in a case where that is the only effective remedy."[1175] Steyn, J., also held that a duty of care did arise,[1176] and that a breach had been established.[1177] Lord Slade, in the Court of Appeal, agreed that the duty of utmost good faith did not arise out of an implied term of the contract, but had its source in the positive rules of law.[1178] However, according to the Lord Justice, the only remedy was, therefore, as indicated in section 17 of the M.I.A. 1906.[1179] In his view, it was not imperative from the view of legal principle to allow damages as a remedy.[1180] The Court of Appeal also did not approve of Steyn, J.'s finding that a duty of care arose. Slade, L.J. found that there was no authority whatsoever in support of a duty to disclose in tort,[1181] and that the insurers were under no duty of care to the banks.[1182] In the House of Lords, Lord Templeman agreed with the judgement in the Court of Appeal,[1183] whilst Lords Bridge and Jauncey noted that if a duty of care could in fact be said to exist, then such a duty could not be more extensive than the duty to disclose.[1184] The result of *La Banque Financière* was, therefore, that avoidance of the policy was established as the only remedy available to the assured where the insurer had breached his duty to act in the utmost good faith. No remedy sounded in damages for breach of the utmost good faith in the pre-contractual context.[1185]

In *The Good Luck*[1186], the Court of Appeal had to deal with a claim for damages by an assignee bank against an insurer for breach of the utmost good faith in the post-contractual context. The Court did not question the proposition that the principle also applied after conclusion of the contract. In following the judgement of the

[1174] Ibid., at p. 94.
[1175] Ibid., at p. 96.
[1176] Ibid., at p. 102.
[1177] Ibid., at p. 103.
[1178] [1988] 2 Lloyd's Rep. 513, at p. 548.
[1179] Ibid., at p. 550; cf. GILMAN: op. cit., Vol. III, par. 579G; RHIDIAN THOMAS, D. (editor): op. cit., p. 31.
[1180] [1988] 2 Lloyd's Rep. 513, at p. 547.
[1181] Ibid., at p. 550.
[1182] Ibid,. at p. 563.
[1183] [1990] 2 Lloyd's Rep. 377, at p. 387.
[1184] [1990] 2 Lloyd's Rep. 377, at pp. 380 and 389; cf. MERKIN, Robert (editor): op. cit., par. 5-11.
[1185] Cf. GILMAN: op. cit., Vol. III, par. 579G.
[1186] See p. 132 *supra*.

Court of Appeal in the *Banque Financière* case, May, L.J. held that damages were not the correct remedy for breach of the utmost good faith.[1187]

It has been firmly established that the principle of utmost good faith and the duty to disclose in particular arises *ex lege*, i.e. outside of the contract.[1188] It is, therefore, irrefutable that damages will not be available as a remedy for non-disclosure based on a breach of an implied contractual term. It has been recently suggested, however, that despite the above-mentioned *dicta* against the recognition of a common law duty of care consistent with the principle of utmost good faith, it is no large step to enforce the principle of utmost good faith by means of a duty of care in tort.[1189] The law of tort, being described as "fluid"[1190], would indeed, be capable of facilitating such a duty in same way as it facilitates liability in tort for fraudulent or negligent misrepresentation. Elsewhere[1191], the same commentator subjected the decision of the Court of Appeal in *Banque Financière*[1192] to thorough criticism. He pointed out that breach of a contractual, tortious, fiduciary or statutory duty is not a prerequisite for the recovery of damages. The only question is whether a duty exists at law, and whether damages should be recoverable for breach of good faith as a matter of principle and policy. Further to this, the fact that section 17 of the M.I.A. 1906 is silent as far as the availability of damages is concerned is no bar to an award of damages. This is so since section 91(2) expressly preserves the common law. Accordingly, "[t]he matter should be left to the general law and exegetical recourse to s. 17 should be eschewed."[1193] In so far as the Court of Appeal has been concerned about an absence of authority for the recovery of damages, the suggestion is that this cannot be a valid reason to refuse a remedy based on sound principle. The law should be able to develop in order that a breach of a well recognised principle such as (utmost) good faith may be remedied. As far as the assured is concerned in the event of breach by the insurer, an award of damages will certainly be much more appropriate to the position of the assured.[1194]

1187 [1989] 2 Lloyd's Rep. 238 at p. 263; also see GILMAN: op. cit., Vol. III, par. 579I.
1188 Cf. p. 132 *supra*.
1189 EGGERS et al.: op. cit., par. 16.125.
1190 Ibid.
1191 C.f. EGGERS: *Remedies for the failure to observe the utmost good faith* [2003] LMCLQ 2, at p. 275.
1192 C.f. fn. 1178 *supra*.
1193 EGGERS: *Remedies for the failure to observe the utmost good faith* [2003] LMCLQ 2, at p. 276.
1194 Ibid., at p. 277.

5.7 TIME OF THE DUTY OF UTMOST GOOD FAITH

The doctrine of utmost good faith and the aspects commonly associated with it, namely the duty to disclose and the duty not to misrepresent material facts, is generally thought to apply only during the contractual negotiations. Accordingly, an insurer cannot require the assured, once the policy has been concluded, to disclose matters that show he has made a bad bargain. Once the risk is accepted, the duty of disclosure does not continue to protect the insurer against what may turn out to be an unfortunate bargain.[1195] This has been established in *Cory v Paton* [1196] where Blackburn, J. put the question before the Court to be –

> "...whether, after the negotiation is complete and the contract made, in fact and in good faith, and the underwriter is under a moral obligation to execute a formal policy, the assured is bound by good faith to give information to the assurer of a matter which would make him aware that his bargain was a bad one, information which ought to have no effect on him, but would expose him to a temptation to break his contract, which, as far as the law is concerned, he may do with impunity, because for fiscal purposes the legislature has forbidden the court, either of law or equity, to enforce the contract."[1197]

The Judge found in favour of the assured, holding that he was not bound to lead his neighbour, i.e. the insurer, into temptation. Three years after that decision, Blackburn, J. confirmed this position in *Lishman and Another v The Northern Maritime Insurance Company.*[1198] He stated the rule to be that the obligation to disclose material facts did not oblige the assured to disclose facts after the underwriter was once bound in honour, since he would then tempt the insurer to break his engagement.[1199] Bramwell, B., presiding in the same case, perceived the rule to be as follows:

> "The obligation that the law attaches to the relation of insurer and insured, viz. that up to the time of the insurance material facts must be communicated, must be taken with this qualification, that when there is previous agreement out of which the policy of insurance substantially arises, by mercantile usage the obligation attaches up to the time of making such agreement only, and not up to the time of making the policy."[1200]

Accordingly, after initialling of a slip "any fresh fact coming to the knowledge of the assured need not be communicated to the underwriters, however material it may be."[1201] In various other English decisions on this point[1202] the duty to make a

---

[1195] BENNET: *Mapping the Doctrine of Utmost Good Faith in Insurance Contract Law* [1999] LMCLQ 165, at pp. 197-198; SOYER: *The Star Sea – a lode star?* [2001] LMCLQ 428, at p. 429; *K/S Merc Scandia v Certain Lloyd's Underwriters (The Mercandian Continent)* [2002] 2 Lloyd's Rep. 563, at p. 570.
[1196] L.R. 7 Q.B. 304.
[1197] Ibid., at p. 309.
[1198] L.R. 10 C.P. 179.
[1199] Ibid., at p. 182.
[1200] L.R. 10 C.P. 179 at p. 182.
[1201] MUSTILL & GILMAN: op. cit., Vol. II, par. 620.

full disclosure, and therefore also the principle of utmost good faith, with which it has more than often been wrongly equated, were held to apply up to the moment when a binding contract of insurance had been concluded.[1203] It has even been said that there is no judicial support for the application of the post-contractual principle of utmost good faith before the enactment of the M.I.A. 1906.[1204] This inference is said to be strengthened i.a. by the fact that section 17 of the Marine Insurance Act is headed by the words "*Disclosure and Representations*", and followed by sections 18-19 which provide expressly for the pre-contractual application of these duties of the assured.[1205]

Moreover, it has been argued that since the imbalance between the knowledge of the insurer and assured does not exist anylonger once the insurance policy is concluded, the reason for the application of the duty of the utmost good faith falls away. Since the parties are then in a contractual relationship, general principles of contract law should apply in cases of fraud. The insurer could also find protection against fraud and alteration of risk by means of express provisions in the contract. Accordingly, the post-contractual application of the duty of utmost good faith contradicts the principle of freedom of contract and affords unnecessary protection to the insurer.[1206] There is, also, nothing in section 17 which compels the operation of the duty of utmost good faith after inception of the contract. Viewed in terms of the harsh remedy of rescission of the contract for breach of the duty in section 17, it has been suggested that section 17 should be limited to the pre-contractual

[1202] E.g. *British Equitable v G.W.R.* (1869) 20 L.T. 422 and *Canning v Farquhar* (1886) 16 Q.B.D. 727, both dealing with life policies including a term to the effect that before tender of premium, the insurer incurs no risk and no insurance will take effect. In both cases a material alteration in the proposer's state of health occurred after acceptance of the proposal but before payment of premium. In both cases the policy was found to be void, i.e. that the insurer was under no obligation to issue a policy; also cf. *Pim v Reid* 6 Man. & G. 1, where the Court of Common Pleas was concerned with a fire policy containing a condition obliging the assured to disclose and not to misrepresent "any circumstance which is material to be made known to the company, in order to enable them to judge of the risk they have undertaken, or are required to undertake..." on pain of nullity. The Court found that the clause did not extend to circumstances after the policy had been effected (*per* Maule, J. at p. 24 and Cresswell, J. at p. 25. On general principles, Tindal, C.J. stated at p. 19 that "a policy of insurance [was] not avoided by an alteration in the trade carried on..."; *Looker v Law Union* [1928] 1 K.B. 554, also concerning life insurance, where a proposer became ill before the payment of the first premium and the policy was issued, notice of the material change in the risk should have been communicated to the insurer, affirming *Canning v Farquhar*, also cf. *Allis Chalmers v Fidelity Deposit* (1916) 32 T.L.R. 263, a case concerning fidelity insurance.

[1203] MERKIN, Robert (editor): op. cit., p. 119.

[1204] SOYER: *Continuing duty of utmost good faith in insurance contracts: still alive?* [2003] LMCLQ 39, at p. 41. This observation is, with respect, wrong, especially in the light of Willes, J.'s statement of the law in *Britton* (cf. on page 194 *infra*).

[1205] SOYER: *The Star Sea – a lode star?* [2001] LMCLQ 428, at p. 429.

[1206] These arguments were advanced by SOYER: *Continuing duty of utmost good faith in insurance contracts: still alive?* [2003] LMCLQ 39, at pp. 41-42.

duty of utmost good faith, and that the continuing duty to observe utmost good faith should be free from the limitations of section 17.[1207]

However, since there is no time restriction contained in section 17 of the MIA 1906, there is no reason why the duty of utmost good faith should be limited to the pre-contractual stage and should not continue throughout the duration of the contract.[1208] Further to this, it has been argued that sections 18 to 20 of the Marine Insurance Act 1906 are merely illustrative of the duty of utmost good faith and therefore not exhaustive, and that section 17, in laying down the general principle of utmost good faith, does not confine the operation of the principle to pre-contractual negotiations.[1209] Therefore the law does not exclude the duty of utmost good faith after the inception of the policy.[1210] This conclusion seems to be supported by a statement by Sir Mackenzie Chalmers in his commentary to the M.I.A. 1906 to the effect that section 17 states the "general principle... in this section because the special sections which follow are not exhaustive".[1211] Continuing along this line of thought, Longmore , L.J. in *The Mercandian Continent*[1212] quoted with approval from the judgement of Staughton, L.J. in *New Hampshire Insurance Co. v Mirror Group Newspapers Ltd.*[1213] where the Lord Justice said the following about the intention of Sir Chalmers in drafting section 17:

> "A novice could be forgiven for thinking that the only duty of disclosure is by the insured and that it only applies before the contract is concluded (which would no doubt include the new contract which is made upon renewal). But the maxim that mention of one of two things excludes the other must be applied with caution when considering the draftsmanship of Sir Mackenzie Chalmers. His method of codification was, at any rate at times, to state the effect of rules decided by the Courts and not to pronounce upon points which had not been decided."[1214]

This method becomes apparent through the extensive citations of authorities in the above-mentioned commentary by Sir Mackenzie Chalmers. Accordingly, section 17 may have been intended to confirm nineteenth century *dicta*[1215] which supported the application of good faith in the post-contractual stage.[1216] Those cases which are normally said to be authority for the proposition that the principle of utmost

1207 Cf. generally BENNET: *Mapping the Doctrine of Utmost Good Faith in Insurance Contract Law* [1999] LMCLQ 165, at pp. 202-207.

1208 SOYER: *The Star Sea – a lode star?* [2001] LMCLQ 428, at p. 429.

1209 GILMAN: op. cit., Vol. III, pars. 579AA-E.

1210 MERKIN, Robert (editor): op. cit., p. 119.

1211 CHALMERS: **Chalmers' Marine Insurance Act 1906** s. 17; SOYER: *The Star Sea – a lode star?* [2001] LMCLQ 428, at p. 429.

1212 *K/S Merc Scandia v Certain Lloyd's Underwriters (The Mercandian Continent)* [2002] 2 Lloyd's Rep. 563.

1213 [1997] L.R.L.R. 24.

1214 [2002] 2 Lloyd's Rep. 563, at p. 570.

1215 See e.g. Willes, J. in *Britton v Royal Insurance Co.* at p. 194 *infra.*

1216 GILMAN: op. cit., Vol. III, par. 579D.

good faith does not apply after conclusion of the contract, are, in fact, authority for a much narrower proposition: the assured does not shoulder a duty to disclose circumstances that come to his knowledge after conclusion of the policy and that would be material to the risk which the insurer already has underwritten.[1217] Similarly, it is authority for the proposition that an innocent misrepresentation, which is material to the risk after the contract has been made, will not avoid the policy.[1218] This is in line with the limits, set in sections 18-20 of the M.I.A. 1906, to the duty to disclose and not to misrepresent material circumstances.[1219] However, in other circumstances such as claims and held-covered clauses, the application of the duties flowing from the general principle in section 17 remains undefined.[1220] A possible explanation for this state of affairs may be the fact that, although the courts recognised the application of the principle in a post-contractual context before the Act, no detailed examination of the duties flowing from it and remedies for their breach had taken place.[1221]

In summary, there is no duty to disclose matters relevant to the making of the contract once the contract has been made.[1222] The disclosure after conclusion of the contract of facts discovered after such conclusion would serve no useful purpose and is not a requirement.[1223] But, by contrast, situations may arise subsequent to the conclusion of the contract where the principle of utmost good faith makes it necessary that there should be further disclosure because the relevant facts are relevant to the later stages of the contract:[1224] "The question is whether the relevant circumstances subsisting at the later time, after the contract has been concluded, are such as to require someone under such a duty to make a further disclosure."[1225]

Although the scope of the principle of utmost good faith beyond the formation of the contract has been said to be unclear,[1226] this does not deduct from the recognition of the existence of duties flowing from the general principle in section 17, since it has now been authoritatively stated that "... the content of the obligation to observe good faith has a different application and content in different situations."[1227] Thus, where some aspects of the principle of utmost good faith may

---

[1217] Ibid.
[1218] Ibid.
[1219] Ibid.
[1220] Ibid., pars. 579D and E.
[1221] Ibid., par. 579E.
[1222] *The Good Luck* [1988] 1 Lloyd's Rep. 437, at pp. 545-546; BENNET: *Mapping the Doctrine of Utmost Good Faith in Insurance Contract Law* [1999] LMCLQ 165, at p 198.
[1223] Ibid.
[1224] Ibid.
[1225] Ibid.
[1226] MERKIN, Robert (editor): op. cit., p. 119.
[1227] Cf. the judgement of Lord Hobhouse in *Manifest Shipping & Co. Ltd. v Uni-Polaris Insurance Co. Ltd. & La Réunion Européene (The Star Sea)* [2001] 1 Lloyd's Rep. 389, at p. 400.

apply before the contract is concluded, other aspects may find application afterwards.[1228] There are especially two main instances in which the principle of utmost good faith is recognised and applied by the courts in England after inception of the contract, i.e. in cases where either the insurer or the assured seeks to vary or renew the contract of insurance, and secondly in cases where the assured pursues a claim or in what has also been called the "claims context".[1229]

5.7.1 Variation of the Insurance Contract

It has been argued that the principle of utmost good faith will be applicable in the post-contractual context in instances where the policy or cover is to be varied and that such would be the case where there is a variation to extend the cover, where the underwriter is entitled to charge an additional premium, where there is a contractual obligation on the assured to disclose information concerning a proposed risk, in cases where the assured wants to rely on a held-covered clause[1230] and, finally, in instances where the assured seeks to renew the contract of insurance.[1231] However, there is no *numerus clausus* of instances where the principle applies and it may very well be relevant in every instance where there is an exchange of information whereupon a decision is to be made, e.g. an application for extended cover.[1232]

The application of section 17 of the M.I.A 1906 in the context of a "held-covered" clause, under which cover is to be extended beyond that originally countenanced by the policy provided notice is given to the insurers,[1233] was first noted in *Overseas Commodities Ltd. v Style.*[1234] The assured took out a policy on canned pork butts for shipment from France to Britain. The policy incorporated the Institute Cargo Clauses (Extended Cover), clause 4 of which provided that the assured was to be

---

[1228] BENNET: *Mapping the Doctrine of Utmost Good Faith in Insurance Contract Law* [1999] LMCLQ 165, at p. 197.

[1229] *K/S Merc Scandia v Certain Lloyd's Underwriters (The Mercandian Continent)* [2002] 2 Lloyd's Rep. 563; SOYER: *The Star Sea – a lode star?* [2001] LMCLQ 428, at pp. 430 and 434.

[1230] "A held covered clause gives an opportunity to an assured to extend the scope of cover on giving notice to insurers and agreeing on additional premium and other terms imposed by insurers." See SOYER: *The Star Sea – a lode star?* [2001] LMCLQ 428, at p. 431; "The function of a held covered clause is to maintain insurance cover notwithstanding circumstances that would otherwise discharge or prejudice that cover." See BENNET: *Mapping the Doctrine of Utmost Good Faith in Insurance Contract Law* [1999] LMCLQ 165, at p. 202. For an example cf. the Institute Time Clauses Hull (1995), cl. 3 which provides as follows: "Held covered in case of any breach of warranty as to cargo, trade, locality, towage, salvage, services or date of sailing, provided notice be given to the Underwriters immediately after receipt of advices and any amended terms of cover and any additional premium required by them be agreed."

[1231] See SOYER: *The Star Sea – a lode star?* [2001] LMCLQ 428, at p. 430; also Longmore, L.J. in *The Mercandian Continent* [2002] 2 Lloyd's Rep. 563, at p. 571.

[1232] MERKIN, Robert (editor): op. cit., p. 119.

[1233] In general, see MERKIN, Robert (editor): op. cit., p. 119; BENNET: *Mapping the Doctrine of Utmost Good Faith in Insurance Contract Law* [1999] LMCLQ 165, at pp. 202-208.

[1234] [1958] 1 Lloyd's Rep. 546.

"[h]eld covered at a premium to be arranged in case of change of voyage or of any omission or error in the description of the interest vessel or voyage." The policy, furthermore, included a warranty that all the tins were to be marked by the manufacturer "with a code for verification of date of manufacture". Some of the tins turned out not to accord with these provisions, and were condemned on import. The assured claimed on the policy, seeking to invoke the held-covered clause in relation to the goods which were not marked in the warranted manner. The assured received two letters from the manufacturers explaining the discrepancy in the marking, of which only the explanation that turned out to be more favourable for the assured was disclosed to the underwriters.

McNair, J. decided in favour of the underwriters, holding that the assured could not rely on the held-covered clause, since in relying on the clause, the assured needed to act with the utmost good faith towards the underwriters. He furthermore held that the principle of the utmost good faith rested on the assured throughout the running of the policy and concluded:[1235]

> "To obtain the protection of the 'held covered' clause, the assured must act with the utmost good faith towards the underwriters, this being an obligation which rests upon them throughout the currency of the policy."[1236]

In coming to this conclusion, however, McNair, J. referred neither to section 17 of the M.I.A 1906, nor to any authority.

In *The Litsion Pride*[1237], the same principles were applied in a controversial case[1238] which concerned a policy against war risks, including a term[1239] that the insurer was to be informed once the insured vessel entered an excluded area, upon which event the insurer was entitled to charge an additional premium. The assured did not give the required notice to the insurer after the ship entered a war zone, and the Judge found that he deliberately failed to disclose this fact in order to slip his vessel in

[1235] Cf. for a discussion of this case SOYER: *The Star Sea – a lode star?* [2001] LMCLQ 428, at pp. 431-432.

[1236] [1958] 1 Lloyd's Rep. 546, at p. 559.

[1237] [1985] 1 Lloyd's Rep. 437.

[1238] The judgement of Hirst, J. in this case has been severely criticised by academic writers (see e.g. BENNET: *Mapping the Doctrine of Utmost Good Faith in Insurance Contract Law* [1999] LMCLQ 165, at p. 206) as well as by other judges (see e.g. the judgement of Lord Hobhouse in *Manifest Shipping & Co. Ltd. v Uni-Polaris Insurance Co. Ltd. & La Réunion Européene (The Star Sea)* [2001] 1 Lloyd's Rep. 389, at p. 405).

[1239] The policy included the War Risk Trading Warranties, the relevant parts of which were in the following terms: "This coverage shall extend worldwide, but in the event of a vessel or craft insured hereunder sailing for, deviating towards, or being within the Territorial Waters of any of the Countries or places described in the Current Exclusions ...additional premium shall be paid at the discretion of insurers hereon. Informations of such voyage or deviation shall be given to insurers as soon as practicable, and the absence of prior advice shall not affect the cover hereon..."

and out of the zone to save paying additional premium. An Iraqi helicopter attacked the vessel as a result of which it caught fire and sunk. The insurer was allowed to avoid the policy. Hirst, J. applied the duty of utmost good faith holding that the insurer was entitled to the information under the warranty to enable them to fix the appropriate premium and to consider reinsurance requirements.[1240]

In the course of his judgement, Hirst, J. in his reading of the cases concerning the order for ships' papers as well as in the *Style*[1241] and *Liberian*[1242] cases found powerful authorities in support of the proposition that the obligation of utmost good faith continued after inception of the insurance contract. He concluded as follows:

> "Consequently, I hold that the duty of utmost good faith applied with its full rigour in relation to the giving of information of the voyage under the warranty."[1243]

This conclusion has been the subject of much criticism. The express terms of the War Risk Trading Warranties were i.a. that "... the absence of prior advice shall not affect the cover..." on the policy. The conclusion of Hirst, J. that the duty of utmost good faith finds application on the facts, are therefore neither reconcilable with the wording of the policy, nor with his own finding that the "...requirement that information of such voyage or deviation should be given to insurers as soon as practicable is not a condition precedent."[1244] It is quite difficult to understand how a right of retrospective avoidance could be established where the policy is construed as dealing with the consequences of a failure of notification and where that construction expressly does not provide for prospective discharge.[1245]

However, the courts will not always be willing to impose the principle of utmost good faith whenever the assured is required to notify the insurer under a clause in the policy. In *Hussain v Brown (No. 2)*[1246] the fire policy on a commercial premises provided amongst other things that the "assured shall as soon as possible give notice in writing to the Underwriters of any alteration likely to increase the risk of or any damage to the insured or Underwriter's liability and shall pay such reasonable premium, if any, as may be required by the Underwriters." The High Court held that the duty of utmost good faith did not attach to the requirement to give notice in this case, and distinguished the facts from *The Litsion Pride* on the ground that the clause in the war policy clearly and precisely distinguished which

---

1240 [1985] 1 Lloyd's Rep. 437, pp. 511-512; For a discussion of this case, see MERKIN, Robert (editor): op. cit., p. 119; and SOYER: *The Star Sea – a lode star?* [2001] LMCLQ 428, at p. 430.

1241 See p. 183 *supra*.

1242 *Liberian Insurance v Mosse* [1977] 2 Lloyd's Rep. 560.

1243 [1985] 1 Lloyd's Rep. 437, at p. 512.

1244 Ibid., at p. 471.

1245 BENNET: *Mapping the Doctrine of Utmost Good Faith in Insurance Contract Law* [1999] LMCLQ 165, at pp. 206.

1246 (1996) Unreported (Q.B.).

facts were to be disclosed, whereas, under the policy before the court, the disclosure obligation was too wide and expressed in technical language requiring what was called "permanent vigilance throughout the entire term of the insurance".[1247]

The decision of *Fraser Shipping Ltd. v N.J. Colton & Ors*[1248] serves as an example of a post-contractual duty of utmost good faith in relation to a variation to extend the cover. The assured needing cover for the last voyage of the "Shakir III", a single voyage under tow to Shanghai, took out a policy with the insurers. The policy incorporated the *Institute Voyage Clauses Hulls.* Soon after departure, she was ordered to Huang Pu instead. The insurers was told of this variation only one month later, at which time she was already waiting to dock after a minor collision with a Chinese vessel in a heavily congested Huang Pu port, with a tug which was unable to anchor the vessel securely, in the course of an approaching typhoon, none of which was disclosed to the insurer. The typhoon got the better of the "Shakir III", breaking the towlines and leaving her on the rocks of an island 45 miles away. Potter, L.J. held that the insurers could avoid the policy as the assured was in breach of the duty of utmost good faith in his failure to disclose facts material to the endorsement of the variation of the policy.[1249]

The basis for the application of the duty of utmost good faith in the abovementioned cases was either expressly or by implication said to be section 17 of the M.I.A. 1906. This seems to follow from the fact that at the time that the notice is required or the held-covered clause is triggered, the policy has already been concluded. Therefore, the only provision that might generate the duty of utmost good faith in this context is section 17.[1250] What is problematic though is that section 17 makes no mention of the requirement of materiality, as may be found in sections 18-20 of the M.I.A. 1906, which in turn only applies before conclusion of the policy.[1251] Similarly, the remedy of avoidance of the contract in section 17 appears to be disproportionate in the post-contractual context.[1252] Despite these, at least *prima facie*, problematic issues, it is now settled that the requirements of materiality and inducement, "which must exist before an underwriter can avoid for lack of good faith pre-contract must also apply, making due allowance for the change of context, where an underwriter seeks to avoid for lack of good faith or fraud in relation to post-contractual matters."[1253]

[1247] *The Star Sea – a lode star?* [2001] LMCLQ 428, at p. 431.
[1248] [1997] 1 Lloyd's Rep. 586.
[1249] [1997] 1 Lloyd's Rep. 586, at p. 597.
[1250] SOYER: *Continuing duty of utmost good faith in insurance contracts: still alive?* [2003] LMCLQ 39, at p. 64.
[1251] Cf. p. 187 *infra*.
[1252] Cf. p. 190 *infra*.
[1253] *The Mercandian Continent* [2001] 2 Lloyd's Rep. 563, at p. 573 *per* Longmore, L.J.

Materiality and inducement

There can be no justification for expecting the assured to disclose during the variation, something more than is required during the pre-contractual stage, i.e. facts which are not material. In *The Litsion Pride*[1254], Hirst, J. considered those circumstances to be material that "...would influence the judgement of a prudent underwriter in making the relevant decision on the topic to which the misrepresentation or non-disclosure relates."[1255]

The definition of materiality in section 18 had been used by the courts in applying the duty of utmost good faith after conclusion of a contract.[1256] In coming to the conclusion that the assureds were in breach of the post-contractual duty of utmost good faith, Potter, L.J. in *Frazer Shipping Ltd. v Colton*[1257] applied section 18 of the M.I.A. 1906. The duty to disclose circumstances material to the risk was held to exist at the time the variation was concluded by means of the signing or "scratching" of the endorsement on the policy. Potter, L.J. approved of the definition of material circumstances applied in the *Pine Top* case[1258], i.e. circumstances that, objectively assessed, would have an effect on the mind of a prudent insurer in estimating the risk proposed, without necessarily having a decisive influence on either his acceptance of that risk or the amount of premium demanded. The information received by the assured from the master of the tug and tow relating to the "anchoring of the vessel, the weather and its possible impact on the tug and tow, and the master's views on the future safety of the voyage as varied..." was accordingly held to be material.[1259]

It has been pointed out that section 18 of the M.I.A. 1906 does not lend itself to an application after the conclusion of the contract.[1260] In this regard, Hobhouse, L.J. stated in *The Star Sea*[1261]:

> "In the pre-contract situation it is possible to provide criteria for deciding what information should be disclosed and what need not be. The criterion is materiality to the acceptance of the risk proposed and the assessment of the premium. This is spelled out in the 1906 Act and was the subject of the Pine Top case. But when it comes to post-contract disclosure the criterion becomes more elusive: to what does the information have to be material? Some instructive responses have been given. Where the contract is being varied, facts must be disclosed which are material to the additional risk being

---

[1254] Cf. p. 184 *supra*.
[1255] [1985] 1 Lloyd's Rep. 437, at p. 511.
[1256] See e.g. *Fraser Shipping Ltd v N.J. Colton & Ors* [1997] 1 Lloyd's Rep. 586.
[1257] See p. 186 *supra*.
[1258] *Pan Atlantic Insurance Ltd. v Pine Top Insurance Ltd.* [1994] 2 Lloyd's Rep. 427.
[1259] [1997] 1 Lloyd's Rep. 586, at p. 594.
[1260] BENNET: *Mapping the Doctrine of Utmost Good Faith in Insurance Contract Law* [1999] LMCLQ 165, at p. 206.
[1261] [2001] 1 Lloyd's Rep. 389.

> accepted by the variation. It is not necessary to disclose facts occurring, or discovered, since the original risk was accepted material to the acceptance and rating of that risk."[1262]

An alternative analysis of the operation of held-covered clauses, doing the rounds in academic circles, is the so-called "distinct contract analysis".[1263] According to this theory, the held-covered clause gives rise to a unilateral and irrevocable offer by the insurer to extend the cover on the terms of the clause. The assured, in turn, by giving notice and agreeing to the terms of the clause and the payment of a reasonable additional premium, accepts the offer and gives consideration. Accordingly, the clause leads to a "distinct and separate contract."[1264] The implication would then be that sections 18-20 of the M.I.A. 1906, dealing with pre-contractual duties of utmost good faith, apply during the operation of the held-covered clause.[1265] Arguably, support for this analysis might be found in *Frazer Shipping Ltd. v Colton*,[1266] where Potter, L.J. referred to section 18 in the context of a held-covered clause.

The problem with this analysis is apparent. The fact is that in reality no new contract comes into existence, nor is the existing contract being reviewed *in toto*. The assured is only requesting the insurer to quote terms for extended cover, or put in another way, the assured is requesting the implementation of an extension of cover to which the insurer has already agreed.[1267] At best, the giving of notice under held-covered clauses can be said to be analogous to the presentation of the risk prior to the conclusion of the policy. The principle of utmost good faith fulfils the same function in both scenarios. Accordingly it should operate in a similar way in both situations, sharing the same strict liability nature.[1268] This is, however, a long way from viewing the extension of cover as a "separate and distinct" contract, attracting the duties in sections 18-20.

It is plain that the concept of materiality should be adapted to the context in which the duty of utmost good faith operates. Accordingly, in those instances where the cover in the policy is being extended or varied, the content of the duty applying to the giving of notice should reflect the fact that the policy is not being reviewed *in toto*.[1269] Where some circumstances relating to the original risk have changed since inception of the contract, but these circumstances have no bearing on the variation,

---

[1262] [2001] 1 Lloyd's Rep. 389, at pp. 400-401.
[1263] This analysis is preferred by SOYER: *Continuing duty of utmost good faith in insurance contracts: still alive?* [2003] LMCLQ 39, at p. 64 *et seq.*
[1264] SOYER: *Continuing duty of utmost good faith in insurance contracts: still alive?* [2003] LMCLQ 39, at p. 64.
[1265] Ibid., at p. 65.
[1266] Cf. p. 187 *supra.*
[1267] BENNET: *Mapping the Doctrine of Utmost Good Faith in Insurance Contract Law* [1999] LMCLQ 165, at pp. 204-205.
[1268] Ibid., at p. 214.
[1269] Ibid., at p. 204.

the duty of utmost good faith, therefore, does not require the assured also to notify the insurer of these circumstances.[1270] Thus, Hobhouse, J. (as he then was) held in *Iron Trades Mutual Ins. Co. Ltd. v Companhia de Seguros Imperio*: –

> "Where there is an addition to a contract, as where it is varied, there can be a further duty of disclosure, but only to the extent that it is material to the variation being proposed. If the addition does not alter the contractual rights there will be no fact that it is material to disclose and the same will apply if a variation is favourable to the insurer. It will only be when the insurer is being asked to take on some additional risk and/or needing to reassess the premium or terms of cover that disclosure of further facts could be material and, even then, the facts to be disclosed are only those which are material to what the insurer is being asked to do ...[A]ny other conclusion would lead to an absurdity; the duty of the utmost good faith does not include giving the insurer an opportunity, after he has accepted the risk and become bound, to escape from his commitment."[1271]

In similar terms, Hobhouse, L.J. remarked in *The Star Sea*[1272]:

> "Where the contract is being varied, facts must be disclosed which are material to the additional risk being accepted by the variation. It is not necessary to disclose facts occurring, or discovered, since the original risk was accepted material to the acceptance and rating of that risk. Logic would suggest that such new information might be valuable to the underwriter. It might affect how hard a bargain he would drive in exchange for agreeing to that variation; it might be relevant to his reinsurance decisions. But it need not be disclosed."[1273]

As to the requirement of inducement, the House of Lords made it clear in *Pan Atlantic v Pine Top* that an insurer would only be allowed to avoid a policy in case of a material non-disclosure or misrepresentation, where he could show that he had been induced to underwrite the risk.[1274] Adapted to the post-contractual context, the insurer would need to show that he was induced to vary the contract due to the non-disclosure or misrepresentation.[1275] As far as the requirement of inducement was concerned in *Frazer Shipping Ltd. v Colton*,[1276] Potter, L.J. accepted the evidence of the underwriters that, had they known of the relevant communications concerning the approaching typhoon and the concerns of the master, of the collision, the congestion at the port and the various delays, they would not have

---

[1270] See p. 179 *supra*, in particular fn. 1195.

[1271] (1990) Unreported (Q.B.), quoted by BENNET: *Mapping the Doctrine of Utmost Good Faith in Insurance Contract Law* [1999] LMCLQ 165, at p.204 and SOYER: *The Star Sea – a lode star?* [2001] LMCLQ 428 at p. 432-433.

[1272] [2001] 1 Lloyd's Rep. 389.

[1273] [2001] 1 Lloyd's Rep. 389, at p. 401.

[1274] Cf. p. 166 ff. *supra*.

[1275] *The Mercandian* Continent [2001] 2 Lloyd's Rep. 563, at p. 573; BENNET: *Mapping the Doctrine of Utmost Good Faith in Insurance Contract Law* [1999] LMCLQ 165, at p. 205; SOYER: *The Star Sea – a lode star?* [2001] LMCLQ 428, at p. 433.

[1276] Cf. p. 186 *supra*.

signed the endorsement. Accordingly he found that the underwriters were led to agree to the endorsement by reason of the non-disclosure.[1277]

The scope of the duty of utmost good faith in the context of held-covered clauses and other variations of the cover, should therefore be confined to those circumstances that can be said to be material to the alteration of the risk, and, furthermore, induced the insurer into agreeing to the alteration.[1278]

Remedy

The correct remedy available to the insurer, who was induced to vary the policy, after a breach of the duty of utmost good faith by the assured, is also a contentious issue. Section 17 of the M.I.A 1906 speaks of avoidance of the policy. Since the duty to disclose material facts in the context of a variation of the contract has been based on section 17, it might be argued that the same remedy of avoidance of the contract should be available for breach of the duty during variation of the risk and other similar cases, e.g. in the context of a held-covered clause. Indeed, Hirst, J. declared in *The Litsion Pride*[1279] that in his judgement, "avoidance" in section 17 meant avoidance *ab initio*. Since this was the case in relation to pre-contract avoidance, he saw no reason for putting a different meaning on the word in relation to post-contractual events.[1280]

This appears to be a very drastic and disproportionate remedy. If the section 17 remedy is available for want of utmost good faith in relation to a variation of the policy, the insurer will be able to avoid the contract and claim from the assured payments which were legitimately made under the policy. In the absence of a held-covered clause, or where the assured does not request a variation of the cover, the insurer will only be able, where indeed the risk had been altered, to avoid liability under the policy prospectively – cover up to that point will not be prejudiced.[1281] The remedy for breach of the duty of utmost good faith in failing to disclose or misrepresenting in the context of a held covered clause, should be tailored according to that context, i.e. the remedy of the insurer should accordingly be limited to avoidance of extension of the cover.[1282]

Hirst, J. circumvented the problem caused by the remedy of avoidance *ab initio* in this context by sticking to the explicit wording of section 17:

[1277] [1997] 1 Lloyd's Rep. 586, at p. 596.

[1278] BENNET: *Mapping the Doctrine of Utmost Good Faith in Insurance Contract Law* [1999] LMCLQ 165, at p. 205.

[1279] See p. 184 *supra*.

[1280] [1985] 1 Lloyd's Rep. 437, at p. 515.

[1281] BENNET: *Mapping the Doctrine of Utmost Good Faith in Insurance Contract Law* [1999] LMCLQ 165, at p. 205.

[1282] Ibid.; SOYER: *The Star Sea – a lode star?* [2001] LMCLQ 428, at p. 433.

> "Section 17 provides that the policy *may* be avoided, not that it *must* be avoided. In the pre-contract situation, no doubt the assured's default necessarily strikes at the very basis of the contract itself, so that when, ...the underwriter affirms the contract, it necessarily follows that he is electing not to rely on default, but the same considerations do not apply in the case of post-contractual default. ...I can find no authority against and much commercial good sense in favour of ...[the] submissions that in the case of post-contract breach it is open to the underwriter simply to defend the claim without avoiding the policy."[1283]

Also the Court of Appeal in *The Star Sea*[1284] was not prepared to permit the policy to be vitiated *ab initio* for breach of the post-contractual duty of utmost good faith. In the course of his judgement, Leggatt, L.J. stated:

> "In relation to amendment a duty of disclosure of facts material to the amendment will exist but the law is not, we think, clear as to whether the remedy is avoidance of the whole contract or merely of the amendment. Since inducement of the actual underwriter is necessary, there seems much to be said for the point of view that avoidance of the amendment is all that should be permitted."[1285]

It has been pointed out, and correctly so, that there can be no justification for permitting avoidance *ab initio* in the event of breach of the duty of utmost good faith which applies to held-covered clauses, or for that matter any other situation where the policy is varied after its inception.[1286] Indeed, it has been authoritatively held that there is no authority for a proposition that "a fraudulent misrepresentation leading to a variation will avoid the original contract as well as the variation."[1287] Once the duty of utmost good faith has been properly discharged with regard to the risk against which the cover had been applied for, the insurer should remain liable for prior casualties. The proper remedy of the insurer should therefore be limited to the avoidance of any extension of cover which was agreed upon on the basis of an improper presentation of that risk. Thus, "observance of utmost good faith with respect to a held-covered clause is a condition precedent to the enforceability of the insurer's promise to maintain the cover, not to the insurer's promise to grant cover in the first place."[1288]

It has been suggested that the distinct contract analysis[1289] would also provide a rational basis for the appropriate remedy for breach of utmost good faith in the context of held-covered clauses *etc.* The argument appears to be that the distinct

---

[1283] [1985] 1 Lloyd's Rep. 437, at p. 515.
[1284] [1997] 1 Lloyd's Rep. 360.
[1285] [1997] 1 Lloyd's Rep. 360, at p. 370.
[1286] BENNET: *Mapping the Doctrine of Utmost Good Faith in Insurance Contract Law* [1999] LMCLQ 165, at p. 205.
[1287] Longmore, L.J. in *The Mercandian* Continent [2001] 2 Lloyd's Rep. 563, at p. 571.
[1288] BENNET: *Mapping the Doctrine of Utmost Good Faith in Insurance Contract Law* [1999] LMCLQ 165, at p. 205.
[1289] See p. 188 *supra*.

contract analysis would allow the application of sections 18-20 of the M.I.A. 1906 and would justify the avoidance of the part of the policy that was varied by the operation of the held-covered clause.[1290] Apart from the reservations mentioned above about this analysis, this explanation seems not to admit the fact that no new contract is entered into once the held-covered clause comes into operation or the cover is varied. All that happens is that the original cover is extended or varied. Since the variation takes place after inception of the policy, sections 18-20, being expressly applicable to the pre-contractual context, cannot apply. Further to this, sections 18-20 do not provide for any separate part of the contract to be avoided.

It is of course true that these situations are very much analogous to the position before conclusion of the contract. In *The Mercandian Continent*, Longmore, L.J. held that instances where there was a variation to the contractual position are not examples of bad faith leading to the avoidance of the contract, but rather –

> "...examples of pre-contract lack of good faith because they arise before variation, renewal or application of the 'held covered' provision in the policy and avoid the variation, renewal or the application of the 'held covered' provision, as the case may be, not the entire contract."[1291]

The insured will only be entitled to rescind the entire contract *ab initio* where the breach of utmost good faith occurred before inception of the policy , as there can be no justification for allowing such an extreme remedy once the contract has been made, or where the insured deliberately does not disclose a variation of the risk to avoid additional premium and then claims[1292] under the policy upon the occurrence of a casualty.[1293]

As far as the remedy of damages is concerned, it is clear after the decision of the Court of Appeal in *Banque Keyser Ullmann SA v Skandia (UK) Ins. Co. Ltd.*[1294] that no damages will be available for breach of the pre-contractual duty of disclosure. The remedy of damages was said to be available only where a term, express or implied, of the contract was breached.[1295] The duty of disclosure was held to derive from the legal rule stated in section 18 of the M.I.A 1906, and not from an implied term, the breach of the duty therefore only giving rise to the remedy of rescission. Since the duty of utmost good faith during the performance of the contract had been

[1290] SOYER: *Continuing duty of utmost good faith in insurance contracts: still alive?* [2003] LMCLQ 39 at p. 66, quoting the *dictum* of Leggatt, L.J. in *The Star Sea* [1997] 1 Lloyd's Rep. 360 referred to above.
[1291] [2001] 2 Lloyd's Rep. 563, at p. 574.
[1292] Such a claim will arguably always be fraudulent.
[1293] BENNET: *Mapping the Doctrine of Utmost Good Faith in Insurance Contract Law* [1999] LMCLQ 165, at p. 205; SOYER: *The Star Sea – a lode star?* [2001] LMCLQ 428, at p. 433.
[1294] [1988] 2 Lloyd's Rep. 513.
[1295] Ibid., at p. 550.

based on section 17 of the M.I.A 1906 and not on an implied term, the remedy of damages should not be available in the post-contractual context either.[1296]

5.7.2 The Claims Context

It was established in older common law cases such as *Levy v Baillie*[1297], *Goulstone v Royal Insurance Co.*[1298] and particularly *Britton v Royal Insurance Co.*[1299] that a rule of law existed, even where there was no express clause in the policy, to the effect that an assured who had made a fraudulent claim forfeited the whole claim and could not recover any lesser claim that he could have honestly made.[1300] At the very latest since the judgement of the House of Lords in *The Star Sea*,[1301] it is now accepted that the principle of utmost good faith prescribed in section 17 of the M.I.A. 1906 is not confined to the pre-contract stage and that its application extends for the duration of the contract. This position was confirmed in subsequent decisions of

---

[1296] Cf. *The Good Luck* [1990] 1 Q.B. 818; [1989] 2 Lloyd's Rep. 238 where it was expressly held that the post-contractual duty of utmost good faith is not based on an implied term; also SOYER: *The Star Sea – a lode star?* [2001] LMCLQ 428, at p. 434; for more on the possibility of damages cf. 5.6.2 Remedy of the Assured *infra*.

[1297] (1837) 7 Bing. 349; Mr. Levy effected a policy of insurance against fire with Mr. Baillie and others. The policy contained a condition that "if there appear fraud in the claim made, or false swearing or affirming in support thereof, the claimant shall forfeit all benefit under the policy." After the premises of Mr. Levy, an upholsterer, were subsequently burnt down, he submitted a claim for loss of stock to the amount of £1,085. The insurers contended that the claim was fraudulent. The jury found for the assured and awarded, however, only £500 damages. The insurers then contended that the verdict was, in effect, a verdict in their favour, pointing out that a claim for £1,085, where an assured had lost only £500, amounted to fraud, which avoided the policy. The Court accepted the insurers' plea and granted a new trial.

[1298] (1858) 1 F. & F. 276; The assured, Mr. Goulstone lived together with his wife in their home. In 1852, the assured's household effects were to be sold in execution. The assured was left only with the pieces of furniture which were his wife's under a deed of settlement concluded at their marriage a few years earlier. Upon becoming insolvent in 1854, the assured declared that the only furniture he had was the pieces belonging to his wife under the settlement and that they had been valued by a broker at £50. After a fire occurred in the family house under dubious circumstances, the assured claimed on an insurance policy against fire, *i.a.* an amount of £260 for loss of private household furniture, linen, china etc. During the trial, the assured admitted that he had not acquired new furniture since his insolvency. Pollock, C.B. stated the law to be as follows: "If the claim was fraudulent the plaintiff cannot recover…" He directed the jury to consider "… whether the claim was fraudulent, i.e., whether it was wilfully false in any substantial respect; for instance as to the private furniture which was sworn to be worth only £50 in 1854, and has not since been added to." The jury delivered a verdict against the assured. Cf. p. 206 *infra*.

[1299] (1866) 4 F. & F. 905; For a discussion of the this case, cf. p. 194 *infra*.

[1300] Cf. Mance, L.J. in *Agapitos and Others v Agnew (The Aegeon)* [2002] 2 Lloyd's Rep. 42; also Hobhouse, L.J. in *The Star Sea* [2001] 1 Lloyd's Rep. 389.

[1301] [2001] 1 Lloyd's Rep. 389: Lord Clyde at p. 392 said that confining section 17 to pre-contractual negotiations "…appears to be past praying for." Hobhouse, L.J., towards the end of p. 399, pointed out without any reservations that there "are many judicial statements that the duty of good faith can continue after the contract has been entered into."

the Court of Appeal.[1302] Although, as will be pointed out below, the common law cases mentioned above acknowledged the application of the principle of good faith to the contract after its inception, they established the fraudulent claim rule before the M.I.A 1906 and section 17 came into force. Moreover, there is no evidence that Sir Mackenzie Chalmers had the earlier authorities on fraudulent claims in mind when he drafted section 17.[1303] The question that arises in this context is whether section 17 can be said to apply in the claims context and, if so, what the relationship would be between the fraudulent claims rule at common law and section 17.[1304]

The fraudulent claims rule

It is agreed among judges and academic writers alike[1305] that the fullest description of the common law rule is to be found in *Britton v Royal Insurance Co.*[1306] The case was concerned with a policy against fire, containing a clause to the effect that the policy should be void in the event of a fraudulent claim. It was alleged that the assured took advantage of the fire to make a fraudulent claim. Mr. Justice Willes stated the legal position to be as follows:

> "Of course, if the assured set fire to his house, he could not recover. That is clear. But it is not less clear that, even suppose that it were not wilful, yet as it is a contract of indemnity only, that is, if the claim is fraudulent, it is defeated altogether. That is, suppose the insured made a claim for twice the amount insured and lost, thus seeking to put the office off its guard, and in the result recover more than he is entitled to, that would be a wilful fraud, and the consequence is that he could not recover anything. This is a defence quite different from that of wilful arson. It gives the go by to the origin of the fire, and it amounts to this – that the assured took advantage of the fire to make a fraudulent claim. The law upon such a case is in accordance with justice, and also with sound policy. The law is that a person who has made such a fraudulent claim could not be permitted to recover at all. The contract of insurance is one of perfect good faith on both sides, and it is most important that such good faith should be maintained. It is the common practice to insert in fire policies conditions such that they shall be void in the

[1302] *K/S Merc-Scandia XXXXII v Certain Lloyd's Underwriters subscribing to Lloyd's Policy no. 25T 105487 and Ocean Marine Insurance Co. Ltd.. And Others (The Mercandian Continent)* [2001] 2 Lloyd's Rep. 563, where Longmore, L.J. considered, at p. 575, that it was not open to the Court of Appeal "to decide that s. 17 of the Act has no application after the formation of the contract." Also: *The Aegeon* [2002] 2 Lloyd's Rep. 42 at p.45 where Mance, L.J. agreed to proceed on that basis, expressing the hope that "the House of Lords judicially or Parliament legislatively might one day look at the point again..." Also see in general GILMAN: op. cit., Vol. III, pars. 579I-M; EGGERS et al.: op. cit., Chapter 10.

[1303] *The Mercandian* Continent [2001] 2 Lloyd's Rep. 563, at p. 571.

[1304] See GILMAN: op. cit., Vol. III, par. 579K, where the author states: "Although powerful arguments in logic can undoubtedly be advanced in favour of the proposition that the duty should apply in its full rigour in those post-contractual contexts where it has been recognised, the potentially undesirable and unsatisfactory consequences of imposing a duty of similar scope, in particular in the context of claims, point to different conclusion."

[1305] *The Aegeon* [2002] 2 Lloyd's Rep. 42, at p. 45; EGGERS, Peter MacDonald *Remedies for the failure to observe the utmost good faith* [2003] LMCLQ 2, at p. 257.

[1306] Cf. fn. 1299 *supra*.

event of a fraudulent claim; and there was such a condition in the present case. Such a condition is only in accordance with legal principle and sound policy. It would be most dangerous to permit parties to practise such frauds, and then, notwithstanding their falsehood and fraud in the claim, to recover the real value of the goods consumed. And if there is wilful falsehood and fraud in the claim, the insured forfeits all claim upon the policy."[1307]

It is clear from this *dictum*, that, whatever the precise girth of the remedy, good faith was meant not only to be relevant before the signing of the policy but also extended after its conclusion. The fact that good faith had to be *maintained* leaves no room for any interpretation other than that the principle had to be maintained throughout the duration of the contract. It is further apparent that the fraudulent claims rule flowed from the application of the principle of good faith in the claims context. Lord Mansfield found in *Carter v Boehm* that good faith was the governing principle in all contracts and dealings and that the "reason of the rule which obliges parties to disclose, is to prevent fraud, and to encourage good faith".[1308] Willes, J.'s statements did not detract from that position. The reason for the rule, as stated by him, which prevents a fraudulent assured from recovering under the policy, was exactly that: to prevent fraud, and to encourage good faith. This goal – the prevention of fraud – is therefore shared by both the pre- and post-contractual duties, also in the claims context, and it has been said to have been the single focus of the courts in applying good faith.[1309]

The definition of fraud proposed by the House of Lords in *Derry v Peek*[1310] has been applied to delineate the scope of the fraudulent claims jurisdiction.[1311] Lord Herschell after a thorough discussion of earlier authorities, found these to show that a fraud would be established if the following is shown:

"First, in order to sustain an action of deceit, there must be proof of fraud, and nothing short of that will suffice. Secondly, fraud is proved when it is shewn that a false representation has been made (1) knowingly, or (2) without belief in its truth, or (3) recklessly, careless whether it be true or false. Although I have treated the second and third as distinct cases, I think the third is but an instance of the second, for one who makes a statement under such circumstances can have no real belief in the truth of what he states. To prevent a false statement being fraudulent, there must, I think, always be an honest belief in its truth. And this probably covers the whole ground, for one who knowingly alleges that which is false, has obviously no such honest belief. Thirdly, if fraud be proved, the motive of the person guilty of it is immaterial. It matters not that

[1307] (1866) 4 F. & F. 905, at pp. 908-909.
[1308] Cf. p. 101 *supra*.
[1309] EGGERS, Peter MacDonald *Remedies for the failure to observe the utmost good faith* [2003] LMCLQ 2, at p. 254.
[1310] (1889) 14 Appl Cas. 337, at p. 374.
[1311] BENNET: *Mapping the Doctrine of Utmost Good Faith in Insurance Contract Law* [1999] LMCLQ 165, at p. 207; *Lek v Matthews* (1927) 29 Ll.L.Rep. 141, at p. 145.

> there was no intention to cheat or injure the person to whom the statement was made."[1312]

Viscount Summers in *Lek v Mathews*[1313], a case dealing with a diamond merchant who submitted what turned out to be a false claim for rare stamps stolen from his collections, considered a claim to be false, not only if it was deliberately invented but also if it was "made recklessly, not caring whether it is true or false but only seeking to succeed in the claim."[1314]

Accordingly three forms of fraudulent claims have been identified. The first form occurs where the assured intends to obtain a benefit out of the policy to which he knows that he is not entitled, and therefore deceives the insurer. This will be the case where the assured deliberately brought about the loss, or where the assured claims a loss which is not real in that no loss was suffered, or similarly, where the assured exaggerates or inflates a claim based on a valid loss.[1315] However, as Hoffmann, L.J. pointed out in *Orakpo v Barclays Insurance Services*,[1316] fraud should not be readily inferred from the fact that an assured submitted a doubtful or even exaggerated claim:

> "In cases where nothing is misrepresented or concealed, and the loss adjuster is in as good a position to form a view of the validity or value of the claim as the insured, it will be a legitimate reason that the assured was merely putting forward a starting figure for negotiation."[1317]

This position seems to be supported by a judgement of Lord Coleridge in *Norton v The Royal Fire and Life Assurance Company*[1318], a case about a grocer who submitted an exaggerated claim for stocks lost in a fire on his premises. Lord Coleridge agreed with the judge at first instance that although the assured submitted an exaggerated claim and although it was wrong to do so, the question the jury had to decide was whether the claim could be said to be fraudulent, in the sense of an intention to deceive and defraud the company and obtain from it money he had no right to and that, that must depend on all the circumstances.[1319]

The question as to what will constitute an exaggerated claim in this context is not an easy one to answer. The Court of Appeal in *Orakpo* did not have to decide this

---

1312 (1889) 14 Appl Cas. 337, at p. 374.
1313 (1927) 29 Ll.L.Rep. 141.
1314 Ibid, at p. 145.
1315 SOYER: *Continuing duty of utmost good faith in insurance contracts: still alive?* [2003] LMCLQ 39, at p. 44.
1316 [1995] L.R.L.R. 443; also BENNET: *Mapping the Doctrine of Utmost Good Faith in Insurance Contract Law* [1999] LMCLQ 165, at p. 205.
1317 [1995] L.R.L.R. 443, at p. 451.
1318 (1885) 1 T.L.R. 460.
1319 Ibid, at p. 461.

point, but was of the opinion that the claim would be fraudulent if it were "*substantially*" exaggerated.[1320] The Court of Appeal in *Galloway v Guardian Royal Exchange (UK)*,[1321] was not of one mind as to what would be a substantial exaggeration where an assured claimed for general goods burgled from his home to the value of £16,000. The assured claimed an additional £2,000 in respect of a computer, which part of the claim was based on a loss that the assured, in fact, did not suffer. Lord Woolf considered a claim to be substantially fraudulent where the fraud was material, which again turned on the relation of the fraud to the claim as a whole.[1322] On the facts, the fraudulent part of the claim amounted to about 10 per cent of the claim as a whole, which was considered to be a substantial amount. The whole claim was, therefore, tainted by fraud. Millet L.J. did not find this solution sensible since it would lead to the "absurd conclusion that the greater the genuine loss, the larger the fraudulent claim which may be made at the same time without penalty."[1323] The correct approach, according to Lord Millet, was to consider the fraudulent claim as if it were the only claim and then to consider whether, taken in isolation, the making of that claim by the insured was sufficiently serious to justify stigmatising it as a breach of his duty of utmost good faith so as to avoid the policy. It has been suggested that a fair decision would be reached if both tests were applied at the same time. A claim would, in accordance with this suggestion, be fraudulent if the exaggeration was substantial either in proportion to the total claim or in absolute terms.[1324] In a recent South African case, Marais, J.A. found in the Supreme of Court of Appeal that mere exaggeration is not a proof of fraud, but that it "must appear at least that it was knowinlgly exaggerated which implies that it was not made *in good faith*."[1325] (Own emphasis)

The second form of fraud is where the assured does not entertain an honest belief in the truth of the claim.[1326] Similarly, the third form would occur where the assured submits his claim recklessly, not caring whether it is true or false, and where the claim is in fact false.[1327] Apart from these three classic forms of fraud, a fourth has recently been identified by the English courts, i.e. where the assured believes that he has suffered the loss claimed, but seeks by some lie to improve or embellish the facts surrounding the claim. Where an assured acts in this manner,

---

1320 Cf. the judgement of Hoffmann, L.J. at p. 451 and that of Sir Roger Parker at p. 452 of the report.

1321 [1999] Lloyd's Rep. I.R. 209; for a discussion of this case, cf. BENNET: *Mapping the Doctrine of Utmost Good Faith in Insurance Contract Law* [1999] LMCLQ 165, at p. 208.

1322 [1999] Lloyd's Rep. I.R. 209, at p. 213.

1323 Ibid., at p. 214.

1324 SOYER: *Continuing duty of utmost good faith in insurance contracts: still alive?* [2003] LMCLQ 39, at p. 46.

1325 *Schoeman v Constantia Insurance Co. Ltd.* 2003 (6) SA 313, at p. 325.

1326 SOYER: *Continuing duty of utmost good faith in insurance contracts: still alive?* [2003] LMCLQ 39, at p. 44.

1327 Ibid.

he is said to use a "fraudulent device".[1328] The concept of fraudulent device was the subject of the judgement of Mance, L.J. in *The Aegeon*.[1329] The assured in that case took out a hull and machinery policy whilst the vessel was undergoing maintenance, including a condition that it was warranted that the LSA[1330] certificate had to be updated before hot works was to commence. Subsequent to a fire causing the loss of the vessel the assured claimed against the policy. The insurers defended the claim for breaches of warranty, i.a. that hot works commenced before the certificate was updated. In disclosure the assured presented sworn statements by two workmen in which they attested that hot works commenced on the vessel earlier than the assured alleged. The insurers subsequently claimed to be entitled to avoid the policy for fraud in that the assured "knowingly, falsely and fraudulently misrepresented that no hot works were carried out..." before the alleged date. The question that Mance, L.J. under these circumstances had to consider was whether the underlying rationale of the fraudulent claims rule should extend to a situation where fraudulent devices were used and invalidate not merely the whole of a claim where part proves good, but the whole of a claim where the whole proves otherwise good.[1331] The Lord Justice answered the question in the affirmative:

> "On the basis (which the cases show and I would endorse) that the policy behind the fraudulent claim rule remains as powerful today as ever, there is, in my view, force in [the] submission that it either applies, or should be matched by an equivalent rule, in the case of use of a fraudulent device to promote a claim – even though at the end of a trial it may be shown that the claim was all along in all other respects valid. The fraud must of course be directly related to and intended to promote the claim (unlike the deceit in The Mercandian Continent)."[1332]

Mance, L.J. pointed out that an assured usually sought to improve or embellish the facts surrounding his claim where he was concerned about his prospects of success and wished to improve his chances. Accordingly, he held that where the fraud was directly related to, and intended to promote, the claim, the policy behind the fraudulent claims rule – namely to prevent the assured from gaining by his own fraud and to encourage good faith – also applied and justified the application of the sanction of forfeiture.[1333] He ventured to formulate a rule to cater for fraudulent devices in the following terms:

> "Tentatively, I would suggest that the Courts should only apply the fraudulent claim rule to the use of fraudulent devices or means which would, if believed, have tended, objectively but prior to any final determination at trial of the parties' rights, to yield a not

[1328] *The Aegeon* [2002] 2 Lloyd's Rep. 42, at p. 49.
[1329] Cf. previous footnote.
[1330] Lloyd's Salvage Association.
[1331] [2002] 2 Lloyd's Rep. 42, at p. 47.
[1332] Ibid., at p. 51.
[1333] Ibid.

> insignificant improvement in the insured's prospects – whether they be prospects of obtaining a settlement, or a better settlement, or of winning at trial."[1334]

Although the whole concept of *fraudulent devices* may be fairly new and perhaps even controversial, the important aspect of the judgement for the purpose of this paragraph is that Mance, L.J. accepted that the fraudulent claims rule was still applicable and that the policy behind the fraudulent claims rule was still the prevention of fraud and the encouragement of good faith.

The Litsion Pride and the application of section 17

It was first suggested by Hirst, J. in *Black King Shipping v Massie, The Litsion Pride*[1335] that the general duty of utmost good faith as required in section 17 of the M.I.A 1906 could be applied to the claims context. This part of the case was concerned with a letter that the assureds concocted in order to deceive the insurer into believing that their failure to notify the insurer of entrance into a war zone was due to an innocent oversight. The judge held that the concocted letter constituted a fraud directly connected to the claim and as a result, was fatal to it.[1336] The insurer averred that, since the test was one of utmost good faith, it was not necessary to establish fraud in this instance, but that proof of "deliberate non-disclosure or ... of misrepresentation, albeit negligent or even innocent..." would suffice.[1337] Hirst, J., after finding that the "general principle requiring utmost good faith must apply" in the context of claims, proceeded to explain the scope of application of section 17 as follows:

> "However, in contrast to the pre-contract situation, the precise ambit of the duty in the claims context has not been developed by the authorities; indeed no case has been cited to me where it has been considered outside the fraud context in relation to claims. It must be right, I think, by comparison with the Style and Liberian cases, to go so far as to hold that the duty in the claims sphere extends to culpable misrepresentation or non-disclosure."[1338]

Hirst, J. saw no reason to limit the scope of fraudulent claims to frauds affecting the genuineness or the amount of the claim, provided that the materiality test was satisfied.[1339] In holding thus, Hirst, J. is said to have been "impelled by his vision of a uniform post-formation duty...."[1340] In order to bring the fraudulent claims rule under the post-contractual duty of utmost good faith that had been established in

---

[1334] Ibid.

[1335] [1985] 1 Lloyd's Rep. 437, at p. 512; see p. 184 *supra*; also see the discussion of this case in GILMAN: op. cit., Vol. III, par. 579L.

[1336] [1985] 1 Lloyd's Rep. 437, at p 507.

[1337] Ibid., at p. 507.

[1338] Ibid., at p. 512.

[1339] [1985] 1 Lloyd's Rep. 437, at p. 513.

[1340] BENNET: *Mapping the Doctrine of Utmost Good Faith in Insurance Contract Law* [1999] LMCLQ 165, at p. 213.

cases like *Overseas Commodities Ltd. v Style*[1341] – which of course did not deal with fraud in any strict sense, but with the giving of notice in relation to held-covered clauses – Hirst, J. had to broaden the scope of the duty in the claims context to include not only fraud, but also what he called "culpability".[1342]

Evans, J. in *The Captain Panagos D.P.*,[1343] where the assured caused its vessel to be a total loss after deliberately running it aground and then setting fire to it, subsequently approved of the judgement of Hirst, J. He was of the opinion that a fraudulent claim, by which he meant a claim based on facts which to the knowledge of the assured were untrue, could be defeated without the assistance of an implied term.[1344] This appears to be a statement of the fraudulent claim rule at common law as pronounced by Willes, J. in *Britton*.[1345] Evans, J. then went on to state that any breach of the duty of the utmost good faith in connection with claims, including fraud, would breach an implied term of the policy, irrespective of any honest part of the claim.[1346] However, since in his own words, these issues did not arise for decision, his remarks in approval of the *Litsion Pride* must be considered to be *obiter*.[1347]

The effect of these *dicta* is that the assured is under a continuing duty in the claims context to observe the utmost good faith, or in the words of Hirst, J. not to make culpable non-disclosures or misrepresentations when submitting a claim. The operation of this duty would therefore be the same as the pre-contractual duty, i.e. the insurer could rely on the duty if the assured failed to disclose or misrepresent material facts.[1348]

This broad interpretation of what would constitute a breach of utmost good faith in the claims context, did not survive later decisions of the Court of Appeal. In *Orakpo v Barclays Insurance Services*[1349] the majority of the Court of Appeal was of the opinion that fraud was necessary in order to breach good faith. The Court decided in favour of the defendant insurer that the policy was voidable since it had been induced by a material misrepresentation by the assured. The insurer's argument that the claim was grossly exaggerated and fraudulent was therefore dealt with *obiter*. Hoffmann, L.J. warned, in his discussion of the fraudulent claim defence, that fraud should not be readily inferred from the fact that the assured made an exaggerated or doubtful claim:

1341 Cf. p. 183 *supra*.
1342 [1985] 1 Lloyd's Rep. 437, at p. 512.
1343 *Continental Illinois National Bank & Trust Co. of Chicago and Xenofon Maritime S.A. v Alliance Assurance Co. Ltd.* [1986] 2 Lloyd's Rep. 470.
1344 Ibid, at p. 511.
1345 Cf. p. 194 *supra*.
1346 [1986] 2 Lloyd's Rep. 470, at p. 511-512.
1347 Ibid., at p. 511.
1348 SOYER: *The Star Sea – a lode star?* [2001] LMCLQ 428, at p. 436.
1349 [1995] L.R.L.R. 443.

"In cases where nothing is misrepresented or concealed, and the loss adjuster is in as good a position to form a view of the validity or value of the claim as the insured, it will be a legitimate reason that the assured was merely putting forward a starting figure for negotiation. But in cases in which fraud in the making of the claim has been averred and proved, I think it should discharge the insurer from all liability."[1350]

Similarly, Sir Roger Parker only spoke of fraud in the claims context as giving the insurer the opportunity to defeat the claim and the policy. Also, in *Galloway v Guardian Royal Exchange (U.K.) Ltd.*.,[1351] there was no support for the contention that anything less than fraud would afford the insurer relief in the claims context. Finally, the House of Lords in *The Star Sea*[1352] confirmed that the pre-contract duty of utmost good faith could not apply in all its broadness after the inception of the policy. Hobhouse, L.J. said:

"It is not right to reason, as the defendants submitted that your Lordships should, from the existence of an extensive duty pre-contract positively to disclose all material facts to the conclusion that post-contract there is a similarly extensive obligation to disclose all facts which the insurer has an interest in knowing and which might affect his conduct. The Courts have consistently set their face against allowing the assured's duty of good faith to be used by the insurer as an instrument for enabling the insurer himself to act in bad faith. An inevitable consequence in the post-contract situation is that the remedy of avoidance of the contract is in practical terms wholly one-sided."[1353]

Further on in his judgement, Lord Hobhouse discussed the judgement of Willes, J. in *Britton*, and made it clear that in that judgement and others before it, the defence to the claim was indeed linked to the observation of good faith, but that it was specifically based upon the actual fraud of the assured in submitting the claim.[1354] In concluding his judgement on that part of the case that dealt with fraudulent claims, Hobhouse, L.J. held that for "the defendants to succeed in their defence under this part of the case the defendants have to show that the claim was made fraudulently."[1355] Although it appears, therefore, as if Hirst, J.'s attempt at establishing a uniform duty of utmost good faith, both before and for the duration of the policy, by opening up its application in the claims context, was not successful,[1356] his suggestion that section 17 applies in this context remains contentious.

1350 Ibid., at p. 451.
1351 Cf. fn. 1321 *supra.*
1352 *Manifest Shipping & Co. Ltd. v Uni-Polaris Insurance Co. Ltd. & La Réunion Européene (The Star Sea)* [2001] 1 Lloyd's Rep. 389.
1353 Ibid., at p. 401.
1354 Ibid., at p. 403.
1355 Ibid., at p. 405.
1356 SOYER: *Continuing duty of utmost good faith in insurance contracts: still alive?* [2003] LMCLQ 39, at p. 53; cf. also BENNET: *Mapping the Doctrine of Utmost Good Faith in Insurance Contract Law* [1999]

In *Orakpo*, Sir Roger Parker was of the opinion that a fraudulent claim allowed the insurer not only to reject the claim, but also to avoid the policy:

> "It appears to me that it is contrary to reason to allow an insurer to avoid a policy for material non-disclosure or misrepresentation on inception, but to say that, if there is subsequently a deliberate attempt by fraud to extract money from the insurer for alleged losses which had never been incurred, it is only the claim which is forfeit."[1357]

Although there is no mention of section 17 in this *dictum*, nor in the rest of Sir Parker's speech, it is clear that by suggesting that the policy should be avoided for a fraudulent claim, he had in mind the remedy for breach of the utmost good faith as stipulated for in that section.[1358]

In *Galloway*,[1359] the Court of Appeal upheld an analysis of the fraudulent claims jurisdiction as falling under the doctrine of utmost good faith.[1360] Especially the judgement of Millet, L.J. was tainted in terms reminiscent of section 17 of the M.I.A. 1906. The Lord Justice said about the fraudulent claim that "the making of that claim by the insured is sufficiently serious to justify stigmatising it as a breach of his duty of good faith so as to avoid the policy."[1361]

In *The Star Sea* Lord Scott,[1362] finding "debatable" the question whether the presentation of a fraudulent claim should be regarded as a breach of the continuing duty of utmost good faith under section 17, entitling the insurer to avoidance *ab initio*, was not prepared to decide this issue. It was not necessary in that case to decide the point since the assured had been held not to have committed a fraud. Hobhouse, L.J. started his discussion of the fraudulent claims rule by stating that although insurance policies often provided expressly for the consequences of a fraudulent claim –

> "...it [was] also possible for principles drawn from the general law to apply to an existing contract – on the better view, frustration [was] an example of this as [was] the principle that a party [should] not be allowed to take advantage of his own unlawful act. It [was] such a principle upon which the defendants [relied] in the present case."[1363]

LMCLQ 165, where the author suggests at p. 214 that "it is difficult to see any reason in principle for the law to adopt a position somewhere between fraud and strict liability."

1357 [1995] L.R.L.R. 443 at p. 406.

1358 BENNET: *Mapping the Doctrine of Utmost Good Faith in Insurance Contract Law* [1999] LMCLQ 165, at p. 210.

1359 Cf. fn. 1321 *supra*.

1360 BENNET: *Mapping the Doctrine of Utmost Good Faith in Insurance Contract Law* [1999] LMCLQ 165, at p. 210.

1361 [1999] Lloyd's Rep. I.R. 209, at p. 214.

1362 [2001] 1 Lloyd's Rep. 389 at p. 413.

1363 Ibid., at pp. 402-403.

He stated the law on fraudulent claims to be as follows:

> "The law is that the insured who has made a fraudulent claim may not recover the claim which could have been honestly made. The principle is well established and has certainly existed since the early 19th century (Halsbury's Laws of England, 4th ed., reissue vol. 25 (1994) p. 284 par. 492, Welford and Otter-Barry Fire Insurance, 4th ed. (1948) p. 289 et seq.). This result is not dependent upon the inclusion in the contract of a term having that effect or the type of insurance; it is the consequence of a rule of law. Just as the law will not allow an insured to commit a crime and then use it as a basis for recovering an indemnity (Berisford v. Royal Insurance Co. Ltd., [1937] 2 K.B. 197), so it will not allow an insured who has made a fraudulent claim to recover. The logic is simple. The fraudulent insured must not be allowed to think: if the fraud is successful, then I will gain; if it is unsuccessful, I will lose nothing."[1364]

While Hobhouse, L.J. based the fraudulent claims rule on a rule of law he stopped short of stating expressly that section 17 did not apply. Nevertheless, his exposition of the law regarding fraudulent claims cannot be faulted.

Whereas the House of Lords did not provide a conclusive answer to the question whether a fraudulent claim would amount to a breach of utmost good faith and in section 17,[1365] Mance, L.J. attempted to clarify the position and ventured where the Law Lords feared to tread in the subsequent matter of the *The Aegeon.*[1366] Although *obiter*, Mance, L.J. considered the relationship between fraudulent claims and the post-contractual duty of utmost good faith. He remarked that it was indicated by the authorities that there were differences between a fraudulent claim to recover a non-existent or exaggerated loss on the one hand, and a breach of the duty of utmost good faith in section 17 on the other.[1367] Recognizing that the state of the law was "imperfect" and "fettered by section 17", he suggested that an acceptable solution would be "to treat the common law rules governing the making of a fraudulent claim (including the use of fraudulent device) as falling outside the scope of section 17."[1368]

It is now said to be settled that section 17 has no application in the fraudulent claims context.[1369] Fraudulent claims, it has been suggested, should therefore be

---

[1364] Ibid., at p. 403.

[1365] Cf. the judgement of Hobhouse, L.J. [2001] 1 Lloyd's Rep. 389, at p. 404 where he held: "As regards the question, academic in the Orakpo case and academic in the present case save as a pleading point, whether the making of a fraudulent claim would entitle the insurer to avoid the contract ab initio, that is a point upon which the judgements in Orakpo cannot be treated as fully authoritative in view of the contractual analysis there adopted."

[1366] *Agapitos and Others v Agnew (The Aegeon)* [2002] 2 Lloyd's Rep. 42.

[1367] Ibid., at p. 50.

[1368] Ibid., at p. 53.

[1369] SOYER: *Continuing duty of utmost good faith in insurance contracts: still alive?* [2003] LMCLQ 39 at p. 59.

dealt with by principles of contract law, even if there is no express term in the policy to this effect.[1370]

Materiality and Inducement in the claims context

The problematic question of what constitutes material facts in the claims context only became relevant after the finding in *The Litsion Pride*[1371] that section 17 applied in the claims context. As far as the fraudulent claims rule was concerned, both Mance, L.J. in *The Aegeon*[1372] and Rix, J. in *Royal Boskalis*[1373] were of the opinion that, as a result of the nature of a fraudulent claim, there was no additional test of materiality, i.e. the test of materiality was built into the concept of a fraudulent claim.[1374] In this regard, Mance, L.J. held:

> "...to the extent that loss claimed is non-existent, the claim will fail anyway and the fraud is clearly material in so far as it amounted to an attempt to recover for non-existent loss. But the real bite of the fraudulent claim rule is to forfeit even the genuine part of any claim; and the fraud by definition is not material in any ordinary sense to the genuine part. Thus, it is sufficient for the rule to apply that the fraud occurs in making a claim and relates to a part of the claim which, when viewed discretely, is not itself immaterial or unsubstantial."[1375]

Hirst, J., applying section 17 to the fraudulent claims rule, held that material facts in this context were facts which might influence the prudent underwriter in his decision to accept, reject or compromise the claim.[1376] Rix, J. in *Royal Boskalis Westminster NV v Mountain*[1377] considered that if section 17 were extended in the manner suggested by Hirst, J., he would formulate the test as follows:

> "If the duty of utmost good faith is to be given a wide scope in the claims context, it seems to me to make sense that the test of materiality should depend on the ultimate legal relevance to a defence under the policy of the non-disclosure or misrepresentation relied on as a breach."[1378]

The House of Lords in *The Star Sea*[1379] did not decide whether the section 17 duty of utmost good faith was to be extended to the claims context. In dealing with this issue, Scott, L.J., referring to the judgement of Rix, J. in *Royal Boskalis*, considered

1370 Ibid.
1371 See p. 199 *supra*.
1372 [2002] 2 Lloyd's Rep. 42.
1373 [1997] L.R.L.R. 523, at p. 599.
1374 [2002] 2 Lloyd's Rep. 42, at p. 51.
1375 Ibid., at pp. 51-52.
1376 [1985] 1 Lloyd's Rep. 437, at p. 513; also see GILMAN: op. cit., Vol. III, par. 579L, and SOYER: *The Star Sea – a lode star?* [2001] LMCLQ 428, at p. 436.
1377 [1997] L.R.L.R. 523.
1378 Ibid., at p. 598.
1379 *Manifest Shipping & Co. Ltd. v Uni-Polaris Insurance Co. Ltd. & La Réunion Européene (The Star Sea)* [2001] 1 Lloyd's Rep. 389; see p. 202 *infra*.

that in the light of the draconian remedy of avoidance *ab initio*, materiality would become highly relevant.[1380] The problem, however, was the yardstick by means of which materiality was to be measured. It was argued by the insurer in *The Star Sea* that the test for materiality should be analogous to the rule that any "document, which, it is not unreasonable to suppose, may tend either to advance the case of the party seeking discovery, or to damage the case of his adversary" needed to be disclosed.[1381] Scott, L.J. said that such a test would lead to a massive duty of disclosure in the claims context and have the result that an assured would have to be advised to swamp his insurer with a mass of facts and information which might have some conceivable relevance to an issue in the case. Such a duty, according to the Lord Justice, had neither commercial justification nor sense.[1382]

In *The Mercandian Continent*,[1383] the Court of Appeal was concerned, not with a fraudulent claim in any strict sense, but with a fraud that was loosely connected with the claim. The assured in this case was a ship-repairer who was liable for negligent repairs carried out on *The Mercandian Continent*. The assured made a claim on its liability insurer, the latter agreeing to take over the defence of the claim against the owners. The assured subsequently provided the insurer's solicitors with a fraudulent document, which it thought might assist them on the issue of jurisdiction in the English Court. The insurer subsequently discovered the fraud and avoided the policy for breach of the section 17 duty of utmost good faith. Although Longmore, L.J. acknowledged that this case was therefore not one where the assured brought a claim, let alone a fraudulent one, the Lord Justice did make important remarks as far as the application of section 17 of the M.I.A. 1906 in the context of fraud was concerned.[1384] Longmore, L.J. stated that it must have been the intention of Parliament that the application of section 17 in the post-contractual context should be subject to the same requirements as before the policy was concluded. It was well recognized that before an insurer could avoid for non-disclosure or misrepresentation before conclusion of the policy, the fact not disclosed or misrepresented must have been material to the knowledge of the prudent underwriter for his assessment of the risk and must have induced the underwriter into underwriting the policy.[1385] He then stated:

> "In my judgement these requirements which must exist before an underwriter can avoid for lack of good faith pre-contract must also apply, making due allowance for the change of context, where an underwriter seeks to avoid for lack of good faith or fraud in relation to post-contractual matters. In particular the requirement of inducement which exists for

[1380] Ibid., at p. 412.
[1381] Ibid., at p. 413.
[1382] Ibid.
[1383] *K/S Merc Scandia v Certain Lloyd's Underwriters (The Mercandian Continent)* [2002] 2 Lloyd's Rep. 563.
[1384] Ibid., at p. 571.
[1385] Ibid., at p. 573.

> pre-contract lack of good faith must exist in an appropriate form before an underwriter can avoid the entire contract for post-contract lack of good faith."[1386]

In order to avoid the application of the extreme remedy of avoidance *ab initio*, Longmore, L.J. consequently set out to limit the application of section 17 in the post-contractual context. He stated that since avoidance *ab initio* was an even more extreme remedy than termination of contract which would be available for repudiatory breach of contract, it would be unjust to allow the insurer to avoid liability for all valid claims previously settled as well as the instant claim without a requirement that the conduct relied upon should be as serious as repudiatory conduct.[1387] Subsequently, Longmore L.J. came to the following solution:

> "Section 17 states that the remedy is the remedy of avoidance but does not lay down the situations in which avoidance is appropriate. It is, in my judgement, only appropriate to invoke the remedy of avoidance in a post-contractual context in situations analogous to situations where the insurer has a right to terminate for breach. For this purpose (A) the fraud must be material in the sense that the fraud would have an effect on underwriters' ultimate liability as Mr. Justice Rix held in Royal Boskalis and (B) the gravity of the fraud or its consequences must be such as would enable the underwriters, if they wished to do so, to terminate for breach of contract. Often these considerations will amount to the same thing; a materially fraudulent breach of good faith, once the contract has been made, will usually entitle the insurers to terminate the contract. Conversely, fraudulent conduct entitling insurers to bring the contract to an end could only be material fraud. It is in this way that the law of post-contract good faith can be aligned with the insurers' contractual remedies. The right to avoid the contract with retrospective effect is, therefore, only exercisable in circumstances where the innocent party would, in any event, be entitled to terminate the contract for breach."[1388]

The requirement of materiality was, moreover, held to be a requirement for the operation of the fraudulent claims rule. Longmore, L.J. referred to *Goulstone v Royal Insurance Co.*[1389] as authority for this finding, in particular the statement of Chief Baron Pollock in that case to the effect that the question was whether a claim on an insurer was fraudulent i.e. whether it was wilfully false in any substantial respect. The assured in *Goulstone* submitted a greatly exaggerated claim in the amount of £260 for private household furniture, linen, china etc. allegedly lost in a fire in the family house. Pollock, C.B. directed the jury that the question that came up for decision was –

> "...whether the claim [had been] fraudulent, i.e., whether it [had been] wilfully false in any substantial respect; for instance, as to the private furniture, which was sworn to be worth only £50 in 1854, and has not since been added to."[1390]

[1386] Ibid., at p. 573.
[1387] Ibid.
[1388] Ibid., at p. 575.
[1389] (1858) 1 F. & F. 276.
[1390] Ibid., at p. 278.

Lord Justice Longmore thought that the Chief Baron was drawing a distinction between, on the one hand, material and substantial fraud in respect of the overvaluation of the furniture, and, on the other, immaterial fraud committed by the assured on his creditors by not declaring the linen and china whilst under execution.[1391] He furthermore agreed with the conclusion of Aikens, J. in *Boskalis* that material facts in this context would be facts that had ultimate legal relevance to a defence under the policy.[1392] However, there is no indication in the speech of Pollock, C.B. that he was considering materiality to be a prerequisite for the operation of the fraudulent claims rule. He merely directed the jury to take into account whether the claim had been substantially exaggerated in deciding whether the claim could be said to have been fraudulent. Pollock, C.B. was not indicating that the fraud should be material, in the sense that the requirement is used in the M.I.A. 1906, in order for the rule to apply.

The decision in *The Mercandian Continent* has been the subject of some criticism. It has been argued that a limitation based on an analogy with a right to terminate a contract for a repudiatory breach is the result of a combination of two completely different concepts: on the one hand there is the law of repudiatory breach, and on the other, the duty of utmost good faith which is *sui generis*.[1393] By limiting the application of section 17 in the post-contractual context to frauds as serious as to amount to repudiatory breaches of contract would deprive the insurer of any real remedy in those instances where the post-contractual fraud was not sufficiently serious to amount to a repudiation.[1394] Furthermore, it has been suggested that if the limitation were to be understood as implied in the language of section 17, the result would be that the same provision would have to be interpreted in two different ways depending on whether the duty of utmost good faith applied before or after the inception of the policy.[1395]

These points of criticism, however, cannot be sustained. First of all, it has been acknowledged by Lord Hobhouse in *The Star Sea*, that "the content of the obligation to observe good faith has a different application and content in different situations."[1396] In the same case, Lord Clyde pointed out that the "substance of the obligation [of good faith] which is entailed can vary according to the context in which the matter comes to be judged."[1397] There is therefore no reason why the general requirement of utmost good faith in section 17 should not be able to

[1391] [2002] 2 Lloyd's Rep. 563, at p. 576.
[1392] Ibid.
[1393] EGGERS, Peter MacDonald: *Remedies for the failure to observe the utmost good faith* [2003] LMCLQ 249 at p. 263.
[1394] Ibid.
[1395] Ibid.
[1396] [2001] 1 Lloyd's Rep. 389 at p. 400; see the reference to Lord Hobhouse's remark at p. 182 *supra*.
[1397] Ibid., at p. 392.

generate different duties, each with its own requirements, depending on the situation on which the principle set out in section 17 is applied.[1398] Due to this nature of the principle of good faith, it is only a logical consequence that the application of section 17 might vary depending on the circumstances. In fact, one should add, each duty flowing from the general principle should have its own remedy. However, in the light of the fact that section 17 limits the remedy for breach of the utmost good faith to avoidance *ab initio*, the duties, arising out of that principle, to which section 17 is to be applied, should be limited as well to those duties for which such an extreme remedy is fitting.

Furthermore, the criticism regarding a lack of real remedy does not seem to take into account the extreme nature of the remedy of avoidance *ab initio*. It has been suggested that the doctrine of utmost food faith should not be "transformed into an instrument of oppression, offending against both justice and the reciprocal nature of the doctrine."[1399] Also, Lord Hobhouse in *The Star Sea* was of the opinion that the section 17 remedy of avoidance *ab initio* in fact was –

> "...appropriate where the cause, the want of good faith, has preceded and been material to the making of the contract. But, where the want of good faith first occurs later, it becomes anomalous and disproportionate that it should be so categorized and entitle the aggrieved party to such an outcome."[1400]

For these reasons, Longmore, L.J. was moving in the right dirctions in trying to limit the application of the remedy in section 17. Even if a situation of post-contractual fraud would occur that would amount to a breach of utmost good faith, but not to a repudiatory breach, the application of section 17 could not be justified and avoidance *ab initio* would not be the correct remedy. Accordingly the solution would not lie under section 17. In *The Aegeon*,[1401] Mance L.J., subscribing to the point of view that the fraudulent claims jurisdiction should fall outside the scope of the section 17 duty of utmost good faith,[1402] carefully distinguished between the fraudulent claims rule and the application of section 17 in this context since the judgement of Hirst, J. in *The Litsion Pride*.[1403] The Lord Justice pointed out that *The Mercandian Continent* was decided on the basis of section 17 of the M.I.A. of 1906, as opposed to any principle governing fraudulent claims.[1404] He recognized the fact that whereas materiality was a relevant requirement in the context of a breach of section 17, that requirement had no application in the context of fraudulent claims:

[1398] Cf. p. 115 *supra*.

[1399] BENNET: *Mapping the Doctrine of Utmost Good Faith in Insurance Contract Law* [1999] LMCLQ 165, at p. 214.

[1400] [2001] 1 Lloyd's Rep. 389, at p. 400.

[1401] *Agapitos and Others v Agnew (The Aegeon)* [2002] 2 Lloyd's Rep. 42.

[1402] Cf. p. 203 *supra*.

[1403] [2002] 2 Lloyd's Rep. 42, particularly at p. 49; for a discussion of *The Litsion Pride*, cf. p. 199 *supra*.

[1404] [2002] 2 Lloyd's Rep. 42, at p. 48.

"to the extent that loss claimed is non-existent, the claim will fail anyway and the fraud is clearly material in so far as it amounted to an attempt to recover of non-existent loss."[1405] Furthermore, it was not relevant to the application of the fraudulent claims rule whether or not the insurers were misled. The rule could only possibly arise for application in those cases where the insurers have *not* been misled into settling the claim. It would be senseless to make it dependent upon proof that the insurer was only temporarily misled.[1406] Mance, L.J. agreed with a *dictum* of Lord Mustill, where the latter stated the general principal in the *Pine Top* case:

> "...the texts and the relevant cases leave no room for doubt that whereas if the representation inducing a contract was either fraudulent or a 'warranty' of the contract its falsehood would invariably give a right to avoid an innocent misrepresentation inducing the contract would give the underwriter a right to avoid only if it was material."[1407]

Accordingly, the fact that the rule applies consequent to the fact that the claim had been fraudulent, and irrespective of any other requirement of materiality, appears to be consistent with this general principal. The difference, however, is that in the pre-contract context, the insurer must have been misled. The only further requirement regarding the fraudulent claims rule stated by Mance, L.J. was that the part of the claim that had been fraudulent, i.e. non-existent or exaggerated, should not itself be immaterial or unsubstantial.[1408]

Remedy

Before the judgement of Mance, L.J. in *The Aegeon*[1409] it appeared to be uncertain whether, where the assured was held to be in breach of the duty, the normal remedy of avoiding the policy would apply, or whether some other remedy might be applicable.[1410] The normal remedy in section 17 of the M.I.A. 1906 of avoidance of the entire policy might have led to the disproportionate effects explained above, in that the insurer would have been able to rescind the policy *ab initio*, undoing everything which might have been perfectly legal in terms of the policy up to the breach.[1411] This was especially so in the light of the statement of Hirst J. in *The Litsion Pride*[1412] that section 17 did not allow of a "halfway-house" remedy, i.e. avoidance going back as far as, but not further than, the loss in respect of which the breach was committed.[1413] However, the judge was of the opinion that where an assured was in breach of utmost good faith post-contract, there was "much commercial good sense" in affording the insurer with an alternative option to

---

1405 Ibid., at pp. 50-51.
1406 Ibid., at pp. 51.
1407 [1994] 2 Lloyd's Rep. 427, at p. 442.
1408 [2002] 2 Lloyd's Rep. 42, at p. 51.
1409 *Agapitos and Others v Agnew (The Aegeon)* [2002] 2 Lloyd's Rep. 42.
1410 MERKIN, Robert (editor): op. cit., p. 119.
1411 SOYER: *The Star Sea – a lode star?* [2001] LMCLQ 428, at p. 435.
1412 [1985] 1 Lloyd's Rep. 476.
1413 Ibid., at pp. 514 and 515; also cf. GILMAN: op. cit., Vol. III, par. 579I.

defend the claim whilst affirming the policy.[1414] This conclusion, however, was not supported by case law, nor was there any principle in English contract law that explained why a fraudulent claim should be severed from the policy.[1415] Furthermore, it has been suggested subsequently that Hirst, J.'s classification of the duty not to submit a fraudulent claim as an implied term[1416] did not accord with the section 17 remedy of rescission *ab initio* of the policy for breach of the utmost good faith.[1417]

In *Orakpo v Barclays Ins. Services*[1418] – a case in which neither the authority to the contrary in *The Good Luck*[1419] nor in *Banque Financière*[1420] were cited – Hoffmann, L.J. also held that the duty not to make fraudulent claims was an implied term of the contract, the breach of which entitled the insurer to be "discharged" from the contract.[1421] The term "discharge" in a contractual context normally envisages the prospective release from the contractual obligations. The effect was, therefore, that earlier honest claims under the policy would be unaffected by the breach of the duty of utmost good faith in the claims context.[1422] Sir Roger Parker in the same case was, in turn, of the opinion that a fraudulent claim allowed the assured the remedy of rescission *ab initio*. He held that it would be paradoxical when the law allowed the insurer to avoid the policy for an innocent breach of utmost good faith before inception of the policy, but merely to reject a claim and keep the policy intact when the assured attempted to defraud the insurer. Furthermore it would be no incentive to honesty to allow a fraudulent assured to recover anything.[1423] Accordingly, as far as the majority of the Court of Appeal in *Orakpo* was concerned, avoidance *ab initio* would be available as a remedy for breach of utmost good faith at the claims stage,[1424] i.e. for a fraudulent claim.

The judgement of the Court of Appeal and the House of Lords in *Banque Financière* does not appear to have been cited in *Orakpo*. In the light of the judgements in the

---

1414 [1985] 1 Lloyd's Rep. 476, at p. 515; also cf. MERKIN, Robert (editor): op. cit., p. 119; BENNET: *Mapping the Doctrine of Utmost Good Faith in Insurance Contract Law* [1999] LMCLQ 165, at p. 209.

1415 SOYER: *The Star Sea – a lode star?* [2001] LMCLQ 428, at p. 435. For the different position in South Africa, c.f. the judgement of Marais, A.J. in *Schoeman v Constantia Insurance Co. Ltd.* 2003 (6) SA 313, at p. 323 where it would appear that the fraudulent part of the claim might indeed be severed if the assured proves that "the claim can and should be separated from the untainted aspects of the claim."

1416 [1985] 1 Lloyd's Rep. 476, at pp. 518-519.

1417 SOYER: *The Star Sea – a lode star?* [2001] LMCLQ 428, at p. 435.

1418 [1995] L.R.L.R. 443.

1419 Cf. p. 131 *supra*.

1420 Ibid.

1421 [1995] L.R.L.R. 443, at p. 451.

1422 Ibid., at p. 452.

1423 BENNET: *Mapping the Doctrine of Utmost Good Faith in Insurance Contract Law* [1999] LMCLQ 165, at p. 210; SOYER: *The Star Sea – a lode star?* [2001] LMCLQ 428, at p. 435.

1424 GILMAN: op. cit., Vol. III, par. 5791.

former case, it would seem as though the remedy of avoidance *ab initio* is not merely *available* in the claims context, but that it is also the *only* remedy available, at least as far as the fraudulent claims rule would be seen as falling under the section 17 duty of utmost good faith.[1425] Support for this point of view is also to be found in *The Good Luck* where the Court of Appeal saw no reason why the remedy for breach of the utmost good faith, should be different after the contract is made, from what it is at the pre-contractual stage.[1426]

One way to clarify the application of the continuing duty of utmost good faith and the question regarding the correct remedy, would be to draw a distinction – as Mance, L.J.[1427] and Hobhouse, L.J.[1428] have done – between the duty of utmost good in the claims context, and the operation of the duty during a variation of the policy.[1429] In the latter case, the duty of utmost good faith is the same as in the pre-contractual period, since a variation extends the scope of the cover, and the conduct of the assured should be judged with the same standard as during the pre-contractual period. The duty arises, therefore, *ex lege*, i.e. out of section 17 of the M.I.A. 1906.[1430] In the claims context, however, the insurer does not take on a new risk. The duty to observe utmost good faith can therefore not be the same as in the pre-contractual period and cannot for that reason arise out of the application of section 17. The basis of the duty of utmost good faith in the claims context should, so the argument goes, be an implied term. This possibility had been mentioned by Slade, L.J. in *Banque Financière de la Cité SA v Westgate Ins. Co. Ltd.*:[1431]

> "[I]t may be that on the particular facts of some cases (though by no means necessarily all) the duty of post contractual disclosure can be said to arise under the terms of the proceeding contract."[1432]

Lord Hobhouse in *The Star Sea* took this argument one step further, stating that –

> "[a] coherent scheme can be achieved by distinguishing a lack of good faith which is material to the making of the contract itself (or some variation of it) and a lack of good faith during the performance of the contract which may prejudice the other party or cause him loss or destroy the continuing contractual relationship. The former derives from requirements of the law which preexist the contract and are not created by it although they only become material because a contract has been entered into. The remedy is the right to elect to avoid the contract. The latter can derive from express or implied terms of

1425 Lord Templeman agreed with the Court of Appeal that a breach of the utmost good faith does not sound in damages and that the only remedy, albeit to the insured in that case, is rescission of the contract ([1990] 2 Lloyd's Rep. 377, at p. 387).
1426 See p. 132 *supra*.
1427 In *The Aegeon* [2002] 2 Lloyd's Rep. 42, cf. p. 203 *supra*.
1428 In *The Star Sea* [2001] 1 Lloyd's Rep. 389, cf. p. 202 *supra*.
1429 SOYER: *The Star Sea – a lode star?* [2001] LMCLQ 428, at p. 435, at p. 440.
1430 Ibid.
1431 [1988] 2 Lloyd's Rep. 513.
1432 Ibid., at p. 548.

> the contract; it would be a contractual obligation arising from the contract and the remedies are the contractual remedies provided by the law of contract. This is no doubt why Judges have on a number of occasions been led to attribute the post-contract application of the principle of good faith to an implied term."[1433]

Bennet proposed that the post-contractual operation of utmost good faith – i.e. in the claims context *and* in the context of a variation of risk – should fall outside the scope of section 17 of the M.I.A. 1906. Although section 17 is sufficiently broad to encompass the post-formation application of utmost good faith, it does not compel it. Furthermore very few judgements expressly held the post-contractual duty of utmost good faith to be founded on section 17. The jurisprudence relating to variation of the risk and fraudulent claims shows, however, that the concept of utmost good faith applies in the post-contractual context. The different approaches in these decisions as to the appropriate standard and remedy applicable, suggest furthermore that the concept of utmost good faith should be applied with a certain amount of flexibility. If the post-contractual duty is severed from section 17, it would allow the courts to mould the appropriate content of the duty and suitable remedy to the particular context. Another result would be that the post-contractual duties flowing from the requirement of utmost good faith may be based upon implied terms, each providing for a specific duty. Again, the content of these terms will be left to the courts to determine.[1434]

In a recent South African case[1435], the Supreme Court of Appeal criticised the implication of a term *ex lege* to the effect that in the face of fraud the entire claim was to be forfeited by an assured, including that part that would have been enforceable otherwise. Marais, J.A. proceeded on the basis of the Roman-Dutch Civil law, which he stated was "basically anti-penal."[1436] The judge found that there was no authority in the Roman-Dutch law for the implication *ex lege* of the term sought for, it being in essence a penal term. He expressed, moreover, that there was no compelling social need in the South African common law for such a doctrine, which was essentially of English manufacture.[1437] The judge particularly referred to the fact that the assured was already burdened with the onus to prove his loss and the value thereof. In the event that an assured is shown to have been fraudulent, it will be particularly difficult for such an assured to prove even that part of the claim that was not tainted by fraud and, further to this, that such part can and should be separated from the fraudulent part. If the assured "fails to satisfy the court on that score the entire claim will of course fail."[1438] According to Marais, J.A., the Roman-Dutch law sanctioned the presentation of a fraudulent

[1433] [2001] 1 Lloyd's Rep 389, at p. 400.
[1434] BENNET: *Mapping the Doctrine of Utmost Good Faith in Insurance Contract Law* [1999] LMCLQ 165, at p. 220.
[1435] *Schoeman v Constantia Insurance Co. Ltd.* 2003 (6) SA 313.
[1436] Ibid., at p. 322.
[1437] Ibid.
[1438] Ibid., at p. 323.

claim by refusing to allow a fraudulent assured to profit by the fraud and by rendering him liable for any loss or expenditure caused by the fraudulent conduct. These remedies were combined with rigorous criminal sanctions.[1439] Marais, L.J.'s suggestions seem to be more in accordance with the objectives of the general principle of good faith, particularly as far as the prevention of fraud and the promotion of equity is concerned. Indeed, punishment does not appear to have been one of those objectives.

Eggers suggests that the harshness of the remedy of avoidance could be ameliorated by recognising a discretion in the courts "to make the remedy... flexible".[1440] The author concedes that there is no reported case of such a discretion, but that it may nevertheless be judicially supported. In English law, the courts normally have a discretion in respect of equitable remedies. Although the right to avoidance is most certainly a common law remedy, *Eggers* argues that there is also an equitable remedy "for all breaches of the duty of good faith".[1441] Whereas there are no other requirements at common law but for the insurer to exercise a right to avoidance, in equity it is the court which grants the remedy. Since equity prevails over the common law in cases of inconsistency, the author argues that the remedy for breach of the utmost good faith should be a discretionary remedy.[1442] Further to this, he points out that the courts have to be wary that the duties relating to the principle of utmost good faith are not employed in such a manner that they become instruments of oppression or fraud in themselves. In the light of the traditional function of equity in the prevention of statutory remedies being used in the promotion of fraud, the courts should have regard to the "oppressive nature of the duty in moulding the remedy for its breach".[1443] Another source of such discretion, is to be found in section 2(2) of the Misrepresentation Act 1967, which allows the court a discretion to award damages in the event of a non-fraudulent misrepresentation instead of rescission. *Eggers* suggests that the following circumstances should be taken into account in order for the court to exercise its discretion:

> "(1) whether or not the remedy is disproportionate to the nature of the breach and the damage done; (2) the public policy in the deterrence and punishment of fraud; (3) the effect of denying avoidance on the innocent party; (4) whether or not any other remedy is available to the innocent party; (5) whether or not the innocent party has so conducted himself as to deprive himself of the right to the remedy...; (6) the effect of the avoidance on the guilty party; and (7) whether or not the interests of third parties have intervened."[1444]

[1439] Ibid., at p. 317.
[1440] EGGERS: *Remedies for the failure to observe the utmost good faith* [2003] LMCLQ 2, at p. 264.
[1441] Ibid., at p. 265.
[1442] Ibid., at p. 266.
[1443] Ibid., at p. 268
[1444] Ibid.

Eggers also makes out a convincing argument in favour of damages as a remedy for the breach of post-contractual duties.[1445] The author suggests that the tort of deceit might be established once fraud had been proved in the presentation of the claim, and moreover, that there might also be a breach of contract insofar as the contract obliged the assured not to present a fraudulent claim. Such an obligation might be the result of either an express or an implicit term of the contract.[1446] No hardship will result to the assured in the event of an award of damages, since the award will normally result in a set-off. The set-off will, therefore, result in a reduction of the claim or an increase of the premium, or an order will be made for payment of an amount that will constitute the value of the change in the terms of the policy on which the insurer would have insisted had there been no breach of duty.[1447]

It is suggested that the section 17 remedy of avoidance is not the correct remedy for breach of good faith in the claims context and that the fraudulent claims rule should fall outside that section, as Mance, L.J. held in *The Aegeon.*[1448] The correct remedy should either be a refusal of the whole claim, including the part that was not tainted by fraud, or – as the position is in South Africa – a mere refusal of the fraudulent part of the claim. The remedy of damages, if applied as discussed above, would also be more in accordance with equity and fairness than a blanket remedy of avoidance. It would also be a move in the direction of uniformity, particularly with the regimes applicable in France and Germany.[1449]

[1445] C.f. fn. 1440 *supra*, at p. 274.
[1446] Ibid.
[1447] Ibid., at pp. 276-277.
[1448] C.f. p. 204 *supra.*
[1449] C.f. 3.2 POST-CONTRACTUAL DUTY OF GOOD FAITH *supra.*

6. CONCLUSION: IN THE MATTER BETWEEN GOOD FAITH AND "UTMOST GOOD FAITH"

Having travelled through centuries of legal thought, we find ourselves, like Little Red Riding Hood after her long walk through the woods, confronting something that *prima facie* appears to be of some antiquity and very familiar too. However, we must not be fooled by the outer man! Firstly, as a matter of etymology, it is clear that the phrase *uberrima fides* was not known in Roman law at all – neither as an independent legal standard, nor as an incidence of *bona fides*. Furthermore, *uberrima fides* was also unknown by the canonists and the civilian jurists. What can be said about the term, is that it was a convenient Latin translation for a legal standard that was described as 'greatest good faith', 'the most abundant good faith', 'the most full and copious good faith', 'perfect good faith' and 'full and perfect faith' in English courts and legal writings in the nineteenth century. The Latin term for the English common law principle of utmost good faith was, therefore, foreign to the civilian legal tradition. It is, at most, a fairly recent Latin translation for a fairly new principle of English contract law and particularly English marine insurance law.

Secondly it is suggested that at no stage did the principle of utmost good faith form part of the development of marine insurance. There appears to be no authority in the early writings on marine insurance in support of a principle of utmost good faith as a special form of good faith. On the contrary, all the civilian authorities on marine insurance law agreed that the contract of marine insurance was a contract to which the principle of good faith or *bona fides* applied.

Thirdly, good faith had various functions in the civilian law of obligations.[1450] It was i.a. a principle of fairness according to *Baldus*,[1451] preventing the parties to any contract whatsoever from obtaining an unfair advantage by misleading each other. In the context of marine insurance law, the application of good faith "as a restraint upon self interest in deference to the interest of others" became particularly relevant.[1452] The old civilian authorities leave no room for doubt that both the assured and insurer had to observe good faith in their mutual dealings, which implied that they were not to mislead each other. As it was stated by Lord Mansfield, good faith "forbids either party by concealing what he privately knows, to draw the other into a bargain, from his ignorance of that fact, and his believing the contrary".[1453]

[1450] Cf. the discussion under 2.1.3 The role of *bona fides* in the writings of the medieval and natural lawyers *supra*.

[1451] Cf. p. 28 *supra*.

[1452] FRIEDMANN, Daniel: *The Transformation of "Good Faith" in Insurance Law* **Good Faith in Contract, Concept and Context** p. 312; cf. p. 15 *supra*.

[1453] Cf. the discussion of *Carter v Boehm supra* under 4.3.3 Lord Mansfield and the remains of *Carter v Boehm*.

Fourthly, good faith dictated that where the equity in a contract had been disturbed in that a person was led to conclude a contract which he would not have concluded otherwise, that person would be allowed to escape entirely from the contract. The civilians also provided for the event that a person was led to contract on less favourable terms, in which case he could demand a reduction of the price if his contractual partner deceived him deliberately. Similarly, the civilian authorities on marine insurance stated that the policy would be annulled where either the insurer or the assured was led to conclude the contract on a misconception of the risk due to a misstatement or concealment of a material fact. *Pothier*, further to this, stated that where the assured had been misled by the insurer, he would still be able to claim on the policy and could claim a return of that part of the premium that was in excess of the real price of the insurance.[1454] Traces of the equitable operation of good faith are still to be found in the marine insurance legislation in Europe today in that provision is made for the correct remedy in different phases of the marine insurance contract, and for different degrees of breach of the duties of disclosure and misrepresentation. The French legislation – in which provision is made for different remedies corresponding to various degrees of fault – is exemplary.

Fifthly, the *dicta* of Lord Mansfield in *Carter v Boehm* have been linked by various jurists to the doctrine of utmost good faith in English marine insurance law. In a recent study on the role of *uberrima fides* in English law,[1455] it has been suggested that Lord Mansfield introduced two principles. The first, it is argued, was the civilian principle of good faith which formed the basis for a pre-contractual duty to disclose in all contracts. The duty applied where one party had access to information which the other did not and failure to observe the principle constituted a fraud. The second principle, or rather duty, recognised by the author, applied only to insurance policies. It was a duty to disclose circumstances that were so central to the risk insured against, that a failure to disclose would result in the actual risk being different to the risk in the contract. In these circumstances the contract would be void without the need of proof of any fraudulent intention on the part of the assured.[1456] According to the author, this latter duty was based on the fact that the insurance contract was – even on the Continent! – subject to "*Treu und Glauben in besonderem Maße*", i.e. utmost good faith.[1457] Ironically, Lord Mansfield never employed that phrase. Also, as was pointed out above, there is no evidence whatsoever of the existence such a principle in the Civilian authorities on marine insurance or of any special form of good faith only applicable in marine insurance. It is suggested that it would constitute an artificial reading of *Carter v Boehm* if one were to detract from the generality of Lord Mansfield's *dicta* in that case. Lord Mansfield set out to introduce the Roman and civilian law standard of good faith in

---

[1454] Cf. text to fn. 358 *supra*.
[1455] SCHNEIDER: ***Uberrima Fides, Treu und Glauben und vorvertragliche Aufklärungspflichten im englischen Recht.***
[1456] Ibid., pp. 51-52 and 59.
[1457] Ibid., pp. 68-69.

general in English contract law, which at that time followed the harsh rules of *caveat emptor*. A natural reading of the case does not allow room for deducing any special rules. That this was in fact so, is not only admitted lately by the English jurisprudence,[1458] but is also supported by the fact that Lord Mansfield was extremely well equipped to do just that, being so well versed in civilian law. Further to this, the very general terms in which he went about explaining the duty of disclosure, suggests that he was in fact not describing a special form of good faith to be applicable in insurance law, but merely applying the standard of good faith, which he opined to be a "governing principle... applicable to all contracts and dealings" to explain why the parties to a marine insurance contract owed the duty of disclosure to each other.[1459]

Sixthly, it is noteworthy that Lord Mansfield did not lay down a hard rule as to what needed to be disclosed, but stated that "[i]t is adapted to such facts as vary the nature of the contract...". It is clear, therefore, that in imposing the positive duty of disclosure in marine insurance in this judgement, Lord Mansfield merely confirmed that a valid contract was based on the principle of good faith. The duty of disclosure did not follow from the fact that the contract was one of marine insurance and that the contract of marine insurance, in turn, was a contract of utmost good faith. The rule was, on the contrary, justified where one of the contracting parties had to rely involuntarily upon the other for information material to his decision to contract and good faith in general required in these circumstances that this information should be disclosed.[1460] Such circumstances may, of course, be present in any contract.[1461] The present position in English marine insurance law, however, is far removed from the principles laid down in *Carter v Boehm*, in that the marine insurance contract is classified from the outset as *uberrimae fidei*, as a result of which it automatically attracts certain duties of disclosure.

Seventhly, the standard of good faith, as known and applied in the civilian tradition, was never received in the general English law of obligations. It had clearly been the intention of Lord Mansfield that it should be so received. English law, however, did not respond well to Lord Mansfield's attempts and remained averse to the principle of good faith in contract. Nevertheless, what English jurists perceived as the fiduciary nature of the marine insurance contract, and the perceived imbalance regarding knowledge of the risk to be insured, required rules which would oblige the parties, and particularly the assured, to disclose facts material to the risk.

1458 See e.g. *Manifest Shipping & Co. Ltd. v Uni-Polaris Insurance Co. Ltd. & La Réunion Européene (The Star Sea)* [2001] 1 Lloyd's Rep. 389, at p. 398 and *Pan Atlantic Insurance Co. Ltd.. and Another v. Pine Top Insurance Co.Ltd* [1994] 2 Lloyd's Rep. 427, at p. 444.

1459 FORTE: *Good Faith and Utmost Good Faith: Insurance and Cautionary Obligations in Scots Law* **Good Faith in Contract and Property** p. 79.

1460 This is, of course, nothing else but a statement of the operation of good faith, as applied on the continent in marine insurance. Cf. 3. GOOD FAITH AND THE MARINE INSURANCE CONTRACT ON THE CONTINENT *supra*.

1461 FORTE: op. cit., pp. 84-85.

Disclosure was not a general requirement in English contract law either, which in itself is no special feature of English contract law, as the rules of *caveat emptor* reigned supreme without the tempering effect of the requirement of good faith. Marine insurance contracts thus became subject to special rules of disclosure and were, as a result, classified as contracts of the utmost good faith, as a distinct type of contract to which the normal rules of *caveat emptor* did not apply in all their vigour. Indeed, the implication is that *Carter v Boehm* had been misinterpreted during the twentieth century, and the English courts "over the years manoeuvred themselves into the position of accepting an unsatisfactory rationale for the existence of the duty of disclosure in insurance contracts, namely the concept of utmost good faith."[1462]

The rules relating to the principle of utmost good faith as applied in English law, in fact, work against fairness in the insurance contract.[1463] Firstly, English decisions like *Bates v Hewitt*[1464] and *Lindenau v Desborough*[1465], and later on *Joel*[1466] set the course for this state of affairs by broadening its scope of application. The reason for this development was the fact that the general principle of good faith had not been received in English law, turning on its head the fine scheme of legal rules relating to that principle: instead of good faith dictating when a contract might be avoided for lack of disclosure or misrepresentation, the condition for the application of the rules relating to non-disclosure and misrepresentation, namely an inequality in the flow of information between the contracting parties, came to be considered a fixed characteristic of marine insurance policies. As a result, the rules relating to non-disclosure and misrepresentation became known by a wonderful name, utmost good faith, but were devoid of the inherent equitable function of good faith.

Secondly, the subsequent development in English marine insurance law of the objective test of materiality, namely the "prudent underwriter", did not improve the legal position either. According to the civilian authorities, the test merely related to facts material to the risk, or as Lord Mansfield suggested, facts that materially varied the object of the contract and changed the risk understood to be run. Admittedly, the introduction of the subjective test for inducement in the *Pine Top* case, did balance the scales again to some extent. It is, nevertheless, submitted that the two-stage test, i.e. objective materiality and subjective inducement, unduly complicates what could be a fairly straight-forward test relating to the variation of the risk.

Thirdly, the entrenchment of the principle in section 17 and the following sections

[1462] FORTE: op. cit., p. 86.
[1463] HODGIN, Ray: **Insurance Law** pp. 174-175; HASSON, R.: *The Doctrine of* Uberrima Fides *in Insurance Law – a Critical Evaluation* (1969) 32 MLR 615.
[1464] Cf. p. 107 *supra*.
[1465] Cf. p. 105 *supra*.
[1466] Cf. p. 109 *supra*.

of the M.I.A. 1906 dealing with pre-contract non-disclosure and misrepresentation did not serve the real objectives of the good faith principle. It wrongly created the impression that observance of the principle of "utmost" good faith did not extend after the conclusion of the contract. Similarly, the fact that these sections only provided for one remedy, i.e. avoidance of the policy, resulted in an inflexible regime, that sometimes worked against equity and fairness, instead of promoting it. This can be clearly seen in relation to the observance of the principle in the post-contractual stage. There can simply be nothing equitable about avoiding the whole policy retrospectively where the "fraud" complained about, did not affect the consensus on which the policy was based. Similarly, restricting an innocent assured to the remedy of avoidance in the case of breach of "utmost" good faith on the part of the insurer cannot be said to promote equity and fairness. On the other hand, the range of remedies available in e.g. the French and German marine insurance legislation for post-contractual breach of good faith is exemplary.

It appears, however, from decisions like *The Star Sea*[1467], *The Mercandian Continent*[1468] and *The Aegeon*[1469] and also to an extent from *The Litsion Pride*[1470], that the English courts are willing to expand the concept of "utmost" good faith from being a mere signifier of a particular kind of contract and providing a basis for sections 18-20 of the M.I.A. 1906, to be a more accurate reflection of the civilian principle of good faith. The courts appear agreeable to attribute content to the principle outside of the restrictions of section 17 of the M.I.A. 1906. One suggestion to provide more flexibility in the application of utmost good faith, which has been discussed above,[1471] would indeed be to sever the duty of utmost good faith as it applies in the post-contractual context from the limitations of section 17 of the M.I.A. 1906.

The same liberating trend is to be observed in current legal writing to the point. Writing in general about the duty of utmost good faith, *Rhidian Thomas* stated:

> "Section 17 makes no attempt to define "utmost good faith', but no fair minded commentator would see this as a defect in the legislation... The concept of good faith is in its nature a flexible, imprecise and evolving concept. It conjures up more a state or attitude of mind, or an outlook, than a dictionary definition... the obligation of utmost good faith demands ... honesty, candour, openness, equal bargaining, fair dealing, assistance, co-operation, protection and disclosure of material facts."[1472]

Bennet, again, wrote the following concerning utmost good faith:

> "The doctrine of utmost good faith must not be transformed into an instrument of

1467 [2001] 1 Lloyd's Rep. 389, *per* Hobhouse, L.J et al.
1468 [2001] 2 Lloyd's Rep. 563, *per* Longmore, L.J.
1469 [2002] 2 Lloyd's Rep. 42, *per* Mance, L.J.
1470 [1985] 1 Lloyd's Rep. 437.
1471 See 5.7.2 The Claims Context, Remedy *supra*.
1472 RHIDIAN THOMAS, D. (editor): op. cit., p. 29.

> oppression, offending against both justice and the reciprocal nature of the doctrine. The fundamental question of policy is how severe a duty is needed and merited at the end of the 20th century to protect insurers against fraudulent claims and also against the risk of paying non-fraudulent claims for which, in truth, the insurer is not liable."[1473]

It has been suggested furthermore by *Bennet* that, since sections 18-20 of the M.I.A. 1906 are restricted in their operation to duties of the assured, any reciprocal duty of the insurer should be founded in the duty of utmost good faith. To the extent that the assured is to observe the utmost good faith in relation to non-material circumstances and correction of mistakes, the insurer will incur a reciprocal duty. Furthermore, he suggests that since at common law a fraudulent misrepresentation will be actionable even if not material, the same should follow for fraudulent non-disclosure, and that this should be based upon the requirement of utmost good faith.[1474]

Also as regards remedies, many legal commentators have recently appealed for the development of remedies other than avoidance of the contract in order to promote the fair and equitable operation of the principle of "utmost" good faith.[1475] This is particularly evident in the application of the principle in the post-contractual context as well as in the situation where the insurer is in breach of his reciprocal duties flowing from the principle. In both instances, English jurists appear to be more willing to expand the scope of application of the principle outside the limitations of section 17 of the M.I.A. 1906, in order to circumvent the draconian remedy of avoidance of the contract. Through this expansion, the duty of utmost good faith is in effect starting to operate in a similar way as the principle of good faith were operating since the early days of marine insurance. Nevertheless, having regard to the equitable influence of good faith in marine insurance on the continent, especially in the context of remedies, it is clear that the principle of utmost good faith, as it presently stands, still lacks the flexibility of good faith. It is suggested that this is due to the fact that section 17 of the M.I.A. 1906, does not reflect the real rationale of Lord Mansfield's decision in the celebrated case of *Carter v Boehm*, and as a result restricted the natural equitable operation of the principle of good faith. Furthermore the courts for a very long time had a restrictive approach to what they called the principle of "utmost" good faith. Nevertheless, it would appear that both the English jurisprudence and legal commentators are moving in the right direction in attributing content to the duty of utmost good faith outside the sphere of section 17.

1473 BENNET: *Mapping the Doctrine of Utmost Good Faith in Insurance Contract Law* [1999] LMCLQ 165, at p. 214.

1474 BENNET: *Mapping the Doctrine of Utmost Good Faith in Insurance Contract Law* [1999] LMCLQ 165 at at p. 165 and also at p. 177, referring to i.a. *Gordon v Street* [1899] 2 Q.B. 641 and *The Bedouin* [1894] 1 P.I. 12; 69 LT 782 (CA).

1475 C.f. EGGERS: *Remedies for the failure to observe the utmost good faith* [2003] LMCLQ 249; SOYER: *Continuing duty of utmost good faith in insurance contractgs: still alive?* [2003] LMCLQ 39; LOWRY and RAWLINGS: *Insurers, Claims and the Boundaries of Good Faith* (2005) 68(1) MLR 82.

6. Conclusion: In the Matter Between Good Faith and "Utmost Good Faith"

In the end, the remains of *Carter v Boehm* might only really be salvaged by the British Parliament or, at the very least, by the bold intervention of a modern incarnation of the great Lord Mansfield.

7. Bibliography

7.1 Essays

BAATZ, Yvonne *Utmost Good Faith in Marine Insurance Contracts* **Marine Insurance at the Turn of the Millennium** Vol 1 Editor: Marc Huybrechts Antwerp, 2000

BENNET, Howard N. *Mapping the Doctrine of Utmost Good Faith in Insurance Contract Law* **Lloyd's Maritime and Commercial Law Quarterly** May 1999

EBKE, Werner F. and STEINHAUER, Bettina M. *The Doctrine of Good Faith in German Contract Law* **Good Faith and Fault in Contract Law** Editors: Jack Beatson and Daniel Friedmann Oxford University Press Inc. New York, 1997

EGGERS, Peter MacDonald *Remedies for the failure to observe the utmost good faith* [2003] **Lloyd's Maritime and Commercial Law Quarterly** 249

FORTE, A.D.M. *Good Faith and Utmost Good Faith: Insurance and Cautionary Obligations in Scots Law* **Good Faith in Contract and Property** Editor: A.D.M. Forte Hart Publishing Oxford, Portland Oregon, 1999

FRIEDMANN, Daniel *The Transformation of "Good Faith" in Insurance Law* **Good Faith in Contract, Concept and Context** Editors: Roger Brownsword, Norma J. Hird and Geraint Howells Darmouth Publishing Co. Ltd. Aldershot, 1999

GORDLEY, James *Good Faith in the Medieval* Ius Commune **Good Faith in European Contract Law** Editors: Reinard Zimmermann and Simon Whittaker Cambridge University Press Cambridge, First edition 2000

GRIGGS, J.S. "*Is the Doctrine of Utmost Good Faith out of Date?*" A Presentation at the Marine Insurance Seminar

HASSON, R. *The Doctrine of* Uberrima Fides *in Insurance Law – a Critical Evaluation* (1969) 32 **Modern Law Review** 615

HUYBRECHTS, Marc A. *Marine Insurance Law: A San Andreas Fault between the Common Law and Civil Law* **The Modern Law of Marine Insurance** Volume Two Editor: D. Rhidian Thomas LLP London, 2002

KOSTKA, Klaus *Marine Transport Insurance in Germany: The General German Cargo Conditions in Coparison to the Institute Cargo Clauses and Recent German Court*

Decisions **Marine Insurance at the Turn of the Millennium** Volume 1 Editor: Marc Huybrechts Antwerp, 2000

LOWRY, John and RAWLINGS, Philip *Insurers, Claims and the Boundaries of Good Faith* (2005) 68(1) **Modern Law Review** 82

McKENDRICK, Ewan *Good Faith: A Matter of Principle?* **Good Faith in Contract and Property** Editor: A.D.M. Forte Hart Publishing Oxford, Portland Oregon, 1999

MILLNER, M.A. *Fraudulent Non-Disclosure* **The South African Law Journal**, 1957, Volume 74

MUSY, Alberto M. *The Good Faith Principle in Contract Law and the Precontractual* (sic) *Duty to Disclose: Comparative Analysis of New Differences in Legal Cultures* **(Unpublished)**

NEHF, James *Bad Faith Breach of Contract in Consumer Transactions* **Good Faith in Contract, Concept and Context** Editors: Roger Brownsword, Norma J. Hird and Geraint Howells Darmouth Publishing Co. Ltd. Aldershot 1999

SCHERMAIER, M.J. *Bona Fides in Roman Contract Law* **Good Faith in European Contract Law** Editors: Reinard Zimmermann and Simon Whittaker Cambridge University Press Cambridge, First edition 2000

SOYER, Bariş *The Star Sea – a lode star?* [2001] **Lloyd's Maritime and Commercial Law Quarterly** 428

SOYER, Bariş *Continuing duty of utmost good faith in insurance contractgs: still alive?* [2003] **Lloyd's Maritime and Commercial Law Quarterly** 39

SPIRO, Erwin *Uberrima Fides* 1961 ***Tydskrif vir Hedendaagse Romeins-Hollandse Reg*** 196

VON ZIEGLER, Alexander *The 'Utmost Good Faith' in Marine Insurance Law on the Continent* **Marine Insurance at the turn of the Millennium** Volume 2 Editor: Marc Huybrecht Antwerp, 2000

WHITTAKER, S and ZIMMERMANN, R *Good faith in European Contract Law: Surveying the Legal Landscape* **Good Faith in European Contract Law** Editors: Reinhard Zimmermann and Simon Whittaker Cambridge University Press Cambridge First edition, 2000

WIGHTMAN, John *Good faith and pluralism in the Law of Contract* **Good Faith in Contract, Concept and Context** Editors: Roger Brownsword, Norma J. Hird and Geraint Howells Darmouth Publishing Co. Ltd. Aldershot, 1999

WILHELMSEN, T-M *Duty of Disclosure, Duty of Good Faith, Alteration of Risk and Warranties* **Comite Maritime International Yearbook** 2000

ZIMMERMANN, Reinhard *Good Faith and Equity* **Southern Cross, Civil Law and Common Law in South Africa** Reinhard Zimmermann and Daniel Visser Clarendon Press Oxford, 1996

7.2 LITERATURE

AMOS, Sheldon **The History and Principles of the Civil Law of Rome** WM. W. Gaunt & Sons, Inc. Florida, U.S.A. Reprint 1989

BEALE, H.G. (General Editor) **Chitty on Contracts** Volume 1 Sweet & Maxwell London Twenty-Ninth Edition, 2004

BENNET, Howard N. **The Law of Marine Insurance** Oxford University Press 1996

BROWNSWORD, Roger HIRD, Norma J. and HOWELLS, Geraint (Editors) **Good Faith in Contract, Concept and Context** Darmouth Publishing Co. Ltd. Aldershot, 1999

BRUCK-MÖLLER ***Kommentar zum Versicherungsvertragsgesetz und zu den Allgemeinen Versicherungsbedingungen unter Einschluß des Versicherungsvermittlerrechtes*** Walter de Gruyter & Co.Berlin, 1961

BEWES, Wyndham Anstis **The Romance of the Law Merchant** Sweet & Maxwell, Ltd. London, 1923

BYNKERSHOEK, Cornelius van ***Quaestiones Juris Privati*** Lugduni Batavorum (Lyon), 1744

CHALMERS, Mackenzie D. Sir, and IVAMY, E.R. Hardy **Chalmers' Marine Insurance Act, 1906** Butterworths London Seventh Edition, 1971

CHESHIRE, G.C. and FIFOOT, C.H.S. **The Law of Contract** Butterworth & Co. (Publishers) Ltd. London Third Edition, 1952

CHORLEY, Lord and BAILHACHE, C.T. **Arnould on Marine Insurance,** in: British Shipping Laws, Volumes 9 and 10, The Law of Marine Insurance and Average Stevens & Sons Limited London, 1961

CICERO, Marcus Tullius ***De Officiis*** Phillip Reclam jun. GmbH & Co. *Durchgesehene und erweiterte Ausgabe*, Stuttgart 2003

CLARKE, Malcolm A. **The Law of Insurance Contracts** LLP Limited London Third Edition, 1997

DE HART, Edward L. and SIMEY, Ralph I. **Arnould on the Law of Marine Insurance and Average** Volume 1 Stevens and Sons; Sweet and Maxwell London Eleventh Edition, 1924

DE JAGER, Theo **The Roots and Future of the South African Law of Marine Insurance** Institute of Marine Law Publication University of Cape Town Publication Number 18, 1993

DE JONGE, H.A.G.J.P. ***De Mededeelingsplicht van den Verzekerde in Theorie en Practijk*** Van Gorcum & Comp. N.V. Assen, 1939

DE SMET, Robert ***Les Assurances Maritimes, Traité Théorique et Pratique de Droit Comparé*** Libraire Générale de Droit & de Jurisprudence Paris, 1934

DORHOUT MEES, T.J. ***Verzekeringsrecht*** N.V. Uitgevers-Maatschappij Zwolle, 1929

DOVER, Victor **A Handbook to Marine Insurance** H. F. & G. Witherby Ltd. London, Sixth Edition, Reprinted, 1962

EGGERS, Peter MacDonald, PICKEN, Simon and FOSS, Patrick **Good Faith and Insurance Contracts** LLP London, 2004

EMéRIGON, Balthazard-Marie ***Traité des Assurance et des Contrats a la Grosse*** Jean Mossy, Imprimeur du Roi, de la Marine, & Llibraire, à la Canebiere Marseille, 1783

EMéRIGON, Balthazard Marie **A Treatise on Insurances,** translated from the French by Samuel Meredith H. Butterworth London, 1850

GILMAN, Jonathan C.B. **Arnould's Law of Marine Insurance and Average** Volume III Sweet & Maxwell London Sixteenth Edition, 1997

GOLDSCHMIDT, L. ***System des Handelsrechts*** Verlag von Ferdinand Enke Stuttgart, *3. Auflage*, 1891

GOUDSMIT, M. Th. ***Geschiedenis van het Nederlandsche Zeerecht*** Martinus Nijhoff 's Gravenhage, 1882

GROTIUS (DE GROOT), Hugo ***De Jure Belli ac Pacis*** Translated from the Latin by A. C. Campbell M. Walter Dunne Publisher New York and London, 1901

GROTIUS (DE GROOT), Hugo ***Inleidinge tot de Hollandsche Rechts-Geleerdeid*** S. Gouda Quint. Arnhem *Derde, herziene en vermeerderde uitgave*, 1926

GROTIUS (DE GROOT), Hugo **The Jurisprudence of Holland,** translated from the Dutch by R.W. Lee Clarendon Press Oxford, 1926

HANSELL, D.S. **Introduction to Insurance** LLP Limited London, 1996

HARE, John **Shipping Law & Admiralty Jurisdiction in South Africa** Juta & Co, Ltd. Kenwyn First edition, 1999

HODGIN, Ray **Insurance Law** Cavendish Publishing Ltd. London, Sydney First Edition, 1998

HOLDSWORTH, William **A History of English Law** Volume 1 Methuen & Co. Ltd. London, Seventh Edition, Revised, 1956

HORN, Norbert ***Aequitas in den Lehren des Baldus*** Böhlau Verlag, Köln, 1968

KARSTAEDT, Rainer ***Grundsätzliche Fragen der Drittzurechnung in den Allgemeinen Deutschen Seeversicherungsbedingungen*** VVW Karlsruhe, 1979

LAY, H.G. **Marine Insurance: A Text Book of the History of Marine Insurance Including the Function of Lloyd's Register of Shipping** Post Magazine London, 1925

LEGH-JONES, Nicholas, BIRDS, John, and OWEN, David (Editors) **MacGillivray on Insurance Law** Sweet and Maxwell London Tenth Edition, 2003

MACGILLIVRAY, E.J., and BROWNE, Denis **MacGillivray on Insurance Law** Sweet and Maxwell London Second Edition, 1937

MACKINTOSH, James **The Roman Law of Sale, with Modern Illustrations, Digest XVIII. 1 and XIX. 1 Translated** T, & T. Clark, Law Publishers Edinburgh, 1907

MAITLAND, F.W. **Equity, a Course of Lectures** Cambridge University Press Cambridge, Second Edition, 1936

MARTIN, Frederick **The History of Lloyd's and of Marine Insurance in Great Britain** Macmillan and Co. London, 1876

MERKIN, Robert (editor) **Colinvaux's Law of Insurance** Sweet and Maxwell London Seventh edition, 1997

MOYLE, J.B. **The Contract of Sale in the Civil Law** Clarendon Press Oxford, 1892

MUSTILL, Sir Michael J. & GILMAN, Jonathan C.B. **Arnould's Law of Marine Insurance and Average** Volume II Stevens & Sons London Sixteenth Edition, 1981

NOLTE, Vincent ***Wilhelm Benecke's System des See-Assekuranz- und Bodmerei-Wesens*** Volume II Perthes Besser & Maute Hamburg, 1852

PARDESSUS, J.M. ***Collction de Lois Maritimes Antérieures au XVIIIe Siècle, Tome Quartième*** *L'Imprimerie Royale* Paris, 1837

PARK, James Allan **A System of the Law of Marine Insurances** Joseph Crukshank Philadelphia Reprinted, 1789

PARK, Semin **The Duty of Disclosure in Insurance Contract Law** Darmouth Publishing Company Ltd. Aldershot, 1996

PLUCKNETT, Theodore F.T. **A Concise History of the Common Law** The Lawyers Co-operative Publishing Company Rochester, N.Y., 1929

POTHIER **A Treatise on the Law of Obligations or Contracts** Translated from the French by William David Evans Volume 1 Robert H. Small Philadelphia, 1826

POTHIER ***Traité des Obligations, Première Partie, Tome Deuxième d'Oeuvres de Pothier*** Cosse et N. Delamotte Videcoq Père et Fils Paris, 1847

POTHIER ***Traité du Contrat d'Assurance, Tome Cinquième d'Oeuvres de Pothier*** Cosse et N. Delamotte Videcoq Père et Fils Paris, 1847

POTTER, Harold **An Historical Introduction to English Law and its Institutions** Sweet & Maxwell, Ltd. London, 1932

POWELL, Raphael **Good Faith in Contracts: An Inaugural Lecture delivered at University college London** Stevens & Sons Ltd. London London, 1956

REINECKE, M.F.B. and VAN DER MERWE, S.W.J. **General Principles of Insurance** Butterworths Durban, 1989

RHIDIAN THOMAS, D.(editor) **The Modern Law of Marine Insurance** LLP London, 1996

RHIDIAN THOMAS, D.(editor) **The Modern Law of Marine Insurance** Volume Two LLP London, 2002

RITTER, Carl ***Das Recht der Seeversicherung: Ein Kommentar zu den Allgemeinen Deutschen Seeversicherung-Bedingungen*** *Erster Band* Cram, De Gruyter & Co. Hamburg, 1967

ROCCUS, Franciscus ***Merkwaardige Aanmerkingen, vervat in twee Tractaaten, waar van het eene is handelende over Schepen en Vragtgelderen, en het andere over Assurantien ofte Verzekeringen*** *Uit het Latyn en Italiaans door Johan Feitema* Francois Changuion Amsterdam, 1737

RöPLING, Gerhard ***Die Geschichte der englischen Seeversicherung*** *Veröffentlichungen des Seminars für Versicherungslehre der Universität Köln, Band 10* René Fischer Verlag Weissenburg/Bayern

SANBOURN, Frederic Rockwell **Origins of the Early English Maritime and Commercial Law** The Century Co. New York, 1930

SCHLEGELBERGER, Franz ***Seeversicherungsrecht, Allgemeine Deutsche Seeversicherungsbedingungen.*** Franz Vahlen G.m.b.H. Berlin und Frankfurt a.M

SCHNEIDER, Nicole ***Uberrima Fides, Treu und Glauben und vorvertragliche Aufklärungspflichten im englischen Recht*** Duncker & Humblot Berlin

SHERMAN, Charles Phineas **Roman Law in the Modern World** Volume 1 Baker, Voorhis & Co. New York Second Edition, 1924

TREITEL, Guenter Sir **The Law of Contract** Sweet & Maxwell London Tenth Edition, 1999

TRÖLSCH, Corinna ***Die Obliegenheiten in der Seeversicherung*** VVW Karlsruhe, 1997

VALIN, René-Josué ***Commentaire sur l'Ordonnance de la Marine*** Poitiers, F.-A Saurin, Imprimeur-Libraire, 1829

VAN DER KEESSEL, Dionysi Godefridi *Theses Selectae Juris Hollandici et Zelandici, ad Suplendam Hugonis Grotii Introductionem ad Jurisprudentiam Hollandicam* Fredericum Muller Amsteldam Editio Nova, 1860

VAN DER LINDEN, Joannes **Regtsgeleerd, Practicaal, en Koopmans Handboek** C.L. van Langenhuysen, Amsterdam Herdruk, (originally of 1806)

VERWER, Adriaen *Nederlants See-Rechten; Avaryen en Bodemeryen* Amsterdam, 1711

VOET, Johannes **Commentary on the Pandects** Translated by Percival Gane Volume Three Butterworth & Co. (Africa) Ltd. Durban, 1956

WILLE, George and MILLEN, Philip **Mercantile Law of South Africa** Hortors Limited Johannesburg Fifth Edition, 1925

WESSELS, Johannes Wilhelmus **The Law of Contract in South Africa** Hortors Johannesburg, 1937

ZIMMERMANN, Reinhard **The Law of Obligations, Roman Foundations of the Civilian Tradition** Juta & Co, Ltd. Kenwyn First Edition, 1990

ZIMMERMANN, Reinhard and WHITTAKER Simon **Good Faith in European Contract Law** Cambridge University Press Cambridge, 2000

7.3 DICTIONARIES

ERLER, Adalbert, KAUFMANN, Ekkehard (*Herausgeber*) ***Handwörterbuch zur deutschen Rechtsgeschichte*** Erich Schmidt Verlag, Berlin, 1971

ALLEN, R.E. (Editor) **The Concise Oxford Dictionary of Current English** Oxford University Press, New York, Eighth Edition, Reprinted, 1990

DIETL, Clara-Erika & LORENZ, Egon **Dictionary of Legal, Commercial and Political Terms/ *Wörterbuch für Recht, Wirtschaft und Politik*** Part II Matthew Bender & Company, Inc. New York, & C.H. Beck'sche Verlagsbuchhandlung München, 1992

FELLERMAYER, Martin, KRüGER, Helga(*Redaktion*) ***Langenscheidts Handwörterbuch, Englisch*** Langenscheidt KG Berlin und München2001

WEIS, Erich (*Herausgeber*) ***Langenscheidts Großwörterbuch, Französisch-Deutsch*** Langenscheidt KG Berlin und München 5. Auflage, 1987

7.4 TABLE OF CASES

- *Aegeon, The* [2002] 2 Lloyd's Rep. 42
- *Agapitos and Others v Agnew (The Aegeon)* [2002] 2 Lloyd's Rep. 42
- *Allis Chalmers v Fidelity Deposit* (1916) 32 T.L.R. 263
- *Anderson v Pacific Fire and Marine Insurance Co.* (1872) L.R. 7 C.P. 65
- *Anemone, The* [1987] 1 Lloyd's Rep. 546
- *Anns v Merton London borough Council* [1978] A.C. 728
- *Arterial Caravans v Yourkshire Insurance* [1973] 1 Lloyd's Rep. 169
- *Bank of Nova Scotia v Hellenic Mutual War Risks Association (Bermuda) Ltd.(The Good Luck)* [1988] 1 Lloyd's Rep. 514
- *Banque Financière de la Cité SA v Westgate Insurance Co. Ltd.* [1990] 2 Lloyd's Rep. 377; [1990] 1 Q.B. 665 (House of Lords)
- *Banque Financière de la Cité SA v Westgate Insurance Co. Ltd.* [1988] 2 Lloyd's Rep. 513 (Court of Appeal)
- *Banque Financière de la Cité v Westgate Insurance Co. Ltd.*[1990] 2 All E.R. 947 (H.L.)
- *Banque Keyser Ullmann SA v Skandia (UK) Insurance Co. Ltd.* [1987] 1 Lloyd's Rep. 69; [1990] 1 Q.B. 665 (Queen's Bench Division)
- *Barber v Fletcher* (1779) 1 Dougl. 305
- *Bates v Hewitt*, (1867) L.R. 2 Q.B. 595
- *Becker v Marshall* (1922) 11 Ll. L. R. 114
- *Becker v Marshall* (1922) 12 Ll. L. R. 413
- *Bedouin, The* [1894] 1 P. I. 12; 69 LT 782 (CA)
- *Bell v Lever Bros Ltd.*[1932] A.C. 161
- *Berger & Light Diffusers Pty. Ltd. v Pollock* [1973] 2 Lloyd's rep. 442
- *Bilbie v Lumley* (1802) 2 East 469
- *Black King Shipping v Massie, The Litsion Pride* [1985] 1 Lloyd's Rep. 437
- *Blackburn Low Co. v Vigors* (1887) 12 App. Cas. 531
- *Brine v Featherstone* (1813) 4 Taunt 869
- *British Equitable v G.W.R.* (1869) 20 L.T. 422
- *Britton v Royal Insurance Co.* (1866) 4 F. & F. 905
- *Brownlie v Campbell* (1880) 5 App. Cas. 925
- *Came v Moye* 2 Sid. 121
- *Canning v Farquhar* (1886) 16 Q.B.D. 727
- *Cantiere Meccanico Brindisino v Janson* [1912] 2 K.B. 112
- *Captain Panagos, The* [1986] 2 Lloyd's Rep. 470
- *Carter v Boehm* (1766) 3 Burr. 1905
- *Clipper Maritime Ltd. v Shirlstar Container Transport Ltd.(The Anemone)* [1987] 1 Lloyd's Rep. 546

- *Container Transport International Inc. v Oceanus Mutual Underwriting Association (Bermuda) Ltd.* [1982] 2 Lloyd's Rep. 178
- *Container Transport International Inc. v Oceanus Mutual Underwriting Association (Bermuda) Ltd.*[1984] 1 Lloyd's Rep. 476 (Court of Appeal)
- *Continental Illinois National Bank & Trust Co. of Chicago and Xenofon Maritime S.A. v Alliance Assurance (The Captain Panagos),* [1986] 2 Lloyd's Rep. 470
- *Cory v Paton (???)* L.R. 7 Q.B. 304
- *Court v Martineau* (1782) 2 Doug. 161
- *Da Costa v Scandret* 2 P. Wil. 170
- *Dalglish v Jarvie* (1850) 2 Mac. & G. 231
- *Davis Contractors Ltd. v Fareham U.D.C.* [1956] A.C. 696
- *Dawsons v Bonnin* [1922] 2 A.C. 413
- *Deposit and General Life Assurance Company v Ayscough* (1856) 6 Ell & Bl 761
- *Derry v Peek* (1889) 14 App Cas 337
- *Donoghue v Stevenson* [1932] A.C. 562
- *Dora, The* [1989] 1 Lloyd's Rep 65
- *Dorset Yacht Co. Ltd. v Home Office* [1970] A.C. 1004
- *Edgington v Fitzmaurice* (1885) 29 Ch. D. 459
- *Ewer v National Employees Mutual* [1937] 2 All E.R. 193
- *Foley v Tabor* (1861) 2 F. & F. 663
- *Fraser Shipping Ltd.v N.J. Colton & Ors* [1997] 1 Lloyd's Rep. 586
- *Friere v Woodhouse* (1817) 1 Holt. 572
- *Gallé Gowns Ltd. v Licenses & General Insurance Co.Ltd.*(1933) 47 Ll.L.Rep. 186
- *Galloway v Guardian Royal Exchange (UK) Ltd.* [1999] Lloyd's Rep. I.R. 209
- *General Reinsurance Corporation v Forsakringsaktiebolaget Fenna Patria* [1982] Q.B. 1022
- *Glasgow Assurance Corporation v William Symondson and Co* (1911) 104 L.T. 254
- *Glicksman v Lancashire and General Assurance Co.* (1926) 26 Ll.L.Rep. 69
- *Godfrey v Britannic Assurance Company, Ltd.* [1963] 2 Lloyd's Rep. 515
- *Good Luck, The* [1988] 1 Lloyd's Rep. 514
- *Good Luck, The* [1989] 2 Lloyd's Rep. 238
- *Good Luck, The* [1990] 1 Q.B. 818
- *Goodwin v Robarts* (1876) L.R. 10 Ex. 337
- *Gordon v Street* [1899] 2 Q.B. 641
- *Goulstone v Royal Insurance Co.* (1858) 1 F. & F. 276
- *Governors of the Peabody Donation Fund v Sir Lindsay Parkinson* [1985] A.C. 210
- *Greenhill v Federal Insurance Co.* [1927] 1 K.B. 65
- *Harrower v Hutchinson* (1870) L.R. 5 Q.B. 584
- *Hedley Byrne & Co. Ltd. v Heller & Partners Ltd.* [1964] A.C. 465

- *Highlands Insurance Co. v Continental Insurance Co* [1987] 1 Lloyd's Rep. 109
- *Hodgson v Richardson* (1764) 1 Wm. B1. 463
- *Horne v Poland* (1922) 10 Ll.L.Rep. 275
- *Hubbard v Glover* (1812) 3 Camp 313
- *Hussain v Brown (No. 2)* (1996) Unreported (Q.B.)
- *Inversiones Maria v Sphere Drake, The Dora* [1989] 1 Lloyd's Rep 65
- *Ionides v Pender* (1874) L.R. 9 Q.B. 531
- *Iron Trades Mutual Ins. Co. Ltd. v Companhia de Seguros Imperio* (1990) 1 Re. L.R. 213
- *Jester-Barnes v Licenses & General Ins. Co. Ltd.* (1934) 49 Ll.L.R. 231
- *Joel v Law Union and Crown Insurance Company* [1908] 2 K.B. 863 (C.A.)
- *K/S Merc Scandia XXXXII v Certain Lloyd's Underwriters subscribing to Lloyd's Policy no. 25T 105487 and Ocean Marine Insurance Co. Ltd. And Others (The Mercandian Continent)* [2002] 2 Lloyd's Rep. 563
- *Lambert v Co-operative Insurance Society Ltd.* [1975] 2 Lloyd's Rep 485
- *Lek v Mathews* (1927) 29 Ll.L.Rep. 141
- *Levy v Baillie* (1837) 7 Bing. 349
- *Liberian Insurance v Mosse* [1977] 2 Lloyd's Rep. 560
- *Life Association of Scotland v Foster* (1873) 11 M 351
- *Lindenau v Desborough* (1828) 8 B. & C. 586
- *Lishman and Another v The Northern Maritime Insurance Company (???)* L.R. 10 C.P. 179
- *Litsion Pride, The* [1985] 1 Lloyd's Rep. 437
- *London General Omnibus Co. Ltd. v Holloway* [1912] 2 K.B. 72
- *Looker v Law Union* [1928] 1 K.B. 554
- *Lynch v Hamilton* (1810) 3 Taunt. 37
- *Macdowall v Fraser* 1 Doug. 247
- *Manifest Shipping & Co. Ltd. v Uni-Polaris Insurance Co. Ltd.& La Réunion Européene (The Star Sea)* [2001] 2 W.L.R. 170 ; [2001] 1 Lloyd's Rep. 389
- *Marc Rich v Portman* [1996] 1 Lloyd's Rep. 430
- *March Cabaret Club & Casino Ltd .v London Assurance* [1975] 1 Lloyd's Rep. 169
- *Marene Knitting Mills Pty. Ltd. v Greater Pacific General Insurance Ltd.* [1976] 2 Lloyd's Rep. 631
- *Mayne v Walter* (1787)
- *Merchants & Manufacturers Ins. Co. v Charles & John Hunt* [1941] 1 K.B. 295
- *Moens v Heyworth* (1842) 10 M. & W. 147
- *Moonacre, The* [1992] 2 Lloyd's Rep 501
- *Mutual and Federal Ins v Oudtshoorn Municipality* 1985 (1) SA 419
- *Mutual Life Insurance Company of New York v Ontario Metal Products Company*

Limited [1925] A.C. 344
- *New Hampshire Insurance Co. v Mirror Group Newspapers Ltd.* [1997] L.R.L.R. 24
- *Newsholme Bros. v Road Transport & Genera* [1929] 2 K.B. 356
- *Noble and Another v Kennoway* (1780) 2 Doug. 510
- *Norton v The Royal Fire and Life Assurance Company* (1885) 1 T.L.R. 460
- *Orakpo v Barclays Ins. Services* [1995] L.R.L.R. 443
- *Overseas Commodities Ltd. v Style* [1958] 1 Lloyd's Rep. 546
- *Pan Atlantic Insurance Co. Ltd. and Another v Pine Top Insurance Co.Ltd.* [1993] 1 Lloyd's Rep. 496
- *Pan Atlantic Insurance Co. Ltd. and Another v Pine Top Insurance Co.Ltd.* [1994] 2 Lloyd's Rep. 427
- *Pawson v Watson* (1778) 2 Cowp. 786
- *Planché and Another v Fletcher* 1 Dougl. 251
- *Pim v Reid* 6 Man. & G. 1
- *Proudfoot v Montefiore* (1867) L.R. 2 Q.B. 511
- *Pryke v Gibbs Hartley Cooper Ltd.* [1991] 1 Lloyd's Rep. 602
- *Rafsanjan Pistachio Producers Co-operative v Bank Leumi (UK) plc* [1992] 1 Lloyd's Rep. 514
- *Re Bradley and Essex Accident* [1912] 1 K. B. 415
- *Regina Fur Company, Ltd. v Bossom* [1957] 2 Lloyd's Rep. 466
- *Rivaz v Gerussi* (1880) 6 Q.B.D. 222
- *Roselodge, Ltd. v Castle* [1966] 2 Lloyd's Rep 113
- *Royal Boskalis Westminster NV v Mountain* [1997] L.R.L.R. 523
- *Rozanes v Brown* (1928) 32 Ll.L.R. 98
- *Schoolman v Hall* [1951] Lloyd's Rep 139
- *Scottish Shire Line Ltd. v London and Provincial Marine and General Insurance Co. Ltd.* [1912] 3 K.B. 51
- *Seaman v Fonnereau* (1734) 2 Str. 1183
- *Seaton v Burnand* [1900] A.C. 135
- *Smart v Wolff* (1789) 3 T.R. 348
- *Smith v Bank of Scotland* (1829) 7 S 244
- *Smith v Kay* (1859) 7 H.L.C. 750
- *Societe Anonyme d'Intermediaries Luxembourgeois v Farex Gie* [1995] L.R.L.R. 116
- *Sprung v Royal Insurance* [1999] Lloyd's Rep. IR 111
- *Star Sea, The* [2001] 2 W.L.R. 170 ; [2001] 1 Lloyd's Rep. 389
- *St. Paul Fire & Marine Insurance Co. (UK) Ltd. v McConnell Dowell Constructors Ltd.* [1995] 2 Lloyd's Rep. 116
- *Tate v Hyslop* (1885) 15 Q.B.D. 368
- *Taylor v Eagle Star Ins. Co.* (1940) 67 Ll.L.R. 136
- *Traill v Baring,* (1864) 4 De G. J. & S. 318

- *Tyler v Horne* Hil. T. 1785
- *Visscherij Maatschappij Nieuw Onderneming v Scottish Metropolitan Assurance Co. Ltd.* (1922) 10 Ll.L.Rep. 579
- *West v National Motor and Accident* [1955] 1 All E.R. 800
- *Wheelton v Hardisty* (1857) 8 E. & B. 232
- *William Pickersgill v London & Provincial Marine and General Ins. Co. Ltd.* [1912] 3 K.B. 614
- *Wilson v Duckett* 3. Burr.1361
- *Wing v Harvey* 5 DE G. M. & G. 265
- *Wittingham v Thornborough* 2 Vern. 206
- *Wolff v Horncastle* (1798) 1 Bos & Pul 316; 126 E.R. 924
- *Woolcott v Excess Insurance* [1978] 1 Lloyd's Rep. 633; [1979] 1 Lloyd's Rep. 231, Court of Appeal; [1979] 2 Lloyd's Rep. 210, Queen's Bench Division (retrial)
- *Zurich General Accident and Liability Insurance Company Ltd. v Morrison* [1942] 2 K.B. 53

Peter Lang · Europäischer Verlag der Wissenschaften

Yuansheng Jiang

Health Insurance Demand and Health Risk Management in Rural China

Frankfurt am Main, Berlin, Bern, Bruxelles, New York, Oxford, Wien, 2004.
XX, 205 pp., num. fig. and tab.
Development, Economics and Policy.
Edited by Franz Heidhues and Joachim von Braun. Vol. 41
ISBN 3-631-52624-5 / US-ISBN 0-8204-7312-X · pb. € 42.50*

Good health is widely believed to be intimately associated with economic growth and development. A number of governments of developing countries have been combating poverty and boosting development through providing adequate access to health care. However, developing countries have been constrained by the limited governmental revenue. Thus, additional resources should be mobilized through appropriate instruments. Health insurance is a highly practical instrument. However, health insurance in rural areas is problematic and the demand for private health insurance and community-based health insurance scheme is inadequate. Taking China as an example, this study estimates the demand for health insurance and analyzes the health risk management of rural households.

Contents: Identifying Determinants of Expanding Demand for Health Insurance · Ways of Establishing and Developing the Rural Cooperative Medical Scheme by Analyzing the Willingness of Rural Households to Pay · Risk Coping Strategies of Rural Households · The Extended Family

Frankfurt am Main · Berlin · Bern · Bruxelles · New York · Oxford · Wien
Distribution: Verlag Peter Lang AG
Moosstr. 1, CH-2542 Pieterlen
Telefax 00 41 (0) 32 / 376 17 27

*The €-price includes German tax rate
Prices are subject to change without notice

Homepage http://www.peterlang.de